The multinational trade

This volume provides new perspectives on the evolution and theory of multinational trading companies. In the history of multinational business, trading companies have played an especially significant and strategic role which continues until the present day, when Japan's *sogo shosha* and giant commodity traders feature among the world's largest global businesses. However the origins and strategies of multinational trading companies are little known compared to those of manufacturing multinationals.

The Multinational Traders features contributions from an international selection of US, European and Asian economists and business historians which demonstrate the importance of trading companies in trade and investment flows in the world economy from the nineteenth century to the present. The authors adopt evolutionary and comparative perspectives to examine diversification strategies and organisational structures. This innovative study is a major contribution to our knowledge of the history and theory of international business.

Routledge international studies in business history
Geoffrey Jones

The multinational traders

Edited by Geoffrey Jones

ROUTLEDGE

London and New York

First published 1998
by Routledge
2 Park Square, Milton Park, Abingdon, Oxon OX14 4RN (UK)

Simultaneously published in the USA and Canada
by Routledge
711 Third Avenue, New York, NY 10017 (US)

First issued in paperback 2013

Routledge is an imprint of the Taylor & Francis Group, an informa business

British Library Cataloguing in Publication Data
A catalogue record for this book is available from the British Library

Library of Congress Cataloguing in Publication Data
The multinational traders / edited by Geoffrey Jones. Papers originally
presented at a conference held at the University of Reading, UK, in
September 1997.
Includes bibliographical references and index.
1. Trading companies – History – Congresses.
2. Export marketing – History – Congresses.
3. International trade – History – Congresses.
4. International business enterprises – History – Congresses.
I. Jones, Geoffrey. HF1416.T693   1998
382′. 6 – dc 21   98 – 18323 CIP

ISBN 0–415–18002–3
ISBN 978-0-415-86261-5 (Paperback)

Contents

Illustrations

FIGURES

TABLES

Contributors

Susan Becker is a Research Assistant at the University of Bonn, Germany. She graduated from the University of Reading with an MA in International Business History in 1992, and in 1994 took her Master's Degree at the University of Bonn. Currently, she is completing her Ph.D. thesis on German and Belgian multinational enterprise before 1914.

Mark Casson is Professor of Economics at the University of Reading in the United Kingdom. His recent publications include *Information and Organization* (1997) and *Culture, Social Norms and Economics* (editor, 1997).

Hélène d'Almeida-Topor is Professor of African Contemporary History at the University of Paris, 1 Panthéon-Sorbonne, France, and member of the African Center of Research (CRA). She is the author of five books and about thirty articles or contributions including *L'Afrique au Xxe siècle* (1993); (with M. Lakroum) *L'Europe et l'Afrique. Un siècle d'échanges économiques* (1994); *Histoire économique du Dahomey 1890–1920* (1995); *Naissance des Etats africains* (1996). She is also co-editor of seven books in the field of economic and social history of Africa including *Les transports en Afrique* (1992); *Les Jeunes en Afrique* (1992); *Echanges franco-allemands sur l'Afrique* (1994); *Interdépendances villes-campagnes en Afrique* (1996). She is president of the Comité français des études africaines.

Hans de Geer received his Ph.D. from Stockholm University in Sweden in 1978. He has specialised in contemporary history and written a number of books and articles on themes such as scientific management, computerisation, industrial relations and business values. From 1991 to 1994 he was Professor in Business and Work Life History at the School of Business, Stockholm University. Since 1995 he has been Professor of Business History and Ethics at the Stockholm School of Economics, and the initiator and director of the Center for Ethics and Economics at the School. At present he is working on a history of Axel Johnson AB.

Robert Greenhill is a member of the Department of Business Studies at London Guildhall University in the United Kingdom. His main fields of interest are British business links with Latin America during the nineteenth and twentieth centuries. In particular, he has published a number of papers on shipping and the commodity trades.

Sébastien Guex is *maître assistant* in contemporary history at the University of Lausanne, Switzerland. He specialises in the economic history of Switzerland, especially Switzerland's role as a financial centre and Swiss government financial policies. His publications include *La politique monétaire et financière de la Confédération suisse 1900–1920* (1993). He is co-editor of the journal *Traverse, Revue d'Historie*.

Jean-François Hennart is Professor of International Business and Director of the Ph.D. programme in International Business at the University of Illinois at Urbana-Champaign in the United States. His main research interest is the transaction cost theory of the multinational firm and of its alternatives, and the theory and empirical analysis of modes of entry into foreign markets. He is the author of *A Theory of Multinational Enterprise* (1982) and of more than 20 articles in journals such as the *Journal of International Business Studies*, *Management International Review, Management Science, Organisation Science*, the *Strategic Management Journal*, the *Journal of Law, Economics, and Organisation*, the *Journal of Economic Behaviour and Organisation, Weltwirtschatfliches Archiv*, the *Journal of Management Studies* and *Business History*. He is US representative on the Board of the European International Business Academy and serves on the Editorial Boards of the *Journal of International Business Studies*, the *Strategic Management Journal, Management International Review* and the *Journal of World Business*.

Geoffrey Jones is Professor of Business History at the Centre for International Business History at the University of Reading in the United Kingdom. He is the author or editor of numerous books and articles on the history of international business, including *The State and the Emergence of the British Oil Industry* (1981); *Banking and Empire in Iran* (1986); (ed. with Peter Hertner), *Multinationals:Theory and History* (1986); (ed.) *Banks as Multinationals* (1990); (ed. with Harm Schröter), *The Rise of Multinationals in Continental Europe* (1993); *British Multinational Banking 1830–1990* (1993); and *The Evolution of International Business* (1996). He is currently completing a book on the history of British-based trading companies from the nineteenth century to the present day. Professor Jones is co-editor of the journal *Business History*, and President of the European Business History Association.

Georgine M. Kryda is a Visiting Assistant Professor of International Business at Oregon State University in the United States. Her research interests include interactions between multinational firms and governments. Her dissertation, *Modelling the Bargaining Game between Multinational Firms and Britain's Office of Fair Trading: An Exploratory Analysis* (1997), took a non-normative look at how expectations regarding consistency, predictability, and transparency are formed by corporate managers and government officials within Britain's highly discretionary system of merger review.

Rory Miller is Senior Lecturer in Latin American Economic History at the University of Liverpool in the United Kingdom. He has published extensively both in the economic history of Peru and on British firms in Latin America. His work includes *Britain and Latin America in the Nineteenth and Twentieth Centuries* (1993) and (ed. with Carlos Dàvila) *Business History in Latin America: the experience of seven countries* (1998). He is also a former editor of the *Bulletin of Latin American Research*.

J. Forbes Munro is the Associate Director of the Centre for Business History in Scotland and the former Clerk of Senate of the University of Glasgow in the United Kingdom. He has published in the fields of African economic history and of maritime history, and is a past joint editor of *The Journal of African History*. He is currently writing a biography of the nineteenth-century Scottish businessman and imperialist, Sir William MacKinnon.

Tom Roehl is Assistant Professor of International Business at the University of Illinois at Urbana-Champaign in the United States, where he teaches courses in international business and the Japanese business system. He does research on interfirm relationships in Japan, to include industrial groups, parts supply relationships and international alliances. In addition to work on general trading companies, he has studied the aerospace industry and the pharmaceuticals industry. His book with Hiroyuki Itami, *Mobilizing Invisible Assets* (1987) was one of the first to develop resource-based theories of corporate strategies.

Keetie E. Sluyterman is senior researcher at the Research Institute for History and Culture of the Utrecht University in the Netherlands and Research Fellow at the Centre for International Business History at the University of Reading in the United Kingdom. She has published widely on Dutch business history, ranging from family firms to multinational companies and from distillers to accountants and banks. She is currently working on the history of Dutch trading companies, including Hagemeyer.

Ken'ichi Yasumuro is Professor of International Business in the department of international business and marketing of the Kobe University of Commerce in Japan. He has published extensively in the fields of Japanese management, international business, and history of multinational enterprises. His contribution to those fields includes studies of Japanese general trading companies and the strategies of Japanese multinational manufacturers.

Preface

There is a vast literature on international business, but multinational trading companies rarely feature in it. Researchers in international business remain preoccupied with manufacturing and, especially, with its high-technology sector, even though services are now by far the most important sector for multinationals. In the history of multinational business, trading companies have played an especially significant and strategic role, which continues until the present day, when Japan's *sogo shosha* and giant commodity traders feature among the world's largest global businesses. This book assembles a uniquely international and interdisciplinary team of leading scholars to assert the importance of trading companies in international business. The authors include specialists in business history, economics and international business and work at universities in France, Germany, Japan, the Netherlands, Sweden, Switzerland, the United Kingdom and the United States.

In order to ensure that the volume was coherent, preliminary versions of chapters were presented at a conference held at the Centre for International Business History at the University of Reading, UK, in September 1997. The conference was funded by the Economic and Social Research Council under Grant No. R006235612. The conference was attended by thirty participants from many countries and their contributions to the discussions have played a major role in the final versions of the chapters presented here. Ph.D. candidates Kenichi Ando, Helen Carrier and Laura Stanciu were especially helpful in the administration of this conference. In preparing the book for publication, Ann Prior has language-edited several chapters, while Margaret Gallagher has undertaken a great deal of word processing in order to get the manuscript into shape.

Geoffrey Jones
Reading, January 1998

1 Multinational trading companies in history and theory

Geoffrey Jones

This book is concerned with the evolution and theory of multinational trading companies. The focus is on the twentieth century. Trading companies in the seventeenth and eighteenth centuries – such as the famous East India Companies – have received much attention from historians, but this is far from the case for their modern successors. Although important studies of individual firms and, especially, of Japanese trading companies have been published, only a handful of wider studies exist. There are two monographs by a French and a Korean published in the mid-1980s (Chalmin 1985; Cho 1987) and two Japanese-sponsored edited volumes (Yonekawa and Yoshihara 1987; Yonekawa 1990). The paucity of literature on trading companies reflects a more general bias in the literature on international business towards the manufacturing sector, even though by the 1990s upwards 50 per cent of world foreign direct investment (FDI) was in services (Enderwick 1989). Nevertheless the neglect of trading companies in the international business literature is especially curious for two reasons.

The first reason is their importance in the world economy, both historically and at the end of the twentieth century. In the nineteenth and early twentieth centuries, as will be shown later in this chapter and in subsequent chapters, trading companies were very significant in world trade in commodities and more generally as vehicles for FDI which, by 1914, had risen to a size relative to world output not to be regained until the 1990s (Jones 1996a: 30). In the 1990s Japan's nine *sogo shosha* – general trading companies – handled over 40 per cent of that country's entire exports and over 70 per cent of its imports. In 1991 their gross sales amounted to a quarter of Japan's nominal GNP. A listing of the world's top 100 multinationals ranked by foreign assets in 1995 included five Japanese *sogo shosha*: Mitsubishi Corporation, Mitsui Co., Itochu, Nissho Iwai and Marubeni (United Nations 1997). Another *sogo shosha*, Sumitomo Corporation (ranked 51 in this listing) lost over £1 billion in unauthorised copper trading in a spectacular scandal in 1996 (*Financial Times*, 21 June 1996). Among other corporate giants in the contemporary world economy are commodity trading companies such as Cargill, the largest private company in the United States, and Glencore International, Switzerland's second largest company by turnover.

The second reason why the neglect of trading companies is curious lies in their inherent interest at a conceptual level. An examination of trading company strategies over time shows them as highly entrepreneurial corporate forms, constantly alert to new opportunities and resourceful in setting up the systems and creating flexible organisations to exploit these opportunities. The history of trading companies shows them as able to 're-invent' themselves generation after generation. Trading companies represent different types of international business than the much more intensely studied manufacturing multinationals (MNEs). They can be seen as knowledge and information-based organisations rather than capital-based. As such, their competencies are of major theoretical interest.

The remainder of this chapter will consider the definitional issues surrounding the study of trading companies, provide a historical overview of their evolution to serve as a context for the subsequent empirical chapters, and rehearse the major theoretical approaches to understanding this type of international firm.

Definitions and typologies

While the identification of Ford and IBM as multinational automobile and computer manufacturers is hardly controversial, the definition of a trading company raises more problems. At its core their business can be described in simple terms as one involving the linking of buyers with sellers. As Casson discusses in Chapter 2, this trade intermediation can be done by broking or reselling. A broker does not assume ownership of the product in which he deals, whereas the reseller does. A multinational trading company engages in trade intermediation between countries, and owns assets in more than one country. It may engage in broking or reselling, or both.

Problems arise because trading companies of all historical periods and nationalities have exhibited tendencies to perform activities other than trade intermediation, strictly defined. They frequently diversify into related services, including shipping and insurance, and into manufacturing and resource exploitation. The resulting companies continue to engage in trade intermediation but perform many other activities also. In Chapter 2, Casson distinguishes between 'pure' and 'hybrid' trading companies which perform other activities beyond trade. Comparatively few trading companies remain 'pure' by this definition. There are, however, numerous types of 'hybrid' trading companies and, if the diversification beyond trade is substantial enough, there comes a point when such firms are better described by another name than trading company. A case in point is the Shell Transport and Trading Company, the British parent of the world's largest oil company, Shell. This originated as a firm of British merchants trading mainly in Asia, which began trading in oil in the late nineteenth century, which then became an oil producer, and which subsequently merged with the Royal Dutch Petroleum Company in 1907 to form the present Anglo-Dutch oil company. At some stage before 1907 Shell is more appropriately described as an 'oil company' rather than a 'hybrid trading company', but precisely when is a matter of subjective judgement. Little can be done about such definitional problems beyond pointing them out. As Casson suggests, the interesting issues concern why some firms remain 'pure' and others become 'hybrids', and why the 'hybrids' take the forms they do.

There are further distinctions which can be made between types of trading company. Trading companies may specialise by product. Becker in Chapter 4 in this book discusses the case of the German metal traders led by Metallgesellschaft. Commodity traders such as Cargill, Bunge and Louis Dreyfus may fall into this category, though the scale of their diversification may put them into another category. For example, Louis Dreyfus, whose annual turnover in 1997 was around $20 billion, was the world's leading trader in cotton and industrial alcohol, but its other interests included shipping, *foie gras*, electricity, the world's third largest orange juice business, the licence to make Ralph Lauren menswear in Europe, and the Four Seasons Hotel in Washington DC. The British-owned ED & F Man provides an example of a major sugar trading company. In 1997 it accounted for 16 per cent of total world cross-border sugar trade, though it also traded in cocoa, nuts, spices, molasses, alcohol and financial services.

A second type of trading firm specialises by region. Most European trading companies in the nineteenth century were specialised by host region, though a handful such as the 'Mackinnon group' discussed by Forbes Munro in Chapter 3 had inter-regional operations. Greenhill and Miller in Chapter 6 and d'Almeida-Topor in Chapter 9 discuss the subsequent evolution of the British companies specialised in Latin America and the French companies specialised in Africa, respectively. The scale of these region-specific firms was sometimes enormous. In 1939 the United Africa Company, the West African trading company owned by Unilever, imported 50,000 types of article, virtually the whole range of goods consumed in the region (Fieldhouse 1994: 411).

General trading companies combine both these region and product-specific features. The most cited examples are Japan's *sogo shosha*, which have been defined 'as a firm that trades all kinds of goods with all nations of the world' (Yoshihara 1987:1). The first *sogo shosha*, the predecessor to Mitsui & Co, dates from 1876, and Japan's nine *sogo shosha* remains today among its largest firms. Chapters 10, 11 and 12 deal with different aspects of these firms in recent decades. Once believed to be uniquely Japanese, Cho showed that by the 1970s and 1980s examples of this form could be found in Korea, Europe and elsewhere (Cho 1987). Certainly in the 1980s a number of European companies, among them Britain's Inchcape and Harrisons & Crosfield, closely resembled *sogo shosha*, although subsequently more focused business strategies have greatly lessened the resemblance.

'Pure' trading companies, therefore, need to distinguished from 'hybrid' firms, and trading companies may be specialised by region or product, or else take the form of general trading companies. Historically, firms have moved within these categories-specialised traders becoming general trading companies, and the reverse process also. While their complexities can make the identification of trading companies difficult, they also present intriguing theoretical challenges to explain differences in the strategies chosen by firms.

Evolution

Pre-1914

Given that the international activities of merchants reached back to antiquity and beyond, the search for the 'first' multinational trading company would be an unrewarding one. When merchants sent their relatives to foreign countries to facilitate trade, they were effectively forming embryonic trading companies. Even the Viking raiding parties of the European Middle Ages may, as de Geer suggests in Chapter 7, be seen as international traders as well as military conquerors.

The European chartered trading companies formed between the sixteenth and eighteenth centuries had more resemblances to modern trading companies than the Vikings, although the extent of the resemblance remains disputed. These companies, which included the English, Dutch, French and Swedish East Indian Companies, the Hudson's Bay Company, and the Muscovy Company, were 'chartered' or given monopoly powers to trade with their regions of specialisation. They became large vertically integrated firms that undertook a range of activities from purchasing products in Russia, Asia, Canada and elsewhere to wholesaling their goods in Europe together with the reverse process of acquiring goods in Europe and shipping and selling them in foreign markets. They undertook hundreds of thousands of transactions annually, which were overseen by managerial hierarchies headquarters based in Europe. They sometimes diversified into production overseas, usually to overcome inefficiencies in supply and quality of goods. The organisational structures were quite complex. In the mid-eighteenth century both the Dutch and the British East Indian Companies had over 350 Head Office administrators. These were 'hybrid' trading companies, although their monopoly privileges and close links with governments limit their resemblances to modern firms. An extreme case was the English East India Company which from the mid-eighteenth century began to take over the government of parts of the Indian subcontinent, then undergoing a period of political instability. Within eighty years the Company was governing much of the subcontinent, an arrangement which continued until 1858. The chartered companies seldom outlived the withdrawal of their monopoly privileges in the eighteenth century. By 1914, the only survivor was the Hudson's Bay Company which evolved into a successful Canadian retailing business (Carlos and Nicholas 1988; Jones and Ville 1996).

From the eighteenth century, as European government monopolies weakened, new types of merchant appeared in the international economy. The Industrial Revolution and the subsequent growth of world trade, and the integration of new countries into the world trading system – partly with the spread of European imperialism – provided great opportunities for trade intermediation. In the eighteenth century individual merchants settled in the ports of the world and major commercial centres such as London, but the importance of information in trade flows meant that these individuals frequently had international ties of families, ethnicity or partnership. When their networks took more permanent form, the result was the emergence of modern-style multinational trading companies.

It is not surprising that British trading companies were pre-eminent in this period. The Industrial Revolution made Britain the world's largest manufacturing country in 1800, and it retained that position until the 1880s when British output was overtaken by that of the United States. British exports, especially of textiles, grew spectacularly fast. In 1860 Britain accounted for 26 per cent of total world trade, and the country's leading industries were highly export dependent. While continental merchants settled in Britain and came to dominate British exports of cotton textiles to elsewhere in Europe, British merchants pioneered new markets for British manufactured goods in Latin America, Asia and other developing markets (Chapman 1992). The extension of British imperial frontiers over large areas of Asia and Africa during the course of the nineteenth century greatly reduced the risks faced by British merchants in establishing branches overseas. A number of British colonial ports, notably Hong Kong and Singapore in Asia, developed as major *entrepots* and centres for British trading companies. Once established in foreign ports, British merchants often became interested in the export of local commodities as well as the import of British goods, and later in other activities such as acting as agents for insurance and shipping companies. Subsequently backward or forward integration strategies were adopted.

This process is discussed for India by Forbes Munro in Chapter 3, and for Latin America by Greenhill and Miller in Chapter 6. These were two of the most important host regions for British trading companies. Both chapters demonstrate the diversification strategies of the firms over time, but also show the great variations between firms. In Latin America, the British companies on the west coast such as Balfour Williamson and Antony Gibbs became highly diversified, while on the east coast there was some tendency to specialise in single commodities, such as coffee. In India, Mackinnon Mackenzie was one of the cluster of British – often Scottish – 'agency houses' which began by importing British textiles and exporting local produce such as tea, and later diversified into plantations and other activities. Again there were considerable variations between firms. The firm of Mackinnon Mackenzie grew within the context of a wider group or network of interrelated firms which by the end of the century included trading operations in the Arab Gulf, East Africa, Australia as well as India, the management of tea plantations, jute mills, coal mines and a cotton factory in India, and control of six steamship companies. This highly diversified trading group became the predecessor to Britain's Inchcape, the closest European equivalent to a *sogo shosha*.

There were different patterns of hybridisation in other regions in which British trading companies operated. In South East Asia, British trading companies largely concentrated on trade until the late nineteenth century, but in the 1900s firms such as Guthries, Harrisons and Crosfield and Bousteads made large investments in the nascent rubber plantation industry in Malaya and surrounding countries (Drabble and Drake 1981). In East Asia, a number of British trading companies were formed which were to prove very durable. Jardine Matheson, which controlled about half of China's foreign trade by the 1830s, originated in a series of partnerships founded from the 1780s by British merchants resident in Canton. The firm's main business before the 1870s was selling Indian opium to China, but by 1914 Jardine Matheson had developed a general trading business in China, with branches in Japan and the United States also. It also managed and partly owned in China and Hong Kong a number of companies engaged in shipping, dockyards, insurance, ice and cold storage, sugar refining and cotton mills. Its major British competitor in the region was John Swire & Sons, which had opened a partnership in China in 1867, but which developed in a different fashion. By 1914 the firm had withdrawn from trading and focused on shipping – it established one of the leading shipping companies in the Far East – dockyards and sugar refineries (Sugiyama 1987). It might perhaps be argued that Swire, whatever its origins, had ceased to be even a 'hybrid' trading company by 1914, although the firm would resume 'trading' in later years.

Diversification by these and other trading companies, especially after 1870, made them important vehicles for British FDI. Britain was the world's largest capital exporter in the period and also its largest direct investor. The existing estimates suggest that Britain accounted for around 45 per cent of total world FDI in 1914, compared to 18 per cent of the next largest home economy, the United States (Dunning 1983). While US FDI was largely undertaken by what may be called 'classic' multinationals, which first grew and developed competencies within their domestic market before investing abroad, much British FDI was undertaken by hundreds or even thousands of firms set up exclusively to operate abroad – usually in a single country and/or product – and with only a small head office located in Britain. Initially these firms were classified as portfolio investment, but the apparent exercise of management control from Britain led to their reclassification as a form of FDI (Houston and Dunning 1976; Svedberg 1978). Subsequently Mira Wilkins described this type of firm as 'free-standing' companies (Wilkins 1986, 1988). Yasumuro in Chapter 10 provides as overview of the subsequent debates on these firms, with whom he finds parallels with contemporary Japanese international business.

While there are numerous uncertainties about the nature of free-standing firms – and consequently the real size of British FDI – it is accepted that free-standing firms were not 'free-standing' in the sense that many nominally independent corporate entities were joined in wider business networks linked by a variety of factors, including cross-directorships, shareholdings, contracts and the provision of services. Wilkins called these groupings 'clusters' (Wilkins 1988), while Chapman developed the concept of 'investment groups' (Chapman 1992). Trading companies formed one of the most important components of Wilkins' 'clusters'. These are also at the centre of Chapman's 'investment groups': Mackinnon Mackenzie and several of the British trading companies active in Latin America and included in his list of '30 leading British based Investment Groups' active between 1900 and 1914 (Chapman 1992). When the British trading companies diversified beyond trading to become 'hybrids', they typically placed the new activity in a company which they promoted on the London (or sometimes local) capital market. However, in many cases the trading company retained a management contract becoming 'managing agents' or 'secretaries' of the new company – and often retained seats on the Board and part of the equity. Subsequently the parent trading company would often provide extensive short-term credit to the company managed by them. This process can be seen when Balfour Williamson, one of the trading companies discussed by Greenhill and Miller in Chapter 6, invested in oil and flour milling before the First World War. Its Californian and Peruvian oil business was conducted by two 'free-standing' companies, Californian Oilfields Ltd (sold to Shell in 1913) and Lobitos Oilfields, while its extensive flour milling business in Chile and Peru was conducted by the Santa Rosa Milling Company (Hunt 1960). It would seem that many of Britain's free-standing companies before 1914 were linked in some fashion to trading companies, which must have accounted for a large – but as yet unknown – proportion of British FDI.

While the British trading companies built large and complex international business systems in the nineteenth century, they were not alone. The French, the Dutch and the Swiss were among the leading houses for trading companies active in developing countries, especially European colonies. The most important French trading companies – headed by the Société Commerciale de l'Ouest Africain (SCOA) and the Compagnie Française de l'Afrique Noire (CFAO) – operated in French colonial Africa (Coquery-Vidrovitch 1975; Bonin 1987; Chalmin 1987). Sluyteman in Chapter 5 discusses the growth of Dutch trading companies in Indonesia, formerly the Dutch East Indies. Like their counterparts, diversification into other activities such as plantations led them into hybridisation. The Dutch companies also often promoted legally separate companies to own plantations, which they either managed, or owned themselves. The Swiss case, discussed by Guex in Chapter 8, is interesting in providing an example of traders from a non-imperial country which became important in the colonies of other European countries, especially British colonies. Before 1914 the role of UTC in the cocoa exports of Ghana (formerly the Gold Coast) and of Volkart in Indian cotton and coffee exports had grown to substantial proportions.

Before 1914 the 'trading' business of the European trading companies active in the developing world involved the import of manufactured goods into their host economies and the export of their primary products. This reflected the pattern of economic specialisation which had developed in the world economy. However, as several chapters in this book demonstrate, other types of trading company were important also. The Netherlands had coal and foodstuffs trading companies involved in intra-European trade. In Sweden the firm of A Johnson & Co. in the 1870s imported coal and coke from Britain and Germany for Swedish industry and exported pig iron, but by 1914 the firm controlled a shipping company and an ironworks. The overseas branches came to buy and sell on behalf of other parts of the group in Sweden, a very different function than that of the British, Dutch and French trading companies, which for the most part did not own businesses in their home economies.

In Chapter 4 Becker discusses the case of another variant of European trading enterprise before 1914 – the trio of German metal trading companies. These firms, especially Metallgesellschaft, diversified into the mining, processing and distribution of copper, lead and zinc, and made large direct investments in the United States and Mexico, as well as Europe. By their control over smelting and refining, and their use of long-term contracts, they were able to control world prices of certain metals including lead, zinc, copper and nickel before the First World War.

The focus on European-owned trading companies before 1914 in this discussion is deliberate. This form of business flourished in nineteenth-century Europe and at its most basic level this reflected Europe's position at the heart of world trade. In 1913 over 60 per cent of world trade was European, consisting both of intra-European trade and European trade with the rest of the world. In contrast, although the United States had replaced Britain as the world's largest economy, its role in international trade was very much less. In addition, US manufacturing and resource firms demonstrated an early tendency to vertical integration rather than using intermediaries to buy or sell for them. Consequently US-owned trading companies played a small role in the growth of US multinational enterprise abroad. Examples of US multinational trading companies before 1914 included the American Trading Company, Arkell and Douglas, and W R Grace & Co., which owed its origins to the Irish partner of a British merchant firm in Peru. By 1914 this had become a genuine American 'hybrid' trading company with diversified activities in plantations, textile mills and railroads in Latin America (Wilkins 1970: 11–12, 176, 193–4, 211; Clayton 1985).

It was Japan rather than the United States where trading companies became and stayed important. Following the Meiji Restoration in 1868 which marked the beginning of Japan's economic modernisation, several dozen trading companies were founded. The country had been isolated from the world economy for over two hundred years which meant that it had an extreme shortage of people with the language and trading skills needed to undertake foreign business. This ignorance of foreign markets probably encouraged Japanese manufacturers to rely on trading companies rather than establish their own distribution facilities abroad. The Japanese government also favoured Japanese-owned trading companies as a means to reduce their country's dependence on western merchants. It facilitated the growth of the first *sogo shosha*, Mitsui Bussan. The latter's growth was also greatly assisted by its position within the Mitsui *zaibatsu*, or diversified holding company, and much of Mitsui Bussan's business involved buying and selling for other Mitsui companies within the *zaibatsu*. By 1914 trading companies handled 51 per cent of total Japanese exports and 64 per cent of total imports, and Mitsui Bussan alone accounted for 20 per cent of Japan's total exports and imports. By 1914 the firm had also diversified into cotton textiles manufacture and flour milling in China (Yonekawa and Yoshihara 1987; Yonekawa 1990; Jones 1996a:150–51).

A final point to emphasise is that there were many examples of trading companies in the international economy before 1914 beyond those discussed in this volume. In Europe, especially important examples were the Greek merchants whose activities and investments stretched from Russia through the Mediterranean to Britain (Minoglou and Louri 1997). These Greek merchants ranged from individuals to very substantial trading companies. An example of the latter was Ralli Brothers, which established its headquarters in London, and moved its main trading business focus from Russia to India over the course of the nineteenth century (Chapman 1992: 153–61, 224–5). In late nineteenth-century South East Asia, intra-Asian trade in many products was conducted by powerful overseas Chinese and Indian trading companies whose contours and significance are only now being explored (Brown 1994).

The late nineteenth century and early twentieth century clearly represents a 'heroic' period for multinational trading companies. They were trade intermediaries at a time when world trade was growing at much higher rates than world output – sometimes more than 60 per cent per decade in the period before the First World War. However, in the conditions of the period they made markets as well as intermediated them. Through engaging in FDI they built and provided transport and financial infrastructure. They developed oil industries in Latin America and plantation agriculture in South East Asia. Certainly in Britain and possibly in the Netherlands, they accounted for a considerable proportion of those countries' total FDI, either as investors themselves or as mobilisers of other people's money.

1914–45

If the world economy before 1914 offered boundless opportunities to multinational trading companies, the era of the world wars and the Great Depression offered a much less hospitable environment. The immediate post-First World War recession seems to have exercised a severe effect on trading companies worldwide. Further serious challenges came in the 1930s, as world trade collapsed as protectionism spread, commodity prices collapsed, and industrialisation by import substitution spread. The international mobility of capital fell sharply with the adoption of exchange controls (Jones 1996a:44–5). By the 1930s the growth of world FDI had stopped or even gone into reverse, as manufacturing and natural resource MNEs opted to participate in international cartels rather than undertake the risks of FDI. The decline of world trade, tariffs, exchange controls and falling commodity prices inevitably had highly adverse effects on the business of many trading companies. For some companies, the wars had disastrous consequences also. Metallgesellschaft and the other German metal traders had their complex international companies broken up as a consequence of Germany's defeat in the First World War, while the French, British, Greek and other trading companies with businesses in Russia lost their assets following the Communist Revolution of 1917.

Against this background, the trading companies discussed in this volume appear rather resilient. British trading companies have long been regarded as going into decline in this period. In part, this has been seen as the result of faltering British trade performance and the growth of competition for its traditional textile industries. In part, these have often been seen as conservative and lacking in flexibility, perhaps because of their retention of the partnership form or family ownership. In inter-war India the British firms in the inter-war years have been seen as excessively focused on their traditional areas of jute, coal and tea, and reluctant to become involved in the new industries developing behind tariff barriers (Misra 1994).

Latin America has often been seen as the worst case of precipitate British decline. Greenhill and Miller mount a considerable revisionist challenge to this interpretation. While the problems faced by the British trading companies in inter-war Latin America were acute, and several major firms collapsed, they show that there was also a more entrepreneurial response than has often been suggested in the literature. They withdrew from certain commodities such as cocoa and nitrates where prospects seemed bleak, while investing more in others such as coffee and meat-packing with brighter prospects. They became involved in import substitution and sought out British manufacturers as joint venture partners, just as did Japanese trading companies, though with less success as they did not belong to a *zaibatsu* group.

There is evidence from other regions to support the Greenhill and Miller hypothesis that British trading companies, or some of them, were more resilient than has been believed, and able to some extent to 're-invent' themselves once more. In South East Asia, Harrisons & Crosfield, which controlled around 40 rubber plantation companies around the time of the First World War as well as a substantial tea trading business, developed in the inter-war years a substantial logging business in North Borneo (now Sabah, Malaysia), began rubber manufacturing in both Malaysia and Britain, and started chemicals distribution from its Canadian branches, originally established to sell tea (Harrisons & Crosfield 1944; Jones 1996b). James Finlay,

which owned very large tea plantations in India as well as manufacturing jute and cotton textiles, opened tea plantations in East Africa and began manufacturing sugar in the inter-war years (Jones 1996b). In East Asia, it is evident that British companies such as Jardine Matheson and Swires were badly affected by Japanese competition to their shipping, sugar refining and other activities, but there was also a strategic response. During the 1920s and 1930s Jardine Matheson entered and expanded its business in engineering, cotton manufacturing and the manufacture and export of dried eggs in the 1920s, and into brewing in the 1930s (Keswick 1982). Not all of these new ventures were 'successful', but they do demonstrate that some British trading companies at least were willing to respond to new circumstances.

This theme of continued flexibility despite adversity in the inter-war years is suggested by other chapters in the book. The Dutch trading companies in Indonesia began to import Japanese products, and to experiment in manufacturing. Swiss companies, aided by their country's neutrality in the First World War and the strength of the Swiss franc, appear to have grown rapidly in the inter-war years. André, for example, established itself as a leading international grain trader in this period, opening branches in Argentina and the United States. Sweden's A Johnson also expanded in this period, opening branches in Britain, the United States, France and Germany and ever-expanding its Swedish interests to include oil-refining, construction, engineering companies and a bus company.

The evidence presented here would not challenge the view that the 'heroic age' of multinational trading companies had passed by the inter-war years. Their relative significance in international business may have fallen as 'classic' multinationals in manufacturing and natural resources expanded abroad. During the 1920s the rapid growth of multinational manufacturing in automobiles and foodstuffs – industries characterised by complex technologies or proprietary brands – may have reduced the opportunities for trading companies, which were arguably a more appropriate organisational form for handling large volumes of standardised and undifferentiated products. However, this effect was heavily influenced by host region-specific factors. During the inter-war years some European trading companies in Asia, Latin America and Africa built up extensive businesses as selling agents for automobile manufacturers, American as well as European, and for branded consumer products such as whisky. These arrangements continued in some markets well into the post-Second World War period and, indeed to the present day. Much research remains to be undertaken on the complex relationships between manufacturers and traders in the twentieth century. Generally the trading companies of the inter-war years manifested a continued ability to 're-invent' themselves. This was especially evident in the case of the Japanese trading companies, for whom the 1920s was a very difficult era which included the bankruptcy of a major *sogo shosha* in 1927. However, they also developed new risk management systems in this period, invested in Japanese manufacturing companies, and in the 1930s greatly expanded the commodities in which they

traded and the countries with which they traded (Sakamoto 1990; Kawabe 1990).

Since 1945

'Commerce is greater than ever', de Geer states in Chapter 7, 'but trading firms are fewer'. To some extent this encapsulates the fate of multinational trading companies in the last fifty years of the twentieth century. From the 1950s world trade, mainly between developed countries, grew rapidly as tariff barriers fell under the influence of GATT, and as regional trading blocs such as the European Union reduced trade barriers within their borders. From the 1950s also world FDI began to grow again rapidly, with new flows dominated by the United States until the late 1960s. Yet even by the 1970s world FDI stock was still far below its relative importance compared to world output in 1914, mainly because of the nationalisation of the huge foreign investments in natural resources in many developing countries, and the exclusion of foreign MNEs from large parts of the world such as the Soviet Russian and Communist China and its restriction in many developing countries. However, from the 1980s the opening of many countries and sectors to international business, and the rapid growth of FDI in services, raised the relative importance of world FDI in world output to something approaching its 1914 level (Jones 1996a). In the re-making of the global economy in the late twentieth century, as de Geer observes, trading companies did not occupy the centre stage in world trade and even FDI that their predecessors had before the First World War. Indeed, in several chapters of this book, the theme of managing decline seems to be the strongest one.

In some respects this is a misleading view. The three last chapters concern Japanese *sogo shosha* and this reflects their great and continued importance in Japanese international business and in the world economy generally. After the Second World War the Allied forces occupying Japan dissolved both the country's *zaibatsu* and *sogo shosha*. Mitsui Bussan was broken into 233 different companies. However, by the late 1950s the former *sogo shosha* had been reconstituted and joined by a number of formerly speciality textiles, steel and machinery trading companies. Ten (nine after a merger in 1977) *sogo shosha* accounted for over 80 per cent of Japan's total imports and exports during the 1960s. Although the *zaibatsu* no longer existed, the *sogo shosha* were central components of the horizontal enterprise groups or *kigyo shudan* which replaced them (Yoshino and Lifson 1986).

The *sogo shosha* were major factors behind the Japanese 'economic miracle' between the late 1950s and 1973. They were major participants in Japan's export growth, exporting the products of many small and medium-sized firms for whom they also provided credit, while searching the world for the raw industrial materials and energy resources needed for Japan's rapid industrialisation. As Yasumuro shows in Chapter 10, they also engaged in FDI in sectors other than trade, much as their European predecessors had done before the

First World War. Indeed, before the 1970s they were the major pioneers in Japanese FDI, typically investing abroad using joint ventures with other Japanese companies and – in developing countries – local partners also.

Despite their size Japanese writers and others, as Roehl observes in Chapter 11, have long predicted the demise of the *sogo shosha*. As Japan developed industries characterised by high technology and brands, some of their manufacturers undertook their own FDI in foreign distribution and later manufacture. The advantages of *sogo shosha* lay in the movement of large quantities of standardised products rather than in these new industries. Yet the *sogo shosha* were very resilient. Roehl draws attention especially to the ability of the Japanese firms to use information embedded in history to explain this resilience. The 1980s and 1990s saw 're-invention' more than demise. The *sogo shosha* sought new opportunities in third-country trade and in the emerging Chinese market. They were important in enabling Japanese firms to adjust to the appreciation of the yen in the mid-1980s. There were shifts in strategies as long-term contracts were used more in overseas resource investments. Hennart and Kryda in Chapter 12 examine the extensive FDI made by Japanese trading companies in manufacturing in the United States in this period designed to create new value chains.

The post-war economy also saw the growth of commodity trading companies on a massive scale. As the case of Metallgesellschaft showed, multinational commodity traders were of major importance in certain minerals before 1914, and in a number of other commodities this was also true. For example, Ralli were major cotton traders, while in grain Louis Dreyfus, André and Bunge and Born were major world traders. However, the real growth of these firms occurred after 1950, partly in response to the intervention of governments in many commodities through the creation of monopoly marketing boards and the nationalisation of mines and plantations in many developing countries. US firms such as Cargill entered world markets at this time and the results in some commodities were startling. In the 1970s six firms – Cargill, Continental, Louis Dreyfus, Bunge and Burn, André and Tuppfer accounted for 96 per cent of US wheat exports, 80 per cent of Argentinean wheat exports, and 90 per cent of European wheat exports (Chalmin 1985; Michie 1996). The sales of the US company Cargill soared from $US1 billion to $42 billion between 1960 and 1990. During the 1970s the firm made large grain sales to the Soviet Union and it diversified into the products and trade of many other foodstuffs, food-processing operations and steel and coal companies (Broehl 1992, 1998).

The special role of Switzerland in the post-war history of commodity trading is discussed by Guex in Chapter 8. André was one of the world's biggest grain traders in the 1990s, perhaps in second place to Cargill. However, Switzerland's use as a base for foreign-owned companies or entrepreneurs was also striking. During the 1950s Cargill centred its international operations in a Geneva-based subsidiary, Tradax. Even more striking was the remarkable growth of Marc Rich, founded in Canton Zug in 1974, to become twenty years later one of the world's largest traders in crude oil and petroleum markets, aluminium and alumina and a variety of agricultural commodities, including being the largest exporter of EU grain to eastern Europe.

The post-1945 experience of the older European trading companies discussed in this book was not one of spectacular growth. In Latin America, Africa and Asia the combined effects of decolonisation, the growth of economic nationalism, government restrictions and the emergence of powerful locally owned competitors was to create great problems for their traditional businesses and necessitate new strategies. From the 1960s the most popular were diversification into other activities and into other regions, including developed countries. Unlike the *sogo shosha*, which had investments in Japanese manufacturing companies as well as belonging to *kigyo shudan*, the European trading companies had few if any assets in their home economies. The outstanding exception was Unilever's ownership of the United Africa Company, and even in this instance the latter operated until the mid-1980s as a virtually independent company with an arms-length relationship to Unilever (Fieldhouse 1994: 3–9). Unfortunately the core competencies of these firms often did not lend themselves to diversification, even in their own home economies, and by the 1990s the survivors had often re-focused on their core business, and/or original host region.

The Dutch trading companies discussed by Sluyterman faced the problems of re-adjustment especially acutely following the independence of Indonesia in 1949 and the subsequent growth of hostility to Dutch business leading to the nationalisation in 1957 of Dutch capital. The Dutch firms tried to transfer their expertise to Africa, without lasting success, and then invested in manufacturing back in the Netherlands. This proved an unsuccessful option for companies such as Hagemeyer. Ironically, a large equity stake was taken in this company in the mid-1980s by a Hong Kong company with a substantial Indonesian shareholding, an arrangement which continued until the Asian financial crisis in 1997/98. By the late 1990s Hagemeyer had re-focused on trading and might even be considered a 'pure' trading company by that stage.

There were many parallels elsewhere in Europe. D'Almeida-Topor discusses the case of the French trading companies in Africa. There was a concentration of activity in larger companies and a withdrawal from the general trading which had featured in their business in earlier decades. The French trading companies withdrew from marketing local produce and focused their importing on consumer products such as automobiles for which they could add value, such as the provision of after-sales service. They also invested in manufacturing in the African host economies. The continued French political influence in many Francophone African states after Independence no doubt facilitated the continued presence of the trading companies.

In contrast to the Dutch and French examples, Greenhill and Miller show that the British trading companies active in Latin America passed into oblivion after the Second World War. It would appear that the management of these firms were very seriously trapped in a mental outlook more appropriate for earlier generations, and were unable to make sufficient adjustments to new circumstances. They did not want, or were not able, to make the capital commitment to become more deeply involved in their local host economies, which included some of the Latin American countries most prone to economic nationalism and currency depreciation.

As Greenhill and Miller remark, there do seem to have been alternatives to the fate of the British traders in Latin America. US traders such as W R Grace survived and continued to evolve, in Grace's case into a speciality chemicals company. A number of other European trading companies continued in the region. An example was the Dutch-owned Ceteco, which is now mainly active in consumer goods and is part of Hagemeyer. There were also British trading companies active in other regions which continued to 're-invent' themselves. An example was the Inchcape group, the successor of the trading and shipping interests built up by William Mackinnon. In 1958 the amorphous collection of shipping and trading companies was merged into the single firm of Inchcape & Co. The firm's shipping and most of its Indian operations were sold off, and a series of acquisitions of British trading companies active in Asia and also elsewhere repositioned the company as a European general trading company, with specialisation in motor vehicles, soft drinks, consumer and industrial products and office equipment, plus shipping services. In 1996 it had a turnover of over $US9 billion, and employed 35,000 people in 72 countries. Its activities ranged from being the world's largest independent importer and distributor of motor vehicles – representing 37 of the world's car manufacturers – to being a Coca Cola bottling franchise in Russia and Chile. However, such diversity was unfashionable with the British capital markets. During 1998 the firm began the process of splitting itself into three parts: a global car distribution business headquartered and quoted in Britain; a South American bottling business based and quoted in Chile; and an Asian and Middle Eastern trading company quoted and based in Asia.

Equally impressive was the post-war renewal and growth of the British trading companies in China, Jardine Matheson and Swires. The Pacific War followed by the Communist Revolution in 1949 left them with little of their business intact and appeared disastrous on a far worse scale than experienced by the British companies in Latin America. Yet their Hong Kong bases became fortuitous as East Asia began to undergo rapid economic growth. From the 1970s Jardine Matheson invested widely in Asian financial services, motor trading, engineering, property, hotels and food retailing, as well as less successfully in Africa and in Britain, where its investment in the shipping and construction conglomerate Trafalgar House in 1992 was sold within five years. By the mid-1990s its turnover was $US11.6 billion and the firm had refocused sharply on Asia, where its main activities were financial services, supermarkets, consumer marketing, engineering and construction, motor trading, property and hotels. Swires established Cathay Pacific Airways after the Second World War which became one of Asia's major airlines, and invested in Australia in the 1950s in freezer transport and warehousing. It re-entered general trading in Hong Kong in 1946, and invested in a range of industries in the British colony including semi-conductor assembly and bottling. Its investment in bottling in Hong Kong led to the growth of Swires into one of the largest bottlers of Coca Cola in both Asia and the United States. By the mid-1990s Swires was a large business group employing over 90,000 people, mostly in Asia-Pacific, but with considerable business in Australia and the United States, and with a portfolio of businesses involved in trading, aviation, marine services, property and manufacturing.

The importance of Japanese trading companies and the renewal and growth of British trading companies such as Jardines and Swires in part suggest that, at least in the post-1945 period, there has been a strong region-specific aspect to the growth of trading companies. Asia, especially East and South East Asia, appears to have provided an especially favourable environment for their continued operation. Significantly Korea was another country in the region where general trading companies grew rapidly in importance from the 1970s. The reasons for this are a matter of speculation but must be related to the high rates of growth, the export orientation of many of the regional economies, and the existence of major free-market entrepots led by Hong Kong and Singapore. This may suggest that as economies are liberalised and government intervention declines in the emerging economies of Latin America, Africa and Eastern Europe, there will be new opportunities for established trading companies or for new types of trading firm.

Explaining trading companies

There are a number of interrelated theoretical questions concerning multinational trading companies. First, and most basically, why are such firms used in trade intermediation? Second, why do they exhibit a constant tendency to diversify? Third, what are their competencies, and how are they able to re-invent themselves? The chapters in this book contain many insights on all three questions.

The answer to the first question involves establishing the conditions where buyers find it more effective to buy and sellers to sell through intermediaries rather than to search directly for contracting partners. Trading companies reduce search, negotiation and transaction costs and seem likely to be employed at least initially when the risks of international trade are high. Consequently, nineteenth-century Western Europeans traded with Latin America, Asia and Africa initially using trading companies because their markets and business cultures were unfamiliar, even if many countries fell under European imperial control. For nineteenth-century Japan, all foreign countries were alien, so trading companies were used to trade with all areas. Subsequently the information acquired by trading companies about the cultures and languages of the countries they dealt with became a major asset with little incremental cost to repeated use, and trading companies were able to offer such information at a much lower cost than individual new firms could obtain them.

Casson in Chapter 2 identifies the obstacles to trade, which relate especially to lack of information and lack of trust. The transactions costs caused by these obstacles can be reduced by the use of intermediaries such as trading companies to link buyers and sellers, though the efficiency of using trading companies depends crucially on the characteristics of the product and the volume of trade. For Casson, it is the reselling rather than broking function that holds the key to understanding the rationale for multinational trading companies; the resellers access to market intelligence enables it to engage in profitable speculation.

Entrepreneurship and speculation feature in both Casson's chapter and many of the empirical chapters. As Casson argues, establishing a trading company is an entrepreneurial activity involving taking 'a gamble that buyers and sellers really do want to trade in the product, and that they would rather do it through a middleman than directly between themselves' (Chapter 2, p. 24, this volume). This entrepreneurial aspect is very evident in the career of, say, William Mackinnon and the other nineteenth-century founders of trading companies. They often operated at the boundaries of the international economy and at the frontiers of empires. The nineteenth-century trading companies were exposed to an continual range of risks – political, exchange rate, commodity price – at a period when information flows were poor because of the state of communications and transport. These risks provided both the danger and the chance of high rewards. In trading, the relation between risk-taking and speculation is ill-defined, for judgements about movements in prices and exchange rates are often at the heart of the business. Trading companies are opportunistic, forever searching for new niches to provide chances for intermediation, and relying on – hopefully – accurate and privileged information and knowledge to give them an edge. Not surprisingly, excessive or ill-judged speculation, or unauthorised speculation by staff, ended the existence of many firms.

The theme of diversification is evident throughout this book. As Casson suggests, standard transaction costs theory can explain diversification into the production, transportation and distribution of the products they traded. Risk reductions and problems of quality control arising from information asymmetry and opportunism are especially important. However, trading companies have also historically integrated into activities unrelated to their principal activities, and this can be related to the public good property of the information they possess. For example, the Dutch trading companies in Indonesia and French companies in Africa possessed region-specific information which represented indivisible assets that reduced the set-up costs of entering entirely new business ventures, so the marginal cost of entry into new activities was low. Once established in a location, trading companies have displayed an almost universal tendency to launch out from their original business into other lines of activity.

The issue of diversification is of central concern to Hennart and Kryda in Chapter 12 who argue that it arises from the central characteristics of their business. Trading companies put buyers and sellers into contact, and as a result their business is always threatened by the possibility that their clients will deal directly with each other. In order to avert this possibility, trading companies can take equity stakes in both suppliers and customers to prevent being dropped or invest in the distribution channels used by buyers and sellers. The promotion of 'free-standing' companies by nineteenth-century British trading companies was a vivid illustration of the former strategy. The new firms were committed by contracts and other means to use the facilities of the parent trading companies.

The fact that their business is always at risk also provides an incentive for trading companies to invest in entirely new activities to create new value added chains. As Hennart and Kryda note, this pattern can be seen in the nineteenth century when European trading companies established rubber plantations in South East Asia, and the model can be applied to many of their pioneering investments of that era. As these authors show, the strategies continue to be followed by contemporary Japanese trading companies, which · invest in both mature and emerging value chains. Yasumuro demonstrates a similar phenomenon, the *sogo shosha* undertaking FDI to create markets. When these markets were created, the trading company divested, and moved to another investment.

The chapters presented here show the creation of both large international businesses and of businesses which 're-invented' themselves from generation to generation, to such an extent that some firms might look radically different from themselves a generation previously. This raises the question of the competencies of trading companies. Analysis of the 'ownership advantages' of multinational manufacturing firms has often pointed to their management and organisation, including their ability to innovate and possession of technological advantages. Following the US business historian Alfred D. Chandler, Jr, the employment of professional management and managerial hierarchies has been seen as essential (Chandler 1990).

The competence of trading companies seems to have been rather different. Japanese *sogo shosha* were noted for their early employment of professional managers and this led the Japanese business historian Shin'ichi Yonekawa to argue that merchants could only grow into general trading companies if they became 'modern managerial enterprises' (Yonekawa 1987: xi). However, what is striking is the importance of continuous family or personal ownership of trading companies, from Sweden's A Johnson to commodity traders such as Marc Rich or Cargill, the latter still owned into the 1990s by the Cargill and MacMillan families. Family ownership might work better in trading than in other sectors because of the variable and risky nature of the business which might alarm a large body of shareholders. Families with a strong identity and vision, and able to deal effectively with problems of generational succession, might be better equipped to compete in such a business than managerial firms, except managerial firms in Japan which possessed stable shareholders within the context of wider enterprise groups. Families differ in their competencies, however. Family ownership and resultant excessive conservatism appears as one of the serious handicaps of British trading companies in South America in the 1950s and 1960s. Yet in Asia, Jardine Matheson and Swires remain to the present day ultimately controlled by the Keswick and Swire families.

It is evident that information and knowledge are at the heart of the competencies of trading companies. They held knowledge about products and regions which was their main asset. It could also be a liability if, as in the case of the European trading companies in the post-colonial period, they sought to diversify geographically when in fact their competence was heavily region-specific. Roehl in Chapter 11 examines the circumstances in which history can either restrict or provide competitive advantages for firms. The importance of information might help to explain why particular ethnic groups – Scots, Greeks, Jews – have featured so strongly in their histories, for the trading companies operated within wider commercial networks which acted as sources of information and business. The successful functioning of such networks rested on high levels of trust which were facilitated by ethnicity.

A striking feature of many trading companies also has been their search for access rather than control. Unlike 'classic' manufacturing multinationals which until recently sought to integrate and control, trading companies have traditionally had more flexible boundaries. The use of contracts and minority equity holdings, and joint ventures pervades their histories, because they were seeking access to trade flows rather than full control of all the value chains. The ability to manage relationships, and to find new relationships, was a crucial area of competence for these firms.

Since the nineteenth-century multinational trading companies have been major forces within international business. They have moved both trade and capital across borders, and through their diversification strategies they have been investors in resources and manufacturing also. The significance of these trading firms has been disguised in part by their often complex corporate structures as well as their predilection for privacy, and in part by the preoccupation of academics with manufacturing, rather than services. However, at the end of this century multinational traders remain important, and the *sogo shosha* and the commodity traders persist as corporate giants. This is a type of multinational business whose history, functions and significance now merit attention.

Acknowledgements

This chapter draws heavily on the discussions during the Reading Conference in September 1997. Keetie Sluyterman made very helpful comments on an earlier draft.

References

Bonin, H. (1987) *C. F.A. O. Cent Ans de Compétition*, Paris: Economica.

Broehl, W. G. (1992) *Cargill. Trading the World's Grain*, Hanover: University Press of New England.

—— (1998) *Cargill. Going Global*, Hanover: University Press of New England.

Brown, R. A. (1994) *Capital and Entrepreneurship in South East Asia*, London: Macmillan.

Carlos, A. M. and Nicholas, S. (1988) "'Giants of an Earlier Capitalism". The chartered trading companies as modern multinationals', *Business History Review*, 62 (3): 398–419.

Chalmin, P. (1985) *Negociants et Chargeurs*, Paris: Economica.

—— (1987) 'The rise of international commodity trading companies in Europe in the nineteenth century', in Yonekawa, S. and Yoshihara, H. (eds) *Business History of General Trading Companies*, Tokyo: University of Tokyo Press.

Chandler, A. D., Jr (1990) *Scale and Scope*, Cambridge, Mass: Harvard University Press.

Chapman, S. (1992) *Merchant Enterprise in Britain*, Cambridge: Cambridge University Press.

Cho, D.-S. (1987) *The General Trading Company*, Lexington/Mass: Lexington Books.

Clayton, L. A. (1985) *Grace. W R Grace & Co*, Ottawa, Illinois: Jameson Books.

Coquery-Vidrovitch, C. (1975) 'L'impact des intérêts coloniaux: SCOA and CFAO dans l'Ouest Africain, 1910–1965', *Journal of African History*, 16 (4): 595–621.

Drabble, J. H. and Drake, P. J. (1981) 'The British Agency houses in Malaysia: survival in a changing world', *Journal of South East Asian Studies*, 12: 297–328.

Dunning, J. H. (1983) 'Changes in the level and structure of international production: the last one hundred years', in Casson, M. (ed.) *The Growth of International Business*, London: George Allen & Unwin.

Enderwick, P. (1989) (ed.) *Multinational Service Firms*, London: Routledge.

Fieldhouse, D. K. (1994) *Merchant Capital and Economic Decolonization*, Oxford: Clarendon Press.

Harrisons and Crosfield (1944) *One Hundred Years of East Indian Merchants: Harrisons & Crosfield 1844–1943*, London: Harrisons & Crosfield.

Houston, T. and Dunning, J. H. (1976) *UK Industry Abroad*, London: Financial Times.

Hunt, W. G. G. (1960) *Heirs of Great Adventure: Balfour Williamson 1901–1951*, London: Balfour Williamson.

Jones, G. (1996a) *The Evolution of International Business*, London: Routledge.

—— (1996b) 'Diversification strategies and corporate governance in trading companies: Anglo-Japanese comparisons since the late nineteenth century', *Business and Economic History*, 25 (2): 103–18.

Jones, S. R. H. and Ville, S. P. (1996) 'Efficient transactions or rent-seeking monopolists? The rationale for early chartered trading companies', *Journal of Economic History*, 56: 898–915.

Kawabe, N. (1990) 'Overseas activities and their organisation', in Yonekawa, S. (ed.) *General Trading Companies*, Tokyo: United Nations University Press.

Keswick, M. (ed.) (1982) *The Thistle and the Jade*, London: Octopus.

Michie, R. C. (1996) 'The international trade in food and the City of London since 1850', *Journal of European Economic History*, 25 (2): 369–404.

Minoglou, I. P. and Louri, H. (1997) 'Diaspora entrepreneurial networks in the Black Sea and Greece, 1870–1917', *Journal of European Economic History*, 26 (I): 69–103.

Misra, M. (1994) 'Entrepreneurial decline and the end of the Empire', unpublished D Phil thesis, University of Oxford.

Sakamoto, M. (1990) 'Diversification: the case of Mitsui Bussan', in Yonekawa, S. (ed.) *General Trading Companies*, Tokyo: United Nations University Press.

Sugiyama, S. (1987) 'A British trading firm in the Far East: John Swire & Sons, 1867–1914', in Yonekawa, S. and Yoshihara, H. (eds) *Business History of General Trading Companies*, Tokyo: University of Tokyo Press.

Svedberg, P (1978) 'The portfolio – direct composition of private foreign investment in 1914 revisited', *Economic Journal*, 80: 763–70.

United Nations (1997) *World Investment Report 1997*, New York: United Nations.

Wilkins, M. (1970) *The Emergence of Multinational Enterprise*, Cambridge, Mass: Harvard University Press.

—— (1986) 'Defining a firm: history and theory', in Hertner, P. and Jones, G. (eds) *Multinationals: Theory and History*, Aldershot: Gower.

—— (1988) 'The free-standing company, 1870–1914: an important type of British foreign direct investment', *Economic History Review*, 41 (2): 259–85.

Yonekawa, S. (1987) 'Introduction', in Yonekawa, S. and Yoshihara, H. (eds) *Business History of General Trading Companies*, Tokyo: University of Tokyo Press.

—— (ed.) (1990) *General Trading Companies*, Tokyo: United Nations University Press.

Yonekawa, S. and Yoshihara, H. (1987) (eds) *Business History of General Trading Companies*, Tokyo: University of Tokyo Press.

Yoshihara, H. (1987) 'Some questions on Japan's sogo shosha', in Yonekawa, S. and Yoshihara, H. (eds) *Business History of General Trading Companies*, Tokyo: University of Tokyo Press.

Yoshino, M.Y. and Lifson, T. B. (1986) *The Invisible Link: Japan's Sogo Shosha and Organisation of Trade*, Cambridge, Mass: MIT Press.

2 The economic analysis of multinational trading companies

Mark Casson

The term 'trading company' signifies companies as diverse as the Dutch and English chartered trading companies of the seventeenth century and after (Carlos and Nicholas 1988), the numerous private trading companies that were active in Asia and Africa during the nineteenth century, and the Japanese trading companies that rose to prominence in the first half of the twentieth century (Jones 1996). Trading companies have played a prominent role in the development of colonies and other dependent areas. Despite their historical importance, however, relatively little research has been done on the theory of the trading firm (Casson 1997, Chapter 9). This chapter attempts to remedy this deficiency. It is structured in three parts. The first six sections develop a static theory of the trading firm. The next three sections discuss the dynamics of the firm, focusing on the pattern of growth and diversification. The chapter concludes with an application to colonial trading companies in the final three sections.

The theory of trade

Trading is a central issue in economics. In neoclassical economic theory, trade is a major source of efficiency gains (Kemp 1964). Trade in finished products allows consumers who possess goods to which they attach little value to exchange them for goods they value more. Trade in labour services allows workers to specialise according to their personal comparative advantage, selling the goods they produce in return for the goods they wish to consume. This promotes a division of labour between industries. Trade also promotes a division of labour within industries – for example, trade in intermediate products promotes specialisation between different stages of production.

The centrality of trade in neoclassical theory makes it surprising that there is no neoclassical theory of the trading company. The reason is that simple neoclassical theory ignores transaction costs. In the absence of transaction costs, there is no real need for institutions such as firms. Workers can trade directly with consumers, and consumers can trade directly with each other. Workers who wish to collaborate in production negotiate directly with each other. In each case, there is no need for a firm to act as 'go-between'.

Table 2.1 Transaction costs incurred in overcoming obstacles to trade

Obstacle	Transaction cost component
Lack of contact	Search and advertising costs
Lack of specification	Display, demonstration
No agreement on price	Price setting
No trust in delivery of specified good	Monitor quantity, quality, punctuality

Source: Casson 1982, Table 9.1.

This changes completely when transaction costs are introduced (Williamson 1975; Buckley and Casson 1976). Table 2.1 summarises the main impediments to trade. The obstacles to trade are shown in the left-hand column, and the means of overcoming them are shown on the right. Real resources must be expended to overcome these obstacles. The resulting expenditures are known as transaction costs. (It is not normally sensible to overcome each obstacle completely – it is better to operate at the margin where further gains from trade are just outweighed by the extra costs involved. The unexploited gains from trade are added to the expenditures described above to obtain an overall measure of transaction cost.)

Most obstacles to trade arise from either ignorance or lack of trust, or a combination of the two. Ignorance is overcome by providing information, while trust is generated by honest individuals building up a reputation. Some individuals are more honest, better informed and enjoy a greater reputation than others. Overall transaction costs are reduced when these individuals specialise in overcoming obstacles to trade on behalf of other people. They act as intermediators, linking buyers and sellers who could not otherwise trade easily between themselves.

Intermediation is a very general principle, and in consequence organised intermediation takes many different institutional forms. In political life, a government intermediates between its citizens, and in social life a leader intermediates between the members of his group. In economic life the principal intermediator is the firm. A firm intermediates in markets by making contact with both buyers and sellers, setting prices, and overseeing the flow of goods between them. This may be termed *market-making intermediation*. A firm that specialises in market-making intermediation may be defined as a *trading firm*.

Intermediation

Intermediation is usually conducted on a recurrent basis. When there are large numbers of buyers and sellers, an intermediator is required as an information hub. The intermediator incurs the costs of searching out and synthesising information on current supply and demand. He then quotes a uniform buying price to sellers, and a uniform selling price to buyers. Each buyer and seller gets a better deal than he could by searching for himself.

In a volatile environment demand and supply conditions are constantly changing, as are the plans of the individuals with whom the intermediator deals. The information collected by the intermediator must therefore be updated on a regular basis. The costs of this routine can be reduced by implementing a division of labour between the people involved in this process. The intermediator therefore establishes an organisation for this purpose.

A trading company requires premises in which to store inventories. Suppliers typically deliver larger lot sizes than customers wish to buy in, so that inventory must be held for break-bulk purposes. If customers expect delivery on demand, without placing orders in advance, then additional inventory must be held to cover peaks and troughs in demand. These peaks and troughs can result either from random fluctuations in individual demands, or from systematic factors – including predictable factors such as seasonal fluctuations and unpredictable factors such as changes in fashion. Inventory may also be held for purposes of display. Even if customers are supplied only on special order, inventory may still be held in a shop or exhibition area so that customers can see for themselves what it is that they are going to get.

All of these costs are covered out of gross profit earned on the intermediation of trade. If the gross profit exceeds the average cost incurred in intermediation then the company earns a net profit, and if it does not then it makes a net loss. Establishing a trading company is an entrepreneurial activity. The salary expended on sales personnel, and the rent paid for warehouses, shops and offices, cannot be recovered if the volume of trade is too low. The founder of a trading company takes a gamble that buyers and sellers really do want to trade in the product, and that they would rather do it through a middleman than directly between themselves. Only if the volume of trade is sufficiently large, and the profit per unit sufficiently high, will the gamble pay off.

A typology of trading firms: brokers *versus* resellers

There are two main kinds of trading firm: the broker and the reseller. The broker does not assume ownership of the product in which he deals, whereas the reseller does. Thus a retailer who buys from a seller (a manufacturer, say) and resells to a buyer (an individual consumer, for example) assumes ownership of the good whilst he passes it on. On the other hand, a broker who finds a buyer in return for a fixed fee paid by the seller is not a reseller because the good remains the property of the seller throughout.

This important distinction is summarised in Figure 2.1. Intermediation is shown by a black square. Brokerage is illustrated at the top of the figure and reselling at the bottom. The product flow is represented by an arrow. The colour of the arrow represents the ownership of the product. A pale grey colour represents the producer and a dark grey colour, the consumer. It can be seen that the broker supervises the change of ownership from producer to consumer, while the reseller actually becomes the owner of the product *en route*.

Reselling involves greater risks than brokerage. The reseller not only assumes the risk of physical damage to the good whilst it is in his possession, but also carries the risk that the value of the good may change between the time at which he buys it and the time at which he sells it on. The greater the lag between purchase and resale, the greater this risk becomes. It is possible to control this risk, but only to a limited extent. When it is difficult for the reseller to find a buyer who requires delivery right away, it may still be possible for him to arrange a forward sale. A forward sale fixes the price in advance of delivery and thereby eliminates the risk relating to price

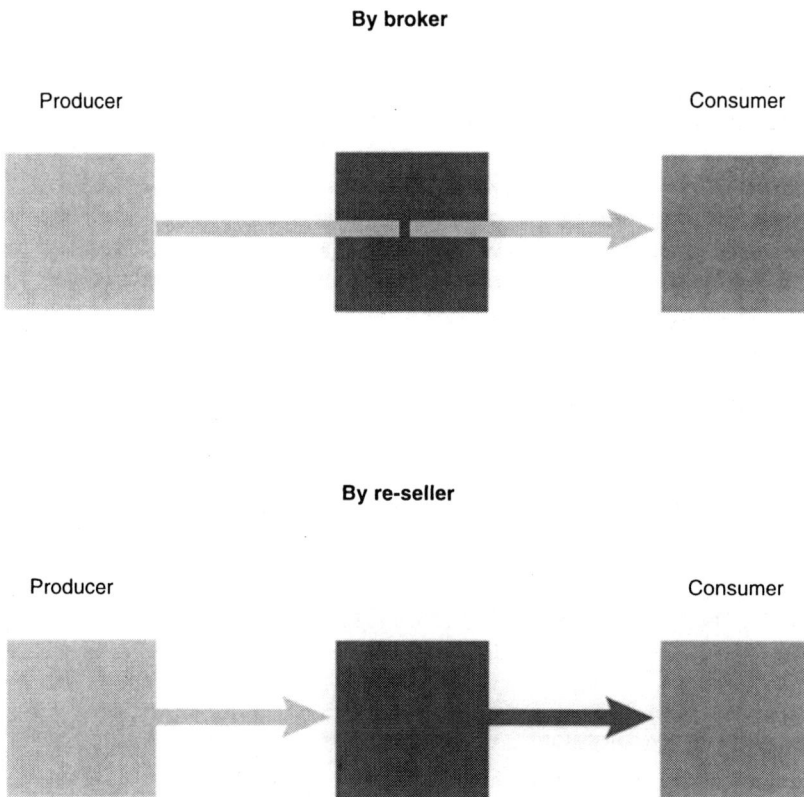

By broker

Producer   Consumer

By re-seller

Producer   Consumer

Figure 2.1 Market-making intermediation in schematic form

fluctuations after the contract has been made. Forward contracts have limited scope as an instrument of risk-reduction, however, because they are often difficult to enforce. In practice, therefore, resellers remain exposed to significant price-related risk.

A reseller must form a judgement about whether a good is likely to appreciate or depreciate in value. He is obliged, in effect, to speculate upon movements in its price. He needs to obtain as much information as possible that is relevant to the future value of the good. Once this information has been acquired, it pays the reseller to exploit it fully. The reseller therefore holds inventory specifically for speculation. He 'buys cheap' when he believes that there is a temporary glut of supplies, and hoards the product until demand recovers and he can 'sell dear'. The success of this strategy depends not only on the quality of information that can be collected, but also on the durability of the product. The more durable the product, the cheaper it is to store for a long period of time, and the more economical it is to pursue a speculative strategy.

Brokers are also exposed to market risks if they operate on a 'no sale, no fee' basis. But because they do not own inventory, they are not exposed to risks on account of the movement of price. The main differences between a broker and a reseller are summarised in Table 2.2.

Because a reseller assumes more risk than a broker does, he requires lower aversion to risk. Different sorts of people will therefore be attracted to different forms of intermediation. People who thrive on excitement, or possess inherited wealth, are most likely to become resellers, while the less adventurous, and the less well off, are likely to become brokers instead.

A reseller also requires a greater capacity for handling information. The effect of formal education is ambiguous in this respect – education enhances the ability to process information, but also biases processing towards the use of conventional formal models which may be of limited use where speculation is concerned. In cases where speculation based on quick untutored wit outperforms the use of complicated formal models, reselling may be discouraged by formal education.

Cultural factors may also be important. For example, religious principles

Table 2.2 Two main methods of market-making intermediation

	Brokerage	*Resale*
Ownership by intermediator?	No	Yes
Intermediator bears risks of matching	Yes (no deal – no fee)	Yes (no margin earned)
Intermediator bears risk of physical loss	No	Yes
Intermediator speculates on price	No	Yes

that condemn gambling will tend to increase risk-aversion, and thereby discourage reselling. On the other hand, a fatalistic belief in divine providence may reduce risk-aversion and so encourage reselling instead.

The nature of the trading environment is important too. Consistently successful speculation by resellers requires them to have privileged access to information. This could be raw information, gathered directly at source, or information synthesised from second-hand sources (such as personal contacts) using judgement that is unique. Some markets have many different sources of volatility, so that there are always gaps in other people's information that a speculator can exploit. Other markets have fewer sources of volatility, so that most people are reasonably well informed, and speculation is therefore more difficult. The availability of mass communication is also a factor. The wider the range of the media (such as the business press), and the cheaper is public access to posts and telecommunications, the more difficult it becomes to speculate successfully. There is no one left to speculate against when everyone has identical information. If there is a long-term secular decline in the cost of communication, therefore, it follows that speculation based on privileged information becomes more difficult to sustain. This suggests that as communications improve, brokerage will tend to drive out speculation.

In practice the same premises may be used for both brokerage and reselling. Thus a reseller that finds it has spare office personnel, or unused warehouse capacity, may diversify into brokerage, whilst a broker with unused capacity may decide to undertake reselling as a sideline. Because the capital requirements of reselling are greater than those of brokerage, some firms may begin as brokers and then develop into resellers when they have accumulated sufficient funds. The accumulation of trading expertise through brokerage may also encourage a firm to diversify into reselling later. Conversely, established resellers faced with intensifying competition from more entrepreneurial entrants may retreat into brokerage later on.

The international dimension

The focus of this chapter is on multinational trading companies (MTCs). According to a commonly accepted definition, a firm is multinational when it owns and controls activities in two or more countries. The rationale for an MTC lies in the intermediation of international trade. Where international trade is concerned, the procurement of a good for export is carried out in one country and its distribution as an import is carried out in another. If both the procurement and distribution activities are carried out by the same firm, then that firm is an MTC. An MTC may be either a broker or a reseller. The two possibilities are illustrated schematically in Figure 2.2.

Intermediation is resolved into three distinct activities in each case: exporting, shipping and importing. A typical brokerage arrangement is shown at the top of the figure. The firm organises exporting for the producer and at the same time organises the importing for the overseas customer. It oversees

Multinational brokerage

| Production | Export brokerage | Shipping | Import brokerage | Consumption |

Multinational reselling

| Production | Export procurement | Shipping | Import distribution | Consumption |

Key — Activity owned by trading company

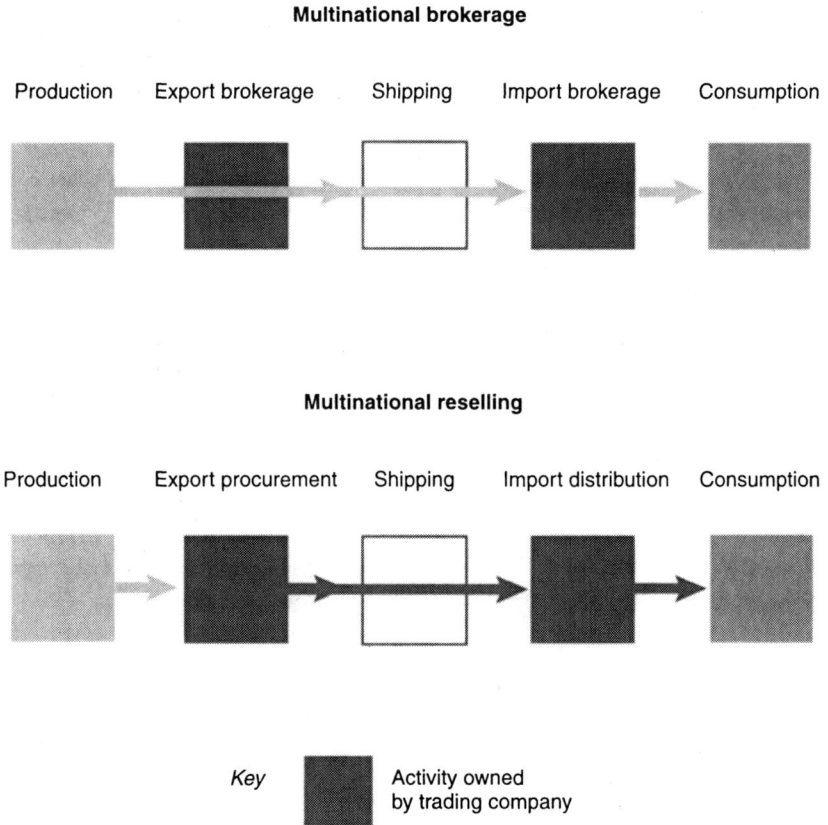

Figure 2.2 Schematic illustrations of pure multinational intermediation

the change of ownership of the product when it is imported. Activities owned and controlled by the MTC are shown in black. Ownership by the producer is indicated by light grey and ownership by the customer by dark grey, as in Figure 2.1. Reselling is illustrated at the bottom of the figure. The firm procures exports, ships them and then distributes them on its own account in the export market.

An international reseller could, in principle, delegate the procurement and resale of his goods to brokers in each country. The reseller would specialise in making speculative judgements about which products were likely to appreciate in price, and leave the physical handling of the products to the brokers instead. In this case the international reseller would not become an MTC. The more heterogeneous the product, however, the more problematic this strategy becomes. Specifying exactly what kind of product to buy becomes difficult. Lags in communication mean that the execution of orders by the brokers may be slow, and so short-term speculative opportunities may be lost. The broker may begin to free ride on the speculator, passing on 'tips' to other people, or buying on his own account. He may also use his opportunity to inspect the product to reserve the best-quality items for himself.

The volume of trade must also be taken into account. If reselling involves only occasional small deals, then there may be insufficient business to keep a clerk fully occupied, or a warehouse reasonably full. In this case delegation to a broker is sensible, since an independent broker can be kept fully occupied with the business of several different customers. Otherwise the reseller may as well carry out the broking functions for himself. Unless the product is homogeneous, therefore, or the consignments small and irregular, resellers will normally handle their consignments for themselves.

Now consider the broker. A broker that procures a product in one country does not necessarily distribute it in the other. There are two main reasons for a broker to become an MTC. The first is that a complete service can be offered to customers in the export and import trades. Transaction costs are reduced when there is only one broker instead of two. A second reason is that the broker may have some transferable skill in the organisation of brokerage. If this skill is difficult to license or franchise, then it is advantageous for the broker to exploit it internally by establishing branches abroad instead. In the former case the broker will tend to establish only operations that are linked to one another by major flows of trade, whereas in the latter case he may establish branches that do very little trade with each other at all.

In practice, neither of these reasons seems particularly compelling. Unless a broker is already familiar with a foreign country, it is unlikely that he can be of much help to his customers there. The overall quality of his 'complete service' may therefore be rather poor. The administration of broking is fairly straightforward, and it seems unlikely that special office procedures could be devised which would provide the company with a significant advantage over other firms. The conclusion must be that reselling holds the key to why most intermediators become MTCs. It is the firm's access to market intelligence, and its consequent ability to speculate, that normally induces the firm to become an MTC. In other words, the *integrated reseller* is the most important type of MTC.

Integration into shipping

The reselling arrangement illustrated in Figure 2.2 highlights the way that even an integrated reseller loses control over the product whilst it is being shipped. To achieve complete control over intermediation, the firm would need to integrate into shipping too.

For example, a trading company involved in the export of fruit may decide that to prevent the bruising of the fruit, and avoid its premature ripening, it will carry all its fruit in its own refrigerated ships. This is because the company lacks confidence in an ordinary contract for the carriage of fruit, which gives it insufficient redress against a negligent carrier. It is not interested in carrying fruit for other companies because it wishes to build a unique reputation for premium quality.

There is one major obstacle to this strategy, however, and that is that few consignments are sufficiently large to keep an entire ship fully occupied. Using a larger number of smaller ships, each dedicated to use by a single firm, would increase costs because ships, being floating containers, exhibit significant economies of scale. Sharing the ownership of a ship with other firms is another solution, but disagreements may arise over who should have priority for their cargoes when capacity is in short supply.

In many cases the best solution is for firms to own ships which do not necessarily carry their own cargoes. This arrangement does not afford operational integration in the shipping of individual consignments, but it nevertheless provides a useful service. Because ships are durable assets with long lags in their construction, the short-run supply of shipping is highly inelastic. Where the shipping of perishable products is concerned, demand is inelastic too. The combination of inelastic demand and inelastic supply creates substantial volatility in shipping rates. By owning its own shipping, an MTC hedges against such risks. Although hedging can be effected through forward contracts too, the transactions costs are often high, particularly where organised charter markets are missing. Integration into shipping means that when shipping rates rise, the profits of intermediation are reduced, but profits on shipping increase to offset this. Conversely, when shipping rates fall, the profits of intermediation rise, but profits on shipping fall. Thus integration into shipping stabilises the profits of the firm, and reduces the risk of bankruptcy.

Integration into production

Shipping is only one of several activities into which an MTC may diversify. It is important to distinguish between those MTCs which are multinational by virtue of their trading activities, and those which are only multinational because of the other activities they have diversified into. The former may be termed pure MTCs and the latter hybrid MTCs.

Two examples of hybrid MTCs are shown in Figure 2.3. The top half of the figure illustrates a reseller that has integrated into shipping, but which still procures its cargoes from an independent producer. The bottom half of the figure shows what happens when the same company integrates backwards into production as well. It can be seen that it is quite difficult to distinguish between a multinational reseller that has integrated backwards into production, and a producer that has integrated forward into marketing its exports.

Integration into production is more likely to take place under reselling than under broking. This is because the reseller is exposed to risks connected with the volatility of the price that he has to pay and the quality of the goods he receives. The reseller may take over the producer so that he can control the

Integration of trading and shipping

Production	Export procurement	Shipping	Import marketing	Consumption

Integration of production, trading and shipping

Production	Export procurement	Shipping	Import marketing	Consumption

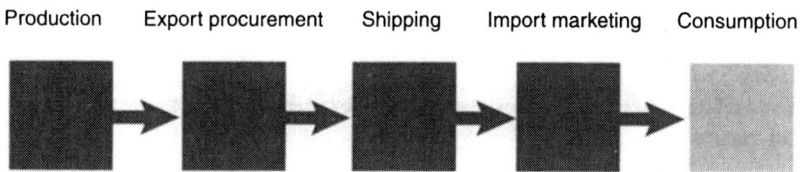

Key — Activity owned by trading company

Figure 2.3 Schematic diagrams of hybrid multinational trading

quality of the goods at first hand. Likewise the reseller faces volatility in downstream demand. He also needs to convince the customer that the quality he delivers is indeed as good as he says that it is. One method is to reassure the customer by taking over his business, so that the reseller bears all the risks connected with the quality of his supplies. Concern over quality may therefore generate both backward and forward integration.

Quality assurance is not the only motive for vertical integration, of course. Table 2.3 summarises the main incentives for vertical integration between intermediation and production. The incentives are not exactly the same as those that apply to vertical integration within a production process itself. Previous discussion of vertical integration in production has tended to assume that bilateral monopoly prevails (Williamson 1985). The theory of intermediation shows, however, that vertical integration can still occur where bilateral monopoly does not exist. Thus an intermediator could integrate into several upstream plants and several downstream plants at the same time, and organise a quite elaborate internal market between them.

In general, pure trading companies are far easier to identify than are hybrid ones. Pure trading companies are a distinctive phenomenon because they are not involved in transport, manufacturing, primary production, or retailing. Hybrid trading companies are not so distinct because they can usually be described in some alternative way. The fact that they allow of an alternative description is unfortunate, but unavoidable. On the other hand, it is reassuring to know that this ambiguity over the terminology is not in fact a sign of any ambiguity in the underlying theory, but is in fact predicted by it. It shows that where trading companies are concerned, it is a mistake to become fixated on questions of terminology. The substantive issues are why some companies remain pure MTCs whilst others become hybrid, and why the hybrid companies take the forms they do.

Diversification by trading companies: product, country and route

The discussion has so far focused upon trade in a single type of good, but it is clearly possible for a trading company to handle several different types of good at once. In some cases all the trade may go in the same direction, with

Table 2.3 Integration of production and reselling

Advantages	Quality control
	Better forward planning with less inventory
	Elimination of monopolistic or monopsonistic price distortions in the wholesale product market
	Improved coordination of irreversible investments
	Better information feedback for product and process development
	Opportunities for tax avoidance through 'transfer pricing' where there are differences in the fiscal regimes of the exporting and importing countries
Disadvantages	Economies of scale in production limited by internal marketing capacity
	Economies of scope in marketing limited by internal production capabilities
	Bureaucracy weakens employee incentives
Potential compromise	Use both internal and external markets

one set of premises in the exporting country handling the procurement of all the goods and the other set of premises in the importing country handling all of the distribution. It is quite possible, though, for trade to go in both directions at once. In this case the premises used to procure an export good may also be used to distribute an import good. However, if the export and import trades have very different operational requirements, then different premises may still be used for each. In this case a trading company involved in two-way trade may have two sets of premises in a given country.

Trading companies can diversify not only in terms of the range of products they handle, but also in terms of the range of countries they serve. So far the emphasis has been placed on bilateral trade, but it is well known that many flows of trade are multilateral. The multilateral nature of trade may well be reflected in the operations of individual trading companies. An integrated reseller involved in multilateral trade will necessarily operate in more than two countries. In triangular trade, for example, the company may export product 1 from country A to country B, export product 2 from B to C, and export product 3 from C to A. Thus in country A it imports product 3 and exports 1, in country B it imports 1 and exports 2, and in C it imports 2 and exports 3. Multilateral trade implies multi-country operation. The situation is illustrated in Figure 2.4. The figure represents triangular trade within a colonial empire, of the kind described later in the chapter on p. 41. The activities controlled by the MTC are shown in black, and activities controlled by others in white.

A company can also specialise according to certain routes. In the example above, the company only trades 'clockwise' from A to B to C, and not in the opposite direction. It could also serve these same three countries using an even more restricted set of routes. Thus it could confine itself to two routes – exporting from A to B and from B to C – without completing the triangle with trade on the third route between C and A. It cannot therefore be inferred from the fact that a trading company operates in a given set of countries that it operates on all the routes between them. In some respects, the pattern of specialisation according to route is more fundamental than the pattern of specialisation according to country, since a knowledge of the routes normally identifies the countries involved more clearly than the set of countries identifies the routes.

Moving from the two-country to the multi-country case makes it necessary to refine the definition of a trading company. This is because the ownership and control of activities may differ according to the products and the routes involved. Thus in the example above the export of product 1 from country A to country B might involve wholly-owned facilities, but the exports of product 2 from country B and product 3 from country C might not. This would be the case if the company owned its own facilities in countries A and B but used an independent broker in country C. Thus, product 1 would be handled entirely by the company, but product 2 would be distributed by the independent broker, and product 3 would be procured by

An example of mangular trade involving
two colonies and their home country

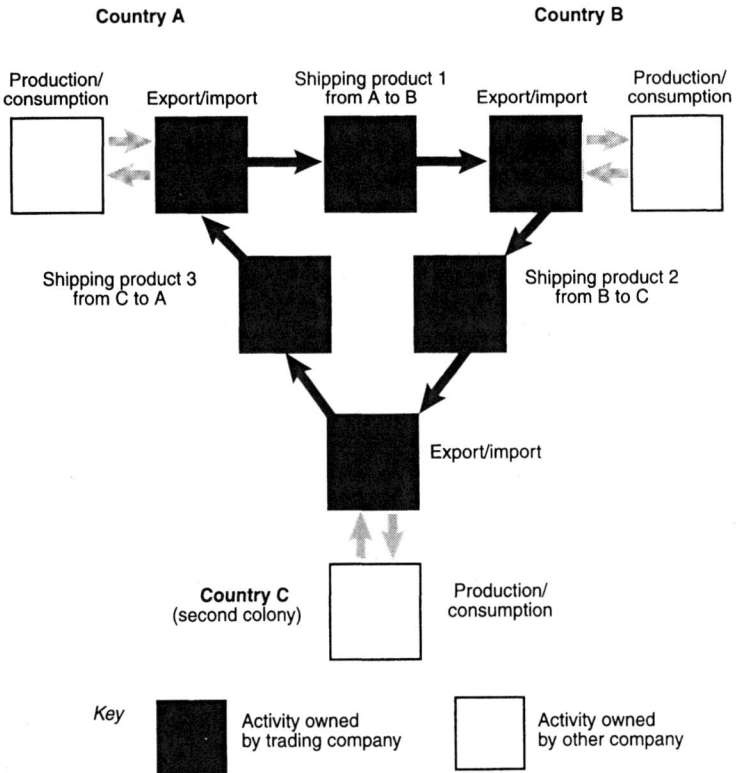

Country A   **Country B**

Production/   Production/
consumption   Export/import   Shipping product 1   Export/import   consumption
                                from A to B

Shipping product 3   Shipping product 2
from C to A   from B to C

                            Export/import

Country C   Production/
(second colony)   consumption

Key   ■ Activity owned   □ Activity owned
            by trading company   by other company

Figure 2.4 Geographical diversification: the use of multiple connected routes to
support multinational trade

the broker too. The most appropriate way to extend the definition is to allow
any company that integrates procurement and distribution on a single route
to qualify as an MTC, whether or not it integrates them on its other routes as
well. This means that in the case described above the multilateral trader is
indeed an MTC.

Information flow and material flow

A trading company does not only handle flows of material goods. It handles
large amounts of information too. In many cases the processing of information will take place at the same locations that handle the goods, but in some
cases information processing may be carried out at different locations instead.
Whether information processing takes place at separate locations depends on
the type of information involved.

Much of the information handled by a trading company is routine information required for procurement and distribution. The company must process customer orders that specify price, quantity, type of product and possibly the time and place of delivery too. It must record the payments made by customers, and place on file any debts that are outstanding. It also needs to requisition goods from its own suppliers, and keep track of any credit that has been supplied. Because this information is closely tied up with procurement and distribution, it is normally efficient for it to be carried out alongside the warehousing facilities for the goods concerned. Indeed, this arrangement was implicitly assumed in the discussion of procurement and distribution earlier on.

The information of greatest strategic significance to a trading company is not routine, however. It relates to the management of the major risks that the company faces. As indicated above, these relate, first, to the estimation of the overall demand for intermediation in the products the company handles, and second, to the opportunity to speculate on, or conversely the need to hedge against, movements in the price of goods that are passing through the company's hands.

Information of this kind tends to come from different sources than does the routine information described above. It is discovered, not through contact with individual customers and suppliers, but from the study of systematic factors in demand and supply which impinge on customers and suppliers as a group. It is necessary for the company to gain access to information from which future movements in these factors can be inferred. Indeed, this type of information is so crucial to the survival and success of the firm that it is usually handled at the headquarters. This implies that the company's headquarters will be located close to where such information is to be found. The distinction is illustrated in Figure 2.5.

Information processing is represented by circles, to distinguish it from the handling of physical product, which continues to be indicated by squares. Information flows are represented by thin lines, and material flow by thick lines (as before). Information of long-term strategic significance is indicated by a slightly thicker line than information which is of only short-term speculative significance. Strategic information is collected from a broader range of sources than speculative information – these are the sources which are close to the underlying factors driving long-term changes in supply and demand. This information is synthesised at a higher level of the organisation than is the strategic information. Some speculative information is passed up to the strategic level, and some of the strategic information filters down to inform speculation. High-level strategic decision-making is likely to be centralised within the firm, but short-term speculation may well be decentralised to the local level.

In most industries there are a wide range of factors that impinge upon the overall balance of demand and supply. The typical trading company does not have sufficient personnel to monitor all of these sources at first hand. Its

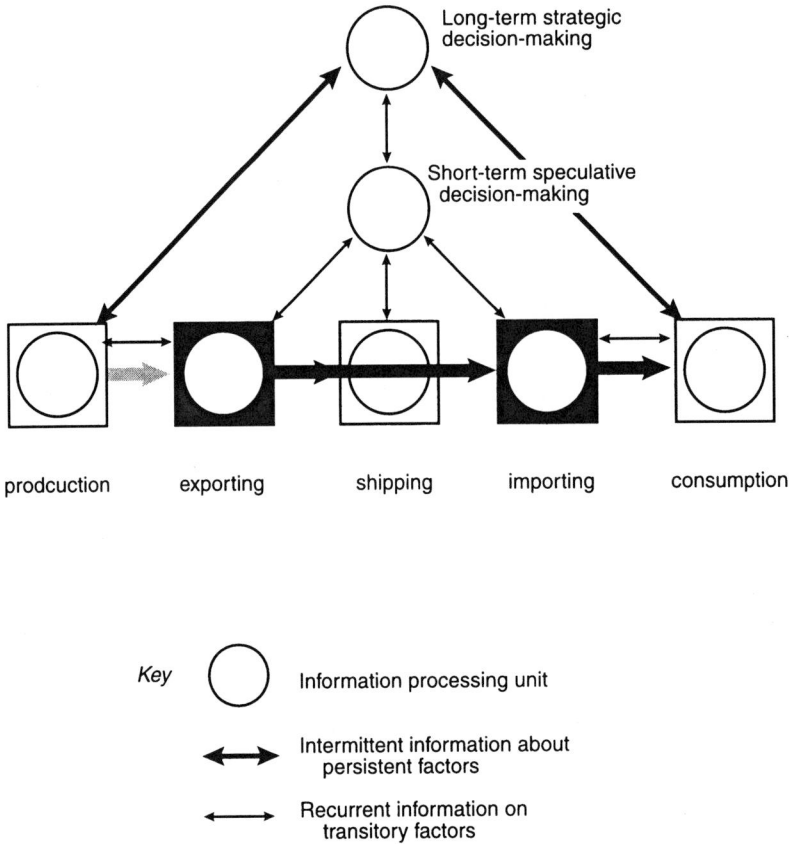

Figure 2.5 Information processing in multinational trading

strategy is therefore to develop a network of contacts through which much of the relevant information can be obtained at second hand. Some of these contacts may be of a personal and confidential nature, but others may simply involve scanning newspapers, journals, and other impersonal sources of published information.

In a competitive environment, the company must be just as alert as its rivals to information of this kind. It is not necessary that the company's forecasts of demand and supply be completely accurate, but it is necessary that they are no worse than those of its rivals. This encourages each company to locate premises at a major information hub – such as a great metropolis – where there is immediate access to a wide range of information. In some cases the company may already have a warehouse in this metropolis, but in many cases it will not. The typical metropolis develops from a port or transhipment point, but once it has gained maturity the rising property values tend to drive out space-intensive port activities to peripheral locations, thereby separating the processing of information from the handling of the goods. A trading company is therefore likely to find that by basing its headquarters at a major metropolis it has separated its strategic information processing from its handling of routine information.

This separation of strategic and routine information processing is of little significance if the company actively trades with the country in which the metropolis is based. It simply means that in the headquarters country the company operates two separate sets of premises instead of just one. It is conceivable, though, that the company does not trade with this country. Consider, for example, a company that trades between two neighbouring colonies in the remote part of an overseas empire. The most crucial factors governing the future development of this trade are government decisions taken in the imperial metropolis. The most up-to-date information is therefore available in the metropolis rather than in the colonies themselves, and so this is where the headquarters will be located. It follows that the company is actually headquartered in a country with which it does not trade.

The main reason for exploring this line of argument is that it bears on the question of whether trading companies can also be free-standing firms, in the sense of Wilkins (1988). A free-standing firm is a company that is headquartered in one country but has all its operations in other countries. It is obvious from what has already been said in the previous paragraph that a trading company can indeed be a free-standing firm.

There is, however, a potential source of confusion which needs to be addressed. Consider, for example, a hybrid trading company which is integrated backwards into mining in an overseas colony. The company exports its mineral production to the home country, where it is distributed to industrial firms. Considered purely as a mining firm, and ignoring its trading activities, this company appears to be a free-standing firm. This is because it does not mine in the country where it is headquartered. Considered as a trading company, however, it is not free-standing because it has a distribution facility in the country in which it is headquartered. This raises the possibility that some of the firms that have recently been described as free-standing firms are in fact only free-standing when regarded purely as mining or manufacturing firms. They are really hybrid trading companies, because their distribution activities in the home country have been overlooked. Once they are correctly classified as trading companies, it becomes clear that they are not really free-standing firms at all.

Integration into finance

A feature of some of the most successful trading companies is their diversification into banking and finance. Typically they become involved in extending long-term credit to small firms in the industries in which they trade. They may eventually evolve into merchant bankers. They reduce their own trading activities and focus on the financing of other firms instead. Some of the creditor firms are typically trading firms (both pure and hybrid), but other creditor firms may be involved purely in agriculture, mining or manufacturing instead.

The explanation of this phenomenon lies in the role of information as an internal public good within the trading firm. The information collected in order to forecast the volume of trade, and to identify opportunities for speculation, may be used for other purposes too. Much of the information collected may be of a general nature, whose implications extend far beyond the particular market in which the company is initially engaged. By synthesising one item of general information with another it may be possible to form judgements about issues with which the company is only indirectly involved. Profit opportunities may be identified which are too remote for the company to exploit itself. The natural way to exploit these opportunities is to encourage others to take them up, and to invest in their enterprises in order to share in their success.

This strategy is particularly appropriate for a diversified trading company. Because it is collecting information that is relevant to several different types of product, it is likely to be scanning a very wide variety of information sources. There is therefore ample opportunity for creative synthesis. At the same time, the company is already diversified as far as its present managerial capacity will allow. To extend the management team any further could result in diseconomies of scale. Only by encouraging managers to solicit investment projects from other people, instead of trying to take on additional projects to manage themselves, can the full potential of their information be realised.

In order to acquire sufficient funds to invest in projects of this kind, the company must of course enjoy the confidence of its own investors. Reinvestment of its own profits is unlikely to be sufficient for this purpose. But in so far as the company has a successful track record, the raising of additional funds is unlikely to be a serious problem.

The company therefore diversifies away from the intermediation of trade flows and refocuses on the intermediation of financial flows instead. It intermediates financial flows using exactly the same principles as it intermediated commodity flows before. It procures funds from investors with whom it has built up a reputation for sound judgement. It distributes these funds to entrepreneurs it has identified as possessing the skills required to exploit the opportunities suggested by its synthesis of information. It 'buys' credit from its investors in return for a relatively low rate of interest and resells this credit to the entrepreneurs for a higher rate of interest, thereby earning a margin which covers the cost of acquiring and processing the information used to identify the opportunities and assess the risks.

Export-led colonial development

A significant proportion of trading companies have been heavily involved in the development of colonial export industries. The theory developed in this paper explains quite naturally why this is so. The illustration given below relates to a settler economy of the British Empire, but the principles apply more widely than this. They apply to any developing country or region which is heavily dependent on a more developed economy for its export markets and its supplies of capital equipment. The argument applies, therefore, to United States involvement in Latin America during the late-nineteenth and early twentieth century, and to Japanese involvement in South East Asia at a slightly later period. It also applies to British involvement in developing countries which, though not British colonies, were nevertheless dependent on Britain and the British Empire so far as international trade, international capital flows and international technology transfer were concerned.

A newly founded colony has little in the way of infrastructure. It is because of this that the trading post occupies a very important role in early colonial life. The trading post is the institution through which imported goods are distributed, and by which export cargoes are consolidated for shipment overseas. In the absence of established law and order it needs to be easily defended, preferably by location within, or near to, a military fort.

In the absence of other institutions, such as local churches and schools, the trading post becomes a focus of local community life. As well as stocking goods, it offers meals and accommodation. The owner of a trading post is in a good position to pick up information about local conditions from the conversations that go on at his store. Synthesising this information with information obtained through correspondence with his import suppliers and export customers enables him to identify new opportunities for local economic development.

A good example of this concerns prospecting for minerals. During the nineteenth century several regions of the expanding British Empire contained mountainous areas where valuable minerals outcropped, or lay near to the surface. Prospectors in these areas needed to buy suitable clothing, equipment and supplies for their expeditions. They would patronise the local trading post to acquire basic items which were too perishable or too heavy to bring with them to the area. News of any discoveries would soon filter back to the trading post. Successful prospectors would return to the post to celebrate their success, to send letters to their family and friends back home and to arrange for the export of their production.

Naturally, when a mining boom gets underway, a local trading post begins to face stiff competition from other more specialised traders, such as saloon bar keepers and stage-coach operators. However, the owner of the trading post can use his privileged information to diversify into some of these more specialised activities himself.

The lack of suitable infrastructure is an obvious constraint on local development in the early years of colonisation. The critical issue is whether the potential volume of export trade is sufficient to warrant investment in roads, railways, harbours and river navigations. The owner of a trading post is in a good position to form a judgement on issues of this kind. Moreover, he stands to benefit both directly and indirectly from successful infrastructure investment. He benefits directly by taking up shares in the new venture, and he benefits indirectly from the increase in trade which the new venture will afford. He may therefore decide to visit the colonial power's metropolis in order to raise funds for infrastructure investment – most probably a railway in the case of mineral development. Although he is totally dependent on others to provide the funds for his scheme, he has an effective monopoly of the kind of local information which is crucial to success and which the financiers lack. He is therefore in a good position to insist that he is allocated shares in the scheme.

Another kind of venture that complements the operation of a trading post is the ownership of land. The reason for this is that a substantial proportion of the gains that accrue from the promotion of colonial trade are likely to accrue, not as the profits of trade, but as an increase in the value of land. For example, a trading post that actively develops an agricultural or mineral export trade will enhance the value of the land on which the production is carried out. Furthermore, if the growth of trade encourages the building of a railway, then access to the railway will enhance the value of land along the route. Indeed, by acquiring ownership of land along the route of the railway, a speculative trader may not only benefit from the increase in land values after the railway is built, but from the opportunity to sell land to the railway to allow it to be built in the first place. The more difficult the terrain, the fewer options there are likely to be regarding the route, and therefore the easier it is for a landowner to hold the railway to ransom over the building of the track.

It is evident, therefore, that the combination of the opportunity for information synthesis, and the advantages of diversification in capturing the economic rents, stimulate the owner of a trading post to pursue a variety of other activities too. The owner becomes involved in a range of activities that complement his role in the development of trade. In this way he becomes an incubator of local economic development.

The development of colonial trade is likely to have implications for the trading post itself. Colonial development normally begins around a convenient natural harbour, and as the colonial population increases, economic activity expands into the hinterland. As the colonial 'frontier' moves into more remote territory, opportunities for additional trading posts are created. The experience gained in operating the first trading post during the early years when conditions were primitive can be transferred to the operation of new trading posts in the hinterland, where conditions are just as primitive as they used to be near the coast. By transferring his expertise to the hinterland, the owner of the trading post becomes the proprietor of a multi-branch enterprise.

The increase in the number of trading posts, supported by the growth of population, increases the volume of the import and export trade. By consolidating import and export traffic from the different branches, the trading company begins to handle a very significant volume of trade. This provides opportunities to extend the managerial division of labour within the company. It is possible to set up special export and import departments, which deal in wholesale rather than retail quantities. As trade expands further, it may be possible for individual managers to specialise in arranging the import and export of particular types of good.

To obtain a better price for exports, the company may decide to set up an export distribution facility in its major overseas market – typically the domestic market of the colonising power. Similarly, to obtain a better selection of imports at a better price, it may decide to set up its procurement facility near to its major sources of supply. Typically these sources are the domestic producers of the colonial power. It is therefore possible, if the company desires, to combine the procurement and distribution activities within a single facility based in the colonial power. By this stage of its evolution, the humble trading post has expanded into a fully fledged trading company, with facilities in two countries, and multiple branches within one of them.

A trading company of this type may expand even further by developing branches in neighbouring colonies. Colonial expansion tends to be a sequential process, with the most accessible parts of newly discovered or newly conquered territories being developed first. As expansion proceeds, new colonies are created. This is because the difficulties of communication means that the optimal size of a newly created colony is usually relatively small. Experience gained in the colonies that are settled first can be transferred to other colonies later on.

This is particularly significant where groups of island colonies are concerned. For geo-political reasons, each island is normally a separate colony. But because they are connected by sea, which affords an easy means of transporting freight, economic ties between neighbouring islands are likely to be strong. Economic logic therefore suggests that an entrepreneur with a flair for trade will set up a network of trading posts in the different colonies. His enterprise becomes a multinational purely because of its inter-colonial links, independent of any links with the colonising country itself. Moreover the trading posts may establish their own distinctive network of internal trade. Goods acquired at each trading post may be consigned to the other trading posts for resale. In this way the integrated trading company promotes the international division of labour between the neighbouring island economies through its own internal trade.

Money and barter

The involvement of trading companies in developing regions helps to explain one notable feature of their operation, namely the relatively high incidence of barter-type transactions. Many trading companies began by establishing trading posts in remote overseas areas, where they bartered imported finished products for raw materials and semi-processed products that they exported back to the home country. The early chartered trading companies typically operated a network of such trading posts in the territories for which they held a statutory monopoly.

The use of barter appears paradoxical, given that the use of money eliminates the need for a 'double coincidence of wants' between buyer and seller and thereby reduces transactions costs between them. The resolution of the paradox lies primarily in the fact that money must be generally acceptable if it is to do its job efficiently. The explanation of the recourse to barter in developing regions is that either there is no established indigenous currency or (more commonly) that the currency used by the indigenous people was not acceptable to the company. Conversely, the settlers' home currency is not acceptable to the indigenous people, at least in the short run. Moreover, even if the indigenous people find the settlers' currency acceptable, they will have had to accumulate significant savings in order to obtain sufficient reserves of the currency to support their part in the export trade.

The combination of barter and credit means that the terms of trade between the current imports supplied to indigenous people and the subsequent purchase of exports from them combines elements of both relative price and the rate of interest. The relative price relates to the number of units of the export that are needed to purchase on a spot basis one representative basket of the imported goods. The rate of interest represents the discount at which a claim on future delivery of the export good stands relative to an immediate claim for the same quantity of the export good. Because the terms of trade combine these two elements, it is possible that indigenous people are unable to infer from the quoted terms of trade exactly what rate of interest that they are being charged.

In cases where the rate of interest is regulated (or in more extreme cases where 'usury' is prohibited) recourse to barter transactions allows a trading company to charge for credit at a higher rate than would otherwise be possible. This indicates that under certain circumstances recourse to barter may reflect not the unavailability or unacceptability of local currency, but rather the existence of restrictions on the rate of interest whose infringement is more difficult to detect when barter is employed. Barter therefore helps to reduce transaction costs in the credit market when the maximum legal rate of interest is below the equilibrium level. When the savings in transactions costs in the credit market outweigh the additional transactions costs incurred in product markets, barter is used instead of money.

The combination of barter and credit is a surprisingly common feature of international trade, even today. Under the name of 'countertrade' it is widely used to export capital equipment to countries with a weak, or internationally unacceptable, currency. In the late 1980s these countries included the heavily indebted developing countries of Africa and Latin America, and the Soviet-type economies of Central and Eastern Europe. It is also used in trade with Islamic countries, in order to circumvent religious prohibitions on interest charges. Implicit interest rates are levied by driving a wedge between relative spot money prices and the barter terms of trade.

Wherever internationally traded goods are bartered, the trading company becomes involved in a two-way product flow. This is illustrated in Figure 2.6.

The MTC's offices and warehouses are handling two-way flows in both the ports. These flows may involve the MTC in dealings with different groups of people. The diagram illustrates the case where the MTC deals with different groups in the home country – namely consumer goods manufacturers and processors of colonial products – but with the same people – namely plantation owners – in the colony.

In the case of the early trading companies, they were involved not only in the procurement of raw materials from overseas colonies, but the procurement of finished goods in the home market for import into the colony. In the

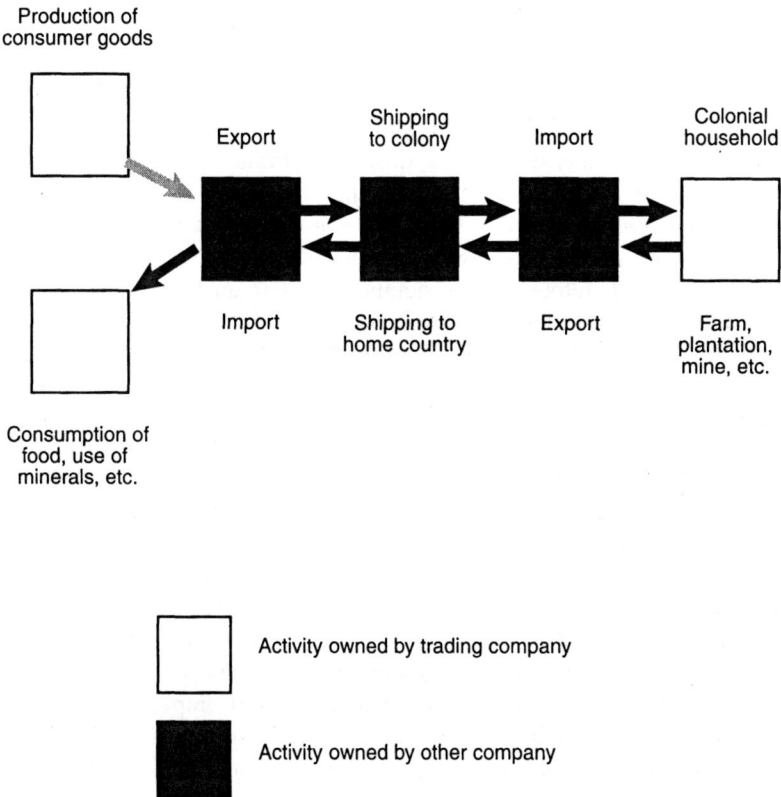

Production of
consumer goods

| | Export | Shipping to colony | Import | Colonial household |

| | Import | Shipping to home country | Export | Farm, plantation, mine, etc. |

Consumption of
food, use of
minerals, etc.

☐ Activity owned by trading company

■ Activity owned by other company

Figure 2.6 Product diversification through barter trading: an example of a colonial trading post dealing in both consumer goods and raw materials

case of countertrade export deals in the 1980s, trading companies were involved not merely in the procurement of high-technology manufactured exports and construction services in the industrialised countries, but the procurement of foodstuffs, footwear and other low-technology products in the developing countries.

Because of the element of credit in these barter-type deals, the trading company concerned becomes involved in the assessment of credit risk. It needs to be sure that the customers who take advances from it in the form of imported goods are capable of generating suitable exports in the future. Sometimes the exports required may be specified in advance, while in other cases the debtors may be given a menu of acceptable products and left to decide which they will produce for themselves.

The involvement of the trading company in risk assessment means that the company takes on some of the functions associated with a bank. Unlike a conventional bank, however, it is not advancing money, but real resources instead. It is also accepting repayment in a different type of commodity from that in which the advance is made. This means that the company is, in fact, undertaking activities that are more sophisticated than those of an ordinary bank. The commodities in which it deals are not only more varied than those of a bank, but each of the commodities is itself less homogeneous than money. Each commodity is subject to quality variation. To maintain its reputation, the trading company must ensure that the goods it advances are of suitable quality, whilst to ensure that it is not defrauded it must accurately assess the quality of the products in which it is repaid. A trading company engaged in barter therefore requires significant skill in quality control.

One way for the trading company to reduce the risk relating to repayment is for it to supply technology to its customers to assist their production of export goods, and to supervise relevant aspects of their production activity. This means that the trading company diversifies into technology transfer and management consultancy. Such diversification adds further ambiguity to the concept of a trading company. For example, a company that is strong in research and development relating to the processing of tropical agricultural products may resort to countertrade in order to sell its machinery to developing countries. Instead of accepting the weak indigenous currency, or insisting on payment in strong Western currencies instead, it may agree to accept payment in kind instead. Some of the payment may even consist of food products that have been processed by the machinery itself. The company therefore combines the export of machinery with the import of foodstuffs, which it sells on into Western distribution channels. In one sense the firm is simply an exporter of high-technology capital equipment, which just happens to use countertrade as an export device, but in another sense it is a trading company exchanging capital equipment for processed foodstuffs, which just happens to produce the capital equipment itself.

The decline of colonial trading companies

The reasons for the decline of a trading company are the obverse of this argument. The trading company is well adapted to effecting a wide-ranging synthesis of general information, but it is not a repository of specialised technical information. So long as it remains relatively small, it can maintain the flexibility of response that is necessary to keep pace with the changing needs of successive stages of colonial development. As it grows larger, however, it may lose this flexibility, without necessarily acquiring more technical expertise.

As the growth of the colonial economy levels off, trading activities become more routine. The company's advantage in identifying new opportunities becomes less significant as the number of new opportunities declines. The low-cost exploitation of known existing opportunities becomes more important instead. Production becomes more sophisticated and complex, and goods are increasingly produced in volumes that permit the exploitation of mass-production techniques. Although the trading company is in a good position to identify these trends, it is not necessarily in the best position to respond to them.

As the ability to optimise routine procedures becomes more important and imaginative, improvisation becomes less important, different personal qualities are required in the management team. But it may be difficult for existing managers to recruit the kind of people who have the qualities they now require. They may have little sympathy with, or understanding of, the technical specialists they need to recruit. They may need to recruit them from different social groups and different types of educational institution. If they choose the wrong people, or fail to assimilate them, then the company's performance suffers as a result. New firms are not hampered by their cultural legacy in this way. Although they are disadvantaged by their lack of trading experience, their access to superior technology and their more professional approach to management gives them a competitive edge. Some established firms may survive by adapting to the new conditions, but those that cannot adapt become extinct. They either shut down, or are taken over by successful entrants and reorganised along different lines.

Summary and conclusion

A trading company has been defined as a special type of intermediator. The latter may be brokers or resellers. A reseller is different from a broker because he owns the goods in which he trades. Brokers and resellers may or may not be multinationals, depending on how far they integrate into activities in different countries. Attention has been focused on MTCs.

MTCs come in pure and hybrid forms. A pure MTC is an international intermediator that owns and controls procurement in one country and distribution in another. The typical MTC is an integrated reseller, although integrated brokerage is also possible.

The incentive to control procurement and distribution depends upon the characteristics of the product and the volume of trade. Complexity of specification, difficulty of quality assurance, stability of supply and demand and a high volume of trade all favour internalisation. Conversely, simplicity of specification, ease of quality assurance, volatility of supply and demand, and low volume all favour delegation to independent brokers instead.

Internalisation also governs the diversification of the hybrid trading company into related activities such as manufacturing, retailing and shipping. Some of these other activities may be operationally integrated with the trading activities, as when the company trades in the products it manufactures itself, retails the products it procures overseas and uses its ships to transport its own cargoes. Internalisation may, however, be prompted entirely by the desire for risk reduction, in which case the operational links may be weak. It is an interesting question for historical researchers as to how far hybrid trading companies restrict their diversification to activities which involve only the production, transportation and distribution of the consignments they handle for the purposes of trade.

Trading companies also integrate into activities such as merchant banking and property ownership which are not directly related to their principal activity at all. This diversification is explained by the public good property of the information that they synthesise for trading purposes. Because of the wide-ranging implications of some of the information collected by a trading company, owners and managers may generate ideas for ventures that are quite remote from its core activities. These ideas cannot be licensed for a fee; direct involvement is necessary in order to appropriate the economic rents from them. Diversification into merchant banking allows the trading company to delegate the management of such ventures to other people selected for this purpose, whilst retaining a financial stake in the ventures themselves. Diversification into land ownership allows the company to appropriate some of the rewards generated by these ventures that would otherwise accrue to other people.

An MTC may be engaged in either monetary trade, or barter trade or both. An MTC engaged in barter trade is exemplified by a firm that operates a network of trading posts in different colonies. Numerous other applications can be developed. The study of trading companies is still at a relatively early stage.

This chapter has concentrated on the most basic issues, such as the most appropriate way of defining a trading company for the purposes of historical research. It has shown how the general principles of transactions costs and internalisation theory apply to the trading company. The boundaries of the trading firm are determined according to the same principles that govern the boundaries of any other type of firm. They manifest themselves in a specific way because of the specific features of trading activity. These specific features include the importance of maintaining a steady volume of procurement and distribution activity, and the strategic importance of exploiting the public good property of information to the full. It has been argued that the long-run dynamics of the growth, diversification and decay of the trading company can be understood in the context of the special needs of local development in a dependent economy. The point has been illustrated in the specific context of a British colony, but the general principles apply more widely than this. As historical research into trading companies gathers momentum, more information will come to light, and it is to be hoped that this will stimulate further theoretical development along the lines set out above.

Acknowledgements

I am grateful to Janet Casson and Geoffrey Jones for comments on an earlier draft of this chapter.

References

Buckley, P. J. and Casson, M. C. (1976) *The Future of the Multinational Enterprise*, London: Macmillan, 2nd edn 1991.

Carlos, A. M. and Nicholas, S. J. (1988) '"Giants of an Earlier Capitalism": chartered trading companies as modern multinationals', *Business History Review*, 62: 399–419.

Casson, M. C. (1982) *The Entrepreneur: An Economic Theory*, Oxford: Martin Robertson; reprinted, Aldershot, Hants: Gregg Revivals, 1991.

—— (1997) *Information and Organization*, Oxford: Clarendon Press.

Jones, G. (1996) 'Diversification strategies and corporate governance in trading companies: Anglo-Japanese comparisons since the late nineteenth century', *Business and Economic History*, 25 (2): 103–18.

Kemp, M. C. (1964) *The Pure Theory of International Trade and Investment*, Englewood Cliffs, NJ: Prentice-Hall.

Wilkins, M. (1988) 'The free-standing company, 1870–1914: an important type of British foreign direct investment', *Economic History Review*, 41 (2): 259–82.

Williamson, O. E. (1975) *Markets and Hierarchies: Analysis and Anti-trust Implications*, New York: Free Press.

—— (1985) *The Economic Institutions of Capitalism*, New York: Free Press.

3 From regional trade to global shipping

Mackinnon Mackenzie & Co within the Mackinnon Enterprise Network

J. Forbes Munro

The revival of interest in the business history, as well as the politics, of British overseas trade and investment during the nineteenth and twentieth centuries has brought a welcome shift of attention back towards the merchant houses and trading companies that were so often the intermediaries between British manufacturers and bankers on the one hand and overseas markets and customers on the other. In particular, Stanley Chapman's identification of British-based 'investment groups' and Mira Wilkins' discovery of clusters of so-called 'free-standing companies' as the active agents of British direct investment across the globe (Chapman 1985; Wilkins 1988) have drawn our attention to the diversification activities of the trading firms which were at the heart of many such groups or clusters. More recently, Geoffrey Jones has compared the diversification strategies and organisational structures of British and Japanese trading companies, and concluded that they had many similarities: 'The challenges centred on access and use of information and the coordination of diverse activities. In both cases networks of enterprises linked by equity, debt, people, trade, and services were preferred to internalization, and relationships were substituted for organization' (Jones 1996: 117). What is also clear from such studies, however, is that the British trading organisations which, between roughly 1850 and 1930, liberally sowed their subsidiary and affiliate concerns across the world, differed one from another in the nature, timing, causes and outcomes of their diversification processes and that, if networks were the common organisational form employed, the specific content of each network varied with the activities which were engaged in. There is therefore a need for the development of a typology of merchant-centred enterprise networks which is solidly based upon detailed case studies, preferably drawn from corporate and public archives, in which a full range of the factors contributing to investment and managerial decisions may be explored. Such a typology might embrace the distinction between organisations engaged in general import–export operations on the one hand and specific commodity trades on the other, resulting in differential opportunities for diversification along backwards and forwards linkages.

Another issue to be explored is whether inter-firm dynamics within a network create opportunities for diversification throughout the system, or alternatively result in some part of the network having to forego opportunities to diversify in the interests of the whole. The firm that does not diversify may be as interesting to study as the one that does. When a trading organisation is entirely independent of outside control, or influences over its managerial strategies, it may be free to give full reign to its instinct for enterprise, and pursue whatever possibilities may emerge for it to enter into new lines of trade, production, finance or transportation connected with its current activities. When, however, it is part of an alliance or grouping of firms, and is linked formally or informally with the needs and interests of others, then its role may preclude it from breaking new ground even when such opportunities exist. Such is the theme – the interplay between opportunity, capability and constraint – taken up in this chapter, which takes as its focus a single trading firm but seeks to avoid the 'limitations of the special case' by taking account of its relationship to other firms with which it collaborated.

The firm and the group

Mackinnon Mackenzie & Co was established in Calcutta in 1847, as a partnership between three men from the West of Scotland. It quickly grew from its very modest beginnings in the import–export trades into one of the city's leading British-owned commercial enterprises, with interests in shipping, jute, tea and cotton manufacturing, and from the 1890s it provided the Bengal Chamber of Commerce with a constant succession of chairmen. Throughout the greater part of its history it retained the private partnership form of organisation, becoming incorporated as a public company in India only in 1951. In 1957 it was sold to P&O, as a consequence of the Inchcape Group's retreat from India. The history of Mackinnon Mackenzie & Co therefore spans most of the period of British commercial relations with India between the free-trade era that opened up in the 1830s and the national development plans of the 1950s. This chapter concentrates upon the first phase of the firm's history, from the 1840s to the 1890s, during which its diversification out of trading operations proceeded most rapidly. At this time it was, in terms of the typologies outlined by Mark Casson in Chapter 2, both a broker and a seller, and took the form of a hybrid trading company.

Mackinnon Mackenzie & Co was in many respects a fairly typical British agency house in nineteenth-century India. Chapman identifies five characteristics of such firms: (1) that they worked on commission, acting as agents for manufacturers or merchants in Britain, although this did not preclude them from trading in their own right; (2) that they diversified into various non-trading activities through 'heavy fixed capital investment in the locality of the overseas station'; (3) that they accepted 'heavy public deposits of savings', thereby acquiring some of the functions of merchant banks; (4) that they had close connections with the City of London, or wealthy families in Lancashire and Glasgow; and (5) that they were 'largely the work of family and clan groups among whom the Scots were particularly prominent' (Chapman 1992:

107–13). Such a description broadly fits Mackinnon Mackenzie & Co, except that the firm accepted outside deposits to only a very limited extent. Furthermore, its links to the City of London or wealthy families in the port cities of north-western Britain were not particularly strong, and were probably less significant for business success than its links to British officials in India, and through them to the Government of India. However, Chapman's stress on family-based enterprise is especially relevant to Mackinnon Mackenzie & Co in that the firm was only one, albeit the single most important one, in a cluster of partnerships and companies created and controlled by the Mackinnon and Hall families from a West of Scotland base. Consequently, its pattern of diversification has to be understood in the context of the activities of the Mackinnon Group as a whole as well as the more specific needs, interests and ambitions of the firm itself.

The Mackinnon Group came into being in the late 1840s through the formation of three small partnerships – in Liverpool (Hall Mackinnon & Co, later Mackinnon Frew & Co), Calcutta (Mackinnon Mackenzie & Co) and Glasgow (W. Mackinnon & Co). By 1890 a second generation of family enterprise had added partnerships in London (Gray Dawes & Co and D. Macneill & Co) and in Calcutta (Macneill & Co). Meanwhile, Mackinnon Mackenzie & Co had grown in size (from three partners with a capital of about £12,000 to eight partners with a capital of about £439,000), had acquired branch houses in Bombay and (for a while) in Karachi, and had outstripped the Liverpool and Glasgow houses to become the leading firm within the family-led cluster. Over the same period, the group's subsidiary interests had increased from ownership of a couple of small sailing ships to control of six steamship companies (including one of the world's largest), the operation of subsidiary agencies in the Persian Gulf, East Africa and Australia, and the management of tea plantations, jute mills, coal mines and a cotton factory in India. It was one of the most geographically extensive and diversified trading groups to be found within the nineteenth-century world economy (Griffiths 1977; Jones 1986; Munro 1988). The Mackinnon Group (which after 1913 was translated into the Inchcape Group) was not a single trading company, with a clearly defined head office which made and enforced the policy for the branches. Instead the organisation was very much looser. Overall leadership and co-ordination was provided by the senior family figures, particularly the patriarchal William Mackinnon, but each partnership and their subsidiary/affiliate firms enjoyed a large measure of independence within the general framework of territorial and/or functional specialisation which was held together by kinship and a recognition of mutual interdependence. It was a flexible – although perhaps in the longer term an unstable – form of organisation. For all that, Mackinnon Mackenzie & Co was not an entirely independent expatriate firm, immune from metropolitan direction, for something of the role of head office was performed from Glasgow by W. Mackinnon & Co, in which the Mackinnon Mackenzie & Co partners had an identical interest until 1870 and substantially overlapping interests thereafter.

How and why did Mackinnon Mackenzie & Co diversify out of trade into other services and into the production of goods in India, and what part did it play in the diversification of the Mackinnon Group interests as a whole? The story can be told in three parts:

Phase 1 (1847–62): a period of vigorous trading activity, with only a modest degree of diversification;

Phase 2 (1862–75): a period of extensive diversification along a relatively broad front; and

Phase 3 (1875–93): a period of no diversification and of concentration upon the non-trading activity which had become the firm's core business, but within a more varied pattern of group interests and activities.

Phase 1 (1847–1862)

The firm of Mackinnon Mackenzie & Co arose on the back of the growth of exports of cotton yarns and piece-goods from the Clyde to India during the 1840s and 1850s. As of 1863 it was one of only seven Calcutta houses to have agents in Glasgow (as compared with 12 houses with Liverpool and seven with Manchester connections). It sold cotton textiles on commission from such Glasgow firms as S.A. Liebert & Co, Salmond Connel & Co, Yates Brown & Howat, Muir Brown & Co and William Stirling & Sons, as well as for Manchester-based concerns with Scottish links, including John Pender & Co, Gunnis & Liebert, and J.J. Bell & Co. It also traded in cotton goods on its own account, employing credit from the City of Glasgow Bank with which many of its constituent firms were associated. It balanced its imports of cottons with joint-venture exports of Indian produce to markets in London and Liverpool, and for a while in the 1850s it pursued the opening-up of a trade in Bengali sugar and rice, and other tropical produce, to the Australian colonies. Around 1862 there would have been little to distinguish this fledgling trading firm from all of the others engaged in dickering with Bengali merchants in the Calcutta bazaar – not even the fact that it had taken its first hesitant steps into the managing agency system.

The managing agency system, whereby ownership was separated from control of business concerns, was the principal tool of diversification employed by British merchant houses in India. It was so closely associated with British enterprise in Asia, at first in India (Tomlinson 1989: 96–100; Kling 1966–7) and then in the port cities of Southeast and East Asia, that there appears to be an assumption that it represented some special adaptation of British business practices to the peculiar economic environment of Asia. However, these methods of financing and managing subsidiary concerns were so well embedded in the British mercantile marine at the beginning of the nineteenth century that their introduction into Asian corporate life probably owed a good deal to the fact that most of the important merchant houses were also shipping agents (and shareholders) and were therefore familiar with the techniques of the managing agency. (Calcutta Customs House records, for example, show that in 1877 some 49 firms, including such well-known names as Jardine Skinner & Co, Gladstone Wyllie & Co, Finlay Muir & Co and Gillanders Arbuthnot & Co as well as Mackinnon Mackenzie & Co, acted as agents for the 1,438 vessels which entered inwards to the port.) At any rate, Mackinnon Mackenzie & Co's earliest diversification came in shipping, and more specifically in local coastal steamshipping. This began in 1856 when the partners promoted the Calcutta and Burmah S.N. Co to conduct regular sailings between Calcutta and the Burmese ports. It was perhaps a natural step for men who already had one foot in shipping between the UK, India and Australia – W. Mackinnon & Co were shareholders in sailing ships managed by Mackinnon Frew & Co of Liverpool as well as in Lewis Potter's Glasgow and Eastern Company, for both of which operations Mackinnon Mackenzie & Co acted as the Calcutta agents.

The initial stimulus for the new coastal steamship concern came from an attempt by leading Glasgow businessmen to wrest the UK–Australia mail contracts away from P&O, and William Mackinnon's related hopes for a connecting line or lines in the Bay of Bengal. The rather unexpected outcome of the initiative was the award of a contract from the Government of India for a steam packet service between Calcutta and Burma. This was an essentially opportunistic act of diversification, which drew a little upon the partners' familiarity with coastal steamshipping in western Scotland and their experience in ship agency work, but also required the mastering of new technology and its application to intra-Asian (as distinct from intercontinental) trades. It did little to support or advance the firm's import–export trades with Britain and Australia. Furthermore, remoteness from the shipyards and coal supplies of Britain made steamshipping in South Asian waters a relatively risky venture at this time, and the enterprise does not appear to have been a particularly profitable one.

Phase 2 (1862–75)

The firm's most significant phase of growth and diversity coincided with a roller-coaster period in British–Indian commercial and financial relations. The boom of 1862–66, brought about by the US Civil War and its impact on Indian produce prices, more especially raw cotton, gave way to the post-war depression of 1866–68 associated with the Overend Guerney crisis in London and the collapse of the Presidency Bank of Bombay. This in turn was followed by the boom – admittedly a somewhat less frenetic one – which followed the opening of the Suez Canal and led to the recovery of business confidence in both Britain and India.

Mackinnon Mackenzie & Co's breakthrough into the front ranks of the Calcutta agency houses occurred between 1862 and 1864, when William Mackinnon successfully interested the Government of India in reallocating existing mail contracts and in funding new mail contracts, which in turn underwrote the development of coastal liner services all around India and as far away as Singapore to the south-east and the Persian Gulf to the north-west. The consequent transformation of the Calcutta and Burma S.N. Co, with paid-up capital of £93,000, into the British India S.N. Co (BI), with a nominal capital of over £1,000,000, took place at a time when capital was freely available, both in India and Britain, for Indian-based ventures, and the Mackinnon and Hall families, by regulating the sale of shares in what was still a private joint stock company, came to control the greatly enlarged concern with less than 25 per cent of the issued capital. In turn, Mackinnon Mackenzie & Co held the managing agency contract on generous terms – 13.5 per cent on gross earnings (that is the ordinary steamer earnings minus direct costs) and a further 5 per cent on net company profits – and as BI's turnover grew over time, more especially during the decade or so after the opening of the Suez Canal (Munro 1990), the contract meant a substantial annual return to the partnership. It also drew Mackinnon Mackenzie & Co more deeply into the economic life of South Asia – as the managers of a system of passenger and freight transport comparable to and complementary with the Indian railway network.

This greater degree of involvement with the Indian economy was also manifest in other acts of diversification. In 1862–3, responding to the 'tea mania' which was Calcutta's equivalent of Bombay's cotton boom, Mackinnon Mackenzie & Co floated the Ramgurgh Tea Company (a rupee company) for the development of tea estates in the hill country of Bihar. Meanwhile, W. Mackinnon & Co in Glasgow promoted the Western Cachar Company (a sterling company) for the same purpose in eastern Bengal, although the managing agency contract went not to the controlling interests' own Calcutta house but to another firm, Begg Dunlop & Co, which William Mackinnon hoped to merge with Mackinnon Mackenzie & Co. The latter firm, however, also gradually acquired its own tea gardens, or management of tea gardens privately owned by its partners, at Chandpore near Chittagong as well as increasingly in Assam – at Nowgong and Mowdie Hill in the mid-1860s, and at Salonah and Bamonee in the early 1870s. By 1873, it had almost 200,000 rupees (or £10,000) of its own capital invested in tea properties (Table 3.1), and managed assets worth considerably more.

This involvement in tea planting was highly speculative, and simply reflected a willingness to follow the investment fashions of the time in the hope of future return – for Mackinnon Mackenzie & Co had no expertise in tea or other types of agricultural production, and initially paid the price of inexperience by acquiring properties, such as those of the Ramgurgh Company, which were not particularly suitable for tea cultivation.

More closely related to the firm's established lines of activity was its entry into jute manufacturing – for the Glasgow Jute Company of 1865, set up to spin jute in Glasgow, would purchase its raw material from Mackinnon Mackenzie & Co in Calcutta and have it transported in Mackinnon Frew's sailing ships, while the India Jute Company of 1866 (also a Glasgow-based

Table 3.1 Mackinnon Mackenzie & Co's investments (thousand rupees)

	1868	1873	1878	1883	1888	1892
EQUITY						
Shipping						
Sailing Ships	3.5	153.5	289.8	104.9	0	0
Steamships	0	91.3	380.9	649.4	937.9	890.8
Other	19.6	4.1	2.6	2.3	42.7	49.4
Shipping Total	23.1	248.9	673.3	756.6	980.6	940.2
Commodities						
Tea	71.4	219.7	12.5	10.0	17.2	16.8
Coal	0.0	14.4	47.6	40.0	0.0	0.0
Saw Mill	4.1	0.0	0.0	0.0	0.0	0.0
Manufacturing						
Cotton	34.9	0.0	234.4	202.4	1.8	1.4
Jute	0.0	159.2	120.1	81.3	1.5	1.7
Urban Property	20.7	13.7	45.5	40.7	64.2	97.7
Bank Shares	36.9	51.5	0.0	0.0	0.0	0.0
Equity Total	191.1	707.4	1,133.4	1,131.0	1,065.3	1,057.8
Shipping % Total	12.1	35.2	59.4	66.9	92.0	88.9
OTHER						
Govt. Securities	67	0	0	600	531	2,052.6
Co. Debentures	0	0	0	0	845	87
Cash in Banks	236.9	160.4	232.5	1,363.60	728.6	1,352.4
Other Total	304	160.4	232.5	1,963.6	2,104.3	3,491.7

Source: Mackinnan Papers, India File 24.

sterling company) would manufacture in Calcutta the gunny bags in which Mackinnon Mackenzie & BI already conducted a lively, if somewhat seasonal, trade with the rice ports of Burma and the sugar ports of the Coromandel Coast. The India Jute Company, which was under Mackinnon Mackenzie & Co's management, was the more successful of these two ventures, its mill at Serampore, up-river from Calcutta, quickly becoming an established part of the city's expanding jute industry. Finally, the partnership also dabbled in cotton-spinning, which the British business community of Calcutta had yet to recognise as an activity which would be more suitably located in Bombay.

Mackinnon Mackenzie & Co took small amounts of shares in several local cotton-spinning ventures, most notably the Goosery Cotton Mill Co, as a way of gaining some knowledge of the business, before it established its own venture, the Garden Reach Cotton Mill Association, in 1874. The mill, owned by a private syndicate of investors but managed by Mackinnon Mackenzie & Co, was set up on property acquired from BI in the riverfront district of Garden Reach, and drew for managerial and technical expertise on William Mackinnon's Lancashire connections, more especially on Eli Lees, an Oldham cotton spinner who had become a significant member of Mackinnon's investment circle. This shift towards import substitution was almost certainly related – perhaps more as a consequence than as a cause – to a decline which had set in the general trading side of the firm's affairs.

The evidence suggests that the Mackinnon and Hall family partnerships carried the process of diversification so far during 1862–75 that it actually undermined the very commercial foundations from which it had grown. Financing a controlling interest in BI (as well as its sister firm NISM, which operated in the Indonesian archipelago), and in the various other new enterprises for which Mackinnon Mackenzie & Co became managing agents, appears to made very heavy demands on the profits of the Glasgow and Calcutta firms – and on the capital of W. Mackinnon & Co in particular. The result was that the two firms withdrew from trade on their own account, and confined themselves to working on commission for others. However, reliance on other people's capital offered no guarantee of success, and various factors conspired to bring yet a further reduction in Mackinnon Mackenzie & Co's import–export business. The difficulties of the Scottish cotton manufacturers during the early years of US civil war and more especially during the post-war depression of 1866–70, which accelerated the long-run decline of the industry within the city of Glasgow (Knox 1995: 17–38), resulted in such a fall in the volume of W. Mackinnon & Co's exports of cotton goods from Glasgow to Calcutta that a decision was taken in 1874 to get out of that business altogether. Although Mackinnon Mackenzie & Co carried on for a while as importers of Lancashire cottons into Calcutta, that too was seen as a declining trade to be replaced by the output of the Garden Reach cotton mill.

Meanwhile the exporting side of the business had been weakened by the closure of two of the Mackinnon Mackenzie & Co's constituents in London during the Overend Guerny crisis of 1866, and by the failure of the Glasgow Jute Co to generate the level of demand for raw jute exports which had been anticipated. The firm's exporting was gradually transformed into a trade in relatively modest quantities of Indian produce to Australia. This was undertaken on behalf of small British (usually Scottish) merchant houses scattered along the necklace of Indian coastal ports served by BI (and who were usually BI agents in these ports as well as dealers in produce). As a consequence of the diversification of its activities, Mackinnon Mackenzie & Co had come to organise itself on a departmental basis, with a partner or senior assistant in

Table 3.2 Mackinnon Mackenzie & Co, Calcutta: departmental earnings (thousand rupees)

30 April	BI Steamers	Other Shipping	Imports	Exports	General	Invest-ments	Interest & Discount	Total	BI % Total
1868	188	78	20	18	73	0	0	377	49.9
1869	353	63	43	37	51	0	0	547	64.5
1870	189	54	86	7	108	0	0	444	42.6
1871	122	40	-36	30	85	0	0	241	50.6
1872	251	66	25	3	178	0	0	523	48.0
1873	328	56	53	8	24	156	83	708	46.3
1874	518	51	-3	39	131	23	139	898	57.7
1875	324	39	22	33	44	24	165	651	49.8
1876	396	80	7	24	42	-130	178	597	66.3
1877	514	114	10	103	50	170	73	1034	49.7
1878	567	65	-8	30	64	-103	104	719	78.9
1879	333	6	3	9	101	-365	484	633	52.6
1880	420	118	2	3	57	-37	123	686	61.2
1881	526	172	1	15	90	71	200	1075	48.9
1882	570	230	0	18	126	0	771	1715	33.2
1883	n.a.	n.a.	n.a.	n.a.	n.a	n.a.	n.a.	n.a.	
1884	n.a.	n.a.	n.a.	n.a.	n.a.	n.a.	n.a.	n.a.	
1885	373	177	0	12	105	44	227	938	39.8
1886	412	272	0	17	61	14	135	911	45.2
1887	522	217	0	16	71	13	241	1080	48.3
1888	570	191	0	15	109	18	187	1090	52.3
1889	697	266	0	13	154	24	231	1385	50.3
1890	685	264	0	16	119	78	107	1269	54.0
1891	744	211	0	16	174	129	403	1677	44.4
1892	704	262	0	35	133	95	570	1799	39.1

Note: because of abscence of supplementary accounts, figures for BI steamers in 1878, 1879 and 1882, and for ships and canal steamers in 1882, are estimates.

Source: Mackinnon Papers, India File 24.

charge of each department, and when figures for departmental earnings first become available, in the financial year 1867–8, the profits from the import and export departments together already constituted as little as 10 per cent of the total, compared with 20 per cent from the intercontinental ship agency department and 50 per cent from managing BI's coastal and intra-Asian steamshipping lines (Table 3.2). It continued on a declining trend thereafter.

Phase 3 (1875–93)

From about 1875, Mackinnon Mackenzie & Co entered a new era in its history, when its diversification energies slackened and it came to focus ever more than before on the shipping agency strand of its business. During this period, the firm acquired no new managing agencies and, while it retained its existing responsibilities for management of the Ramgurgh Tea Co, the India Jute Co, the Garden Reach cotton mill and various scattered tea gardens, it took every opportunity to reduce its equity holding in these enterprises. This occurred particularly during the enlargement of the partnership in 1878 and the reconstruction of the firm in 1884–85, when the Garden Reach Cotton Co and the Kondoli Tea Co were incorporated. Between 1873 and 1888 (see Table 3.1), Mackinnon Mackenzie & Co investments in commodity production and manufacturing in India fell from about 55 per cent to about 2 per cent of its total equity investments. Conversely, its shareholdings in ships and shipping companies increased almost five-fold in value, and rose from 35 per cent to 92 per cent of its total equity holdings. The firm continued to be profitable, and to grow, but it checked its penetration into the agricultural and industrial sectors of the Indian economy and reduced its exposure to the risks of shareholding in these sectors. Furthermore, Mackinnon Mackenzie & Co's increased investment in shipping was not into the British India S.N. So, for which it had special responsibility as managing agents, but went instead into shipping concerns which were managed by other parties in the UK. There was, in short, a substantial disinclination towards further engagement with the Indian economy.

What explains this pattern of events? The answer lies partly in change in the general economic environment. The decline in the rupee's value against the pound sterling (part of the general world devaluation of silver-standard currencies against gold-standard currencies) brought about a shift in the rate of exchange from about 2/- to the rupee in the early 1870s to about 1/3d to the rupee in the early 1890s. The progressive loss of up to 37 per cent in the value of rupee profits on sterling investments made in India acted as a general disincentive to further British investment in the subcontinent – this was a time, for example, when the birth rate of new jute mills in Calcutta declined – and the sterling companies under Mackinnon Mackenzie & Co's management suffered, like all the others, from a fall in the value of remittances received from India. However, currency problems cannot be the whole explanation since it remained open to Mackinnon Mackenzie to diversify by way of the creation of rupee companies floated in India. Furthermore, members of the Mackinnon and Hall families *were* investing in India during this period – but with the difference that they were doing so outside Mackinnon Mackenzie & Co.

Personal circumstances also contributed to Mackinnon Mackenzie & Co's step back from diversification. Almost all of the expansion in the firm's portfolio of activities between 1862 and 1875 had been brought about by the entrepreneurial endeavours of William Mackinnon, who by the early 1870s was the only surviving senior partner in the firm. Between 1847 and 1873 William Mackinnon had alternated periods of residence in Glasgow, at the head of W. Mackinnon & Co, with periods of residence in Calcutta, at the head of Mackinnon Mackenzie & Co. However, on returning to the UK in 1873, having secured the consolidation of BI's contracts with the Government of India into a single ten-year contract, William Mackinnon began to translate his business activities from Glasgow to London, and to work more through the junior partnerships within the Mackinnon Group to the relative neglect of those he had founded in Glasgow and Calcutta. He never returned to his seat in the Calcutta office – partly because his wife refused to go back to the city – and instead he devoted his talents for opportunistic business initiatives to a range of international adventures – from land for orange groves in Florida, to a meat-packing plant in Queensland, and to railway promotion in Western India and in East and Central Africa. Had he remained the effective head of Mackinnon Mackenzie & Co, it is probable that the pattern of broad diversification by the firm would have continued after 1875. Instead, for the men who took over the running of the Calcutta office – first his cousin Duncan Mackinnon, then Peter Hall, and eventually, after something of an inter-regnum, James Lyle Mackay – William Mackinnon's presence in the UK came to be a negative force, more capable of blocking initiatives he did not like than of seizing opportunities as they presented themselves locally in India. This is seen most explicitly in his attempts to prevent Mackinnon Mackenzie & Co from re-entering import–export trades on their own account. When, in 1877, the firm went in for large (and, as it turned out, profitable) exports of raw jute, William Mackinnon let his displeasure be known:

> We must not become speculators in produce. It will only lose money & give trouble. Our sound commission business is large enough to tax the energies of all . . . and I trust we will have no more produce operations. If you had as much experience of such things as I have you would not think on such business . . .

> (Nat. Lib. Acc. 6168/7)

The same philosophy led to his decision to sell off Mackinnon Mackenzie's Karachi branch (set up in 1878 following the closure of BI's agents there), when it was discovered that the commissions on BI business were not enough to cover the costs of operations and that any agency in that port would need to be combined with general trade. Although no examples can be found of opportunities for fresh diversification into commodity production or manufacturing being put to him and being turned down, the messages emanating from the Burlington Hotel in London and the Balinakill estate in Argyll were broadly that local initiatives by Mackinnon Mackenzie & Co's junior partners in India were not particularly welcome.

However, this was not simply a matter of William Mackinnon becoming more conservative as he grew older. It must also be understood in the context of the rise of the second generation of family firms within the group, and consequent shifts in the location and nature of functions conducted within the group (see Figure 3.1). By the 1870s, two new focal points for enterprise had emerged within the family-run network of investment. The first was Gray Dawes and Co of London, which was established on William Mackinnon's initiative by his nephew, Archie Gray, and a partner, Edwyn Dawes. Gray Dawes & Co combined trade in the Persian Gulf and East Africa and the conduct of BI agencies in these regions with ship agency and maritime insurance work in the Port of London. It became, in practice if not in name, the managing agents for the Mackinnon Group's ventures into deep-water intercontinental steam shipping from the mid-1870s onwards. The initial reactions of the Mackinnon–Hall family partnerships to the opening of the Suez Canal had been to invest in strengthening BI's position in South Asian waters and to modernising the small sailing ship fleet managed by Mackinnon Frew of Liverpool, in the expectation that there would still be profitable bulk trades for sailing ships between the UK and India around the Cape. This latter decision is reflected in the rise in the value of Mackinnon Mackenzie & Co's investment in sailing ships to a peak of 289,833 rupees in 1878 (see Table 3.1).

However, by the mid-1870s it had become clear that steamships via the canal would be the dominant force in trade between Europe and India, and the group commenced its own steamship line to Calcutta. This operated out of London rather than Liverpool and Glasgow, was owned by a private syndicate of family members together with a few selected outsiders, and was managed by Gray Dawes & Co. Much of the immediate strain of financing this initiative fell on Mackinnon Mackenzie & Co, and is reflected in the rise in the value of its investments in steamships to 649,400 rupees in 1883 (Table 3.1) and to the losses made by the firm's investments department in the late 1870s (Table 3.2). Even if other diversification opportunities had presented themselves in Calcutta at that time, the firm would have been hard-pressed to finance them out of retained profits. Investment in the British India Associated Steamers benefited Mackinnon Mackenzie & Co, in that it had the agency for the steamers in Calcutta, and the group's success in London–Calcutta steamshipping encouraged other shipping enterprises, like Wilsons of Hull, to appoint the firm as their agents in Calcutta. Nevertheless, something of a shift was taking place in the investment patterns within the group.

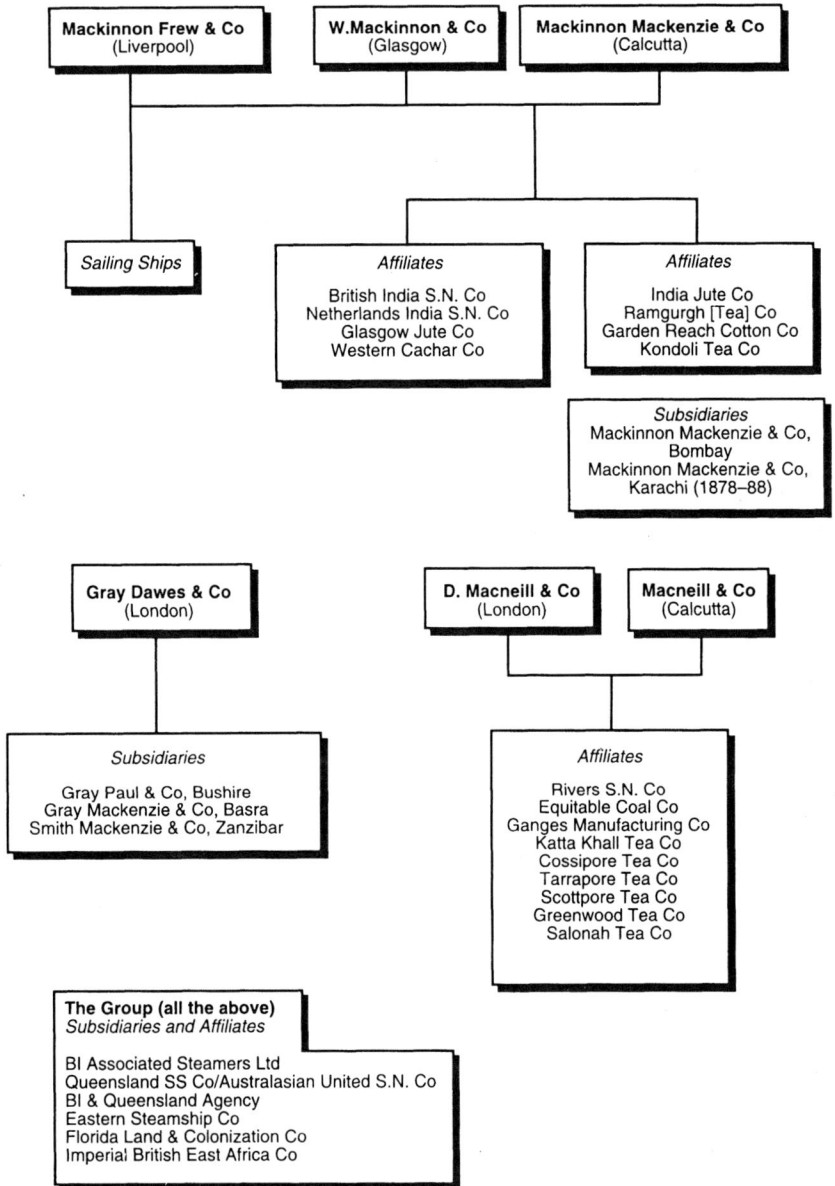

Figure 3.1 The Mackinnon Group, 1860–93

Before 1875 Mackinnon Mackenzie & Co was the principal beneficiary of shipping investments made mainly from the UK end of the group's Glasgow–Liverpool–Calcutta axis, more especially through the establishment of BI; after 1875 it was expected to be a major contributor to shipping operations based in London and from which it derived increasingly fewer benefits. This was particularly true in the 1880s, when British India Associated Steamers Ltd (incorporated in 1885) developed services from London to Java and Queensland which completely by-passed Calcutta, and when Mackinnon Mackenzie was called upon to assist the group's acquisition of a coastal shipping company in Australia as well as a controlling interest in the Eastern Steamship Co (the Ducal Line) which was diverted from UK–India to UK–Australia shipping routes (Munro 1991). Resentment at Mackinnon Mackenzie & Co's conversion into something of a handmaiden to Gray Dawes & Co in shipping matters surfaced among the Calcutta-based partners from time to time. However, William Mackinnon's dominant one-third share in the firm ensured compliance to the overall strategy.

The twin houses of Macneill & Co, Calcutta, and Duncan Macneill & Co, London, represented the second new growth point within the group. These firms were set up in the early 1870s by Duncan Macneill and John Mackinnon, respectively a nephew and a cousin of William Mackinnon's, who left the Calcutta firm of Begg Dunlop & Co, in which they had previously been placed with a view to amalgamating that firm with Mackinnon Mackenzie & Co. They took with them some of Begg Dunlop & Co's agencies and picked up others when that firm went into temporary liquidation in 1873. Rather than bring the younger men and their interests within the Mackinnon Mackenzie & Co partnership, William Mackinnon and other family members gave them every assistance to establish their own firms – lending them money, extending them credit and investing in the concerns for which Macneill & Co became managing agents. By 1875, these included a river steamship company, a coal company, a jute mill, three tea companies and some other tea estates. Macneill & Co became a junior ally of Mackinnon Mackenzie & Co, with much the same spread of diversified interests as the older Calcutta house. The two firms were mutually supportive – it was of considerable assistance to Macneill & Co's Equitable Coal Company, for example, that Mackinnon Mackenzie & Co's British India S.N. Co was the largest purchaser of Bengali coal in Calcutta, while Macneill & Co's Rivers S.N. Co conducted services on the Brahmaputra river as far as Assam, where both firms had tea estates under their management. Tea shipments from the two firms were exported from Calcutta on vessels of BI Associated Steamers, and were sold on arrival in London by the tea-broking house of Duncan Macneill & Co.

Of the two firms in Calcutta, Macneill & Co already had by 1875 the larger stake in tea planting and related services, and after that date it appears to have become the policy of the family-led group to concentrate its further investments in tea into the Macneill & Co/Duncan Macneill & Co firms, while leaving Mackinnon Mackenzie & Co to focus upon shipping. At least three new tea companies – the Scottpore, Greenwood and Salonah – were floated between 1875 and 1885 with Macneill & Co as managing agents, and at the same time as Mackinnon Mackenzie & Co was reducing its equity investment in the tea companies it still managed. (At his death in 1893, William Mackinnon had over £53,000 of his personal estate invested in the tea companies promoted and managed by Macneill & Co.) Family capital also went into the Rivers S.N. Co's takeover in 1888 of the river fleet of a rival firm, the Assam Railways and Trading Company, so as to secure Macneill & Co's continuing dominance in transport and communications between Calcutta and the Assam tea districts.

The reasons for such an emerging division of labour within the group, between the respective landward and maritime sections of the India tea trade, appear to lie in the politics of the shipping industry. Tea freights were a crucial factor in the liner trades between London and Calcutta, which from 1875 was regulated by the world's first major shipping conference (or cartel). Tea was a fine freight, with a high value-to-bulk ratio, and was therefore an ideal cargo for steamship liners combining passenger and cargo traffic. William Mackinnon was well aware that access to the large shipments of tea made by Mackinnon Mackenzie & Co and Macneill & Co gave his BI Associated Steamers an edge in securing and maintaining a share of the liner market. On the other hand, if Mackinnon & Co, as Calcutta agents for the shipping line, were seen to have too large a direct stake in tea shipments and were seen to be in danger of putting their own interests before those of other shippers of tea, the liners could lose market share to other members of the conference. It therefore made good commercial sense after 1875 to place the group's growing tea planting and related service activities under the wing of the legally separate Macneill firms.

In essence, then, the standstill in Mackinnon Mackenzie's diversification activities between 1875 and 1893 took place in the interests of the diversification of the group as a whole. Poised between the newer family interests in London and Calcutta, its role became ever more focused upon steamship management and agency work, and its profits from these activities became a source of ready capital to meet the immediate needs of other parts of the enterprise group of which it was a major component. Mackinnon Mackenzie & Co was a highly profitable firm – between 1868 and 1893 its return on capital employed averaged 26.1 per cent per annum – but these earnings were largely redeployed elsewhere, either in the form of short-term purchases of shares in new shipping ventures for subsequent transfer to the ownership of the partners and their associates or through the direct withdrawal of partners' capital. William Mackinnon's share in the firm, for example, increased in value from £62,000 in 1867 to £243,000 in 1892 (in current rates of exchange), but in the meantime he had also withdrawn £185,300 (in 1870 rates of exchange) to finance both his investments in other group activities and his own more private speculations.

Conclusion

Between 1862 and 1893, Mackinnon Mackenzie & Co moved from a pattern of diversification across a broad front within its adopted territory to one of greater specialisation of function within India as part of a larger process of group diversification on an international scale. As the Mackinnon family interests in Britain extended their activities to the Middle East, Africa and Australia, Mackinnon Mackenzie & Co lost something of its former role as the flagship firm around which all new investment initiatives took place, and became instead merely the manager of one part of the group's interests in India as well as a major source of funding for the globalisation of the group's operations. This empirical case study, therefore, highlights the potential analytical significance of the distinction which has been drawn by Geoff Jones between 'regional specialization' and 'geographic diversification' (Jones 1996: 116–17). Initially the Glasgow–Calcutta axis of W. Mackinnon & Co/Mackinnon Mackenzie & Co appears to have diversified in much the same way as that other, and better-known, Glasgow–India axis represented by the firm of James Finlay & Co – with comparable investments in jute, tea and shipping (the Clan Line in the Finlay case) focused upon the South Asian region. Over the longer term, however, the Mackinnon Group evolved more in the direction of the enterprise network associated with Matheson & Co of London, Jardine Matheson & Co of Hong Kong and Jardine Skinner & Co of Calcutta – that is it became a group with interests and investments in more than one major world region. In the process, the Mackinnon-Hall and Jardine-Matheson groups burst through the territorial limits of Britain's formal, and even 'informal', empire to become truly international, or global, players.

Associated with this greater geographic spread there also appears to be some distinction in organisational forms – the Mackinnon-Hall and Jardine-Matheson enterprise groups were networking organisations *par excellence*, whereas the Finlay's system of management and control, operated from a single head office, located them further along the spectrum towards the internalised hierarchic firm. James Finlay & Co had commenced their trading operations in India in the 1830s very much in a networking mode, but moved fairly quickly to the adoption of the head-office/branch-office mode, with the establishment of branch firms in Bombay (1862), Calcutta (1870), London (1871), Karachi (1890) and Chittagong (1901), and the incorporation of the firm itself in 1909 ([Brogan] 1951). This introduction of a hierarchic structure and the deepening commitment to the South Asian region coincided with, and was made possible by, the improvement of communications between Britain and India – more especially the arrival of the intercontinental telegraph and the speedier postal communications following the opening of the Suez Canal. The growing ability to manage operations in India more directly and immediately from Britain could well have pointed the Mackinnon Group in the same direction. But its trajectory was a different one – outwards from

India, and continuing to employ networking methods. Such divergence may be explained by factors specific to the two organisations – Finlay's origins in cotton manufacturing gave it a much stronger ongoing commitment to the marketing of piece goods in India than W. Mackinnon & Co possessed. Or more personal circumstances may have come into play – William Mackinnon knew and admired Hugh Matheson of Matheson & Co, and seems to have been inclined from 1875 onwards to model his business behaviour on that of his fellow financial supporter of the Free Church of Scotland. What is also possible, however, and remains to be tested by examination of a wider range of case studies, is that the transformation in communications and improved information flows of the second half of the nineteenth century may have encouraged both regionally intensive and geographically extensive patterns of diversification within the world economy at the same time, but were not themselves sufficiently strong to bring about internalising organisational processes among those firms which had or acquired global interests. It would take the telephone, radio and air travel of the twentieth century to bring about that change.

'Regional specialisation' versus 'geographic spread', however, can only partly account for the role played by Mackinnon Mackenzie & Co within the group – for there was further specialisation *within* the South Asian arena. What was unusual within the wider history of British agency houses in India was the rise of Macneill & Co in Calcutta – for no other family-led expatriate enterprise group spawned a second, and ostensibly competitive, firm in the same location as a more established house. Although, in the slightly longer term, the growth of Macneill & Co alongside Mackinnon Mackenzie & Co proved to be a convenient means of handling potentially divergent interests, the origins of the arrangement, in the years between 1869 and 1873, lay deep within the family itself. We shall probably never know how or why the other partners in Mackinnon Mackenzie & Co dissuaded William Mackinnon from merging the emergent Macneill & Co with his own Calcutta firm, something he still hankered after as late as 1878, but whatever the reasons they remind us that 'families may choose to diversify their economic interests in a number of ways, which may or may not involve growth of their original firm' (Jones and Rose 1993: 10).

References

Published texts

[Brogan, C.] (1951) *James Finlay & Company Limited*, Glasgow: Jackson Son & Company.
Chapman, S. (1985) 'British-based investment groups before 1914', *Economic History Review*, 2nd series, 38: 230–251.
—— (1992) *Merchant Enterprise in Britain*, Cambridge: Cambridge University Press.
Griffiths, Sir P. (1977) *A History of the Inchcape Group*, London: Inchcape & Co Ltd.

Jones, G. (1996) 'Diversification strategies and corporate governance in trading companies: Anglo-Japanese comparisons since the late nineteenth century', *Business and Economic History*, 25, (2): 103–18.

Jones, G. and Rose, M. B. (eds) (1993) 'Family capitalism', *Business History*, 35, no. 4.

Jones, S. (1986) *Two Centuries of Overseas Trading: The Origins and Growth of the Inchcape Group*, London: Macmillan.

Kling, B.B. (1966–7) 'The origin of the managing agency system in India', *Journal of Asian Studies*, 26: 37–47.

Knox, W.W. (1995) *Hanging by a Thread: The Scottish Cotton Industry, 1850–1914*, Preston: Carnegie Publishing.

Munro, J. F. (1988) 'Scottish overseas enterprise and the lure of London: the Mackinnon Shipping Group, 1847–1893', *Scottish Economic and Social History*, 8: 73–7.

—— (1990) 'Suez and the shipowner: the response of the Mackinnon Group to the opening of the canal, 1869–1884', in L. R. Fischer and H. W. Nordvik (eds) *Shipping and Trade*, Pontefract: Lofthouse Publications.

—— (1991) '"The gilt of illusion": the Mackinnon Group's entry into Queensland shipping, 1880–1895', *International Journal of Maritime History*, III, (2): 1–37.

Tomlinson, B. R. (1989) 'British business in India, 1860–1970', in Davenport-Hines, R. P.T. and Jones, G. (eds) *British Business in Asia since 1860*, Cambridge: Cambridge University Press.

Wilkins, M. (1988) 'The free-standing company, 1870–1914: an important type of British foreign direct investment', *Economic History Review*, 2nd series, 41: 259–82.

Manuscript sources

Nat.Lib.Acc. 6168/7: Papers of Duncan Mackinnon, National Library of Scotland, Edinburgh, William Mackinnon to Duncan Mackinnon, 23 March 1877.

Mackinnon Papers: Papers of Sir William Mackinnon, Library of the School of Oriental and African Studies, London.

Inchcape Papers: Records of the Inchcape Group of Companies, Guildhall Library, London.

4 The German metal traders before 1914

Susan Becker

An outstanding feature of the international trade in non-ferrous metals before 1914 was the importance of German companies. This chapter aims at an explanation of the factors which contributed to the German metal traders' international success. After the examination of the German metal traders' expansion abroad, special attention will be paid to vertical integration and long-term contracts, which appear to have been an efficient alternative to full-scale integration. Moreover, the German metal traders' attitude towards cartelisation will be examined, as it had a considerable bearing on their business. To begin with, their management will be described.

Intermediation between production and consumption – which is considered the basic definition of trade (cf. Casson, Chapter 2, this volume) – rested overwhelmingly on:

> Metallgesellschaft, Frankfurt/Main;
> Aron Hirsch & Sohn, Halberstadt;
> Beer, Sondheimer & Co., Frankfurt/Main.

Aron Hirsch & Sohn was founded in 1805 by Aron Hirsch. Metallgesellschaft was incorporated under the leadership of Wilhelm Merton in 1881 as the successor of the firm of Philipp Abr. Cohen. Beer, Sondheimer & Co. was established in 1872 by two former assistant managers (*Prokuristen*) of the firm of Cohen.

In 1913, there were more than 550 companies engaged in the non-ferrous metal trade in Germany (Prinz 1984: 173). Yet, most of them remained insignificant compared to Metallgesellschaft, Aron Hirsch & Sohn and Beer, Sondheimer & Co., which seem to have dominated not only the national, but also the international stage.[1] They were able to gain such importance at the expense of their competitors because of their superior organisational, financial and technological capabilities. There were only a few serious competitors to them, like the London-based Brandeis Goldschmidt & Co. and the giant American organisations (Adey 1930: 38, 39, 43).[2] The German metal traders' dominance might well be illustrated by the fact that the British Government issued the Non-Ferrous Metal Industry Act (1917) explicitly in order to oust the Germans from the business, especially in the British sphere of interest (PRO/1).

There were two fundamental factors of influence in the international non-ferrous metal trade prior to the First World War. On the one hand, preconditions for trade were favourable as Germany and Europe as a whole became increasingly dependent on imported non-ferrous minerals and metals because overseas sources increasingly replaced domestic ones while, at the same time, domestic consumption had risen since the nineteenth century. On the other hand, there was a strong tendency prevailing among producers and consumers of non-ferrous minerals and metals to deal directly with each other so that the scope for the independent non-ferrous metal trade was perpetually threatened to diminish. The establishment of syndicates reinforced this threat. The company history of Metallgesellschaft, for example, suggests that it would have developed even better if agencies of American corporations had not been established in Europe (MGA/1: 68).

There remains comparatively little historical research on the German non-ferrous metal trade. Responsibility for this rests mainly on the absence of primary sources. Owing to the fact that only the records of Metallgesellschaft have survived, this company will perforce provide the main empirical data in the following study. This bias is partly justified by the fact that Metallgesellschaft was the most important of the German metal traders at the time and stands as a representative for the other two. Even though a single case study cannot provide insights invariably applicable to the entire group, it is nevertheless valuable in order to reveal the working mechanisms.

Management

Metallgesellschaft, Aron Hirsch & Sohn and Beer, Sondheimer & Co. can be considered family firms in the sense that they were not only owned, but also managed by family members. Whereas Aron Hirsch & Sohn and Beer, Sondheimer & Co. were *Personalgesellschaften*, Metallgesellschaft was founded as a joint-stock company. Yet, the overwhelming majority of shares was held by members of the founding families, i.e. by Ralph and Wilhelm Merton and by Leo Ellinger.[3] By issuing personal shares, Metallgesellschaft's founders restricted their interchangeability (MGA/1: 8).[4] Moreover, Metallgesellschaft's shares were not quoted on the stock exchange. Consequently, Metallgesellschaft very much preserved the character of a family-owned company despite its legal framework.

This is even more interesting if one considers that, in retrospect, Wilhelm Merton claimed to have chosen the legal shape of a joint-stock company because it offered greater advantages in order to attract outside capital. Yet, at the same time, Wilhelm Merton was a strong advocate of the principle of Metallgesellschaft's financial independence of outside capital and banks. His opinion was strongly influenced by his desire to keep managerial control for himself, which is shown by the fact that he was authorised to act on behalf of the entire board of directors (MGA/1: 9, 21). This motivation also surfaces in his reluctance to admit new partners, which was very often necessary when private partnerships wanted to attract leading personnel (MGA/1:7). Summing up, one can conclude that, on the one hand, Wilhelm Merton wanted to provide Metallgesellschaft with a broader capital basis in order to satisfy its financial requirements. That is the reason why he chose to organise it as a joint-stock company. On the other hand, he was unwilling to take the step to the stock exchange because he wanted to maintain full managerial control. That's why most of Metallgesellschaft's shares were held by the founding families. Consequently, the organisational principles of Metallgesellschaft show some kind of compromise typical of German family firms of that era.

From the beginning Metallgesellschaft was able to rely on self-finance through retained and and reinvested earnings so that it remained independent of any outside bank (MGA/1: 21, 22, 46). Originally, Beer, Sondheimer & Co. had made use of the financial backing of Mitteldeutsche Kreditanstalt (APC 1919: 65; Auerbach 1965: 198). Their rapidly developing business soon enabled them to do without and become financially independent, too. This, however, did not preclude that each of the German metal traders fostered relations with one or another bank (United States Federal Trade Commission 1916: 359; PRO/2).

There was, however, some kind of division of labour in the management. Metallgesellschaft was managed by a 'triumvirate' consisting of Wilhelm Merton, Leo Ellinger and Zacharias Hochschild. Wilhelm Merton was *primus inter pares*, as he was responsible for business strategy and organisation, whereas Leo Ellinger was in charge of the day-to-day running of the company and Zacharias Hochschild of outward representation and international relations (MGA/1: 12). Aron Hirsch & Sohn exhibits a similar kind of specialisation of its management as Benjamin Hirsch devoted most of his activity to the international business while Aron Hirsch, the founder's grandson, applied himself to the industrial development (Zielenziger 1930: 201–4; Mosse 1987: 55).

Usually, the founders' sons were admitted to the management after they had passed some kind of apprenticeship, which usually also took them to foreign affiliates of the family firm or to friendly related companies (Ratz 1994: 187; Hirsch 1967: 47–58). While Aron Hirsch & Sohn could rely entirely on having family members in the upper management, the owner families of Metallgesellschaft and Beer, Sondheimer & Co. were gradually supported by 'outsiders'. Zacharias Hochschild had no shareholding in Metallgesellschaft but he was tied to the owner families through family bonds as he was married to the daughter of Leo Ellinger. Moreover, Zacharias Hochschild had been assistant manager in the firm of Cohen, so that a high degree of trust can be presupposed for his relationship to the company owners. When, after the turn of the century, the scope of Metallgesellschaft's business had increased to such an extent that other non-family members were co-opted as junior managers, the Merton family still maintained managerial control (MGA/1: 50).The cohesion within the management was facilitated by the fact that all non-family members of Metallgesellschaft's executive were recruited from long-time staff, so that there were no real 'outsiders' in the management. Family ties were established between the senior management and its successors, too. A daughter of Zacharias Hochschild married one of the future members of Metallgesellschaft's executive in 1903 (MGA/1: 9; Prenzel 1972: 290). Gradually, the partnership of Isaac Leopold Beer and Moses Tobias Sondheimer was also reinforced by non-family members. Their number, however, did not rise above two against five members of the founders' families until the 1920s, so that the character of a family firm was preserved, too. Louis Feist, one of the outsiders who became a partner in the firm, was succeeded by his son so that they established some kind of family tradition of their own (Auerbach 1965: 198, 199).

Metallgesellschaft, Beer, Sondheimer & Co. and Aron Hirsch & Sohn were Jewish-owned companies. This is no coincidence but rather reflects the fact that 70 per cent of all known German non-ferrous metal trading companies were Jewish just before the First World War (Prinz 1984: 173). While Wilhelm Merton was converted to Christianity in 1890 and also raised his sons as Christians, Leo Ellinger and Zacharias Hochschild maintained their Jewish faith. The families of Hirsch, Beer, and Sondheimer also remained closely affiliated with the Jewish religious community.The religious affiliations of the management of these companies resulted in certain repercussions. Neither Aron Hirsch & Co. nor Beer, Sondheimer & Co. would have taken a Gentile into partnership, while Leo Ellinger and Zacharias Hochschild continued not to work on Saturdays and Jewish holidays (Auerbach 1965: 189). It would be very informative to find out about business contacts rooted in the metal traders' affiliation to the Jewish religious community and its business networks. However, only a very general statement can be made here. The Jewish merchants' success appears to have been based rather on their cosmopolitan receptivity for new stimuli than on their international contacts *per se* (Prinz 1984: 143; Mosse 1987: 55).

As far as Metallgesellschaft is concerned, great care was devoted to the training of the personnel which, for example, was subjected to job rotation (MGA/1: 23, 24). By thorough education, Metallgesellschaft sought, on the one hand, to establish a high standard of job qualification, whilst on the other hand, it tried to assure itself of the loyalty of its employees either by granting them a percentage of the profit (*Tantiemen*) or by allowing them to acquire a small number of shares in the company (MGA/1: 22). The underlying ratio-nale was to educate its personnel and Metallgesellschaft was then able to use them as its representatives or as leading managers at the Frankfurt headquar-ters or in one of its foreign subsidiaries (MGA/1: 14, 15, 23, 24; MGA/3: 3; Auerbach 1965: 196). In order to reduce the risk associated with foreign investments in particular, Metallgesellschaft usually delegated trustworthy employees in responsible positions. Curt Netto, a well-known German metal-lurgist and one of Metallgesellschaft's directors, became a member of the

Conseil d'Administration of Metallgesellschaft's most important industrial venture, Usine de Désargenation at Hoboken (Belgium). Jacob Langeloth, a former member of Metallgesellschaft's executive, became President of Metallgesellschaft's American subsidiary, the American Metal Co. Ltd. He was joined by Berthold Hochschild, who was a brother of Zacharias Hochschild, as Director of Finance. Two of Wilhelm Merton's sons spent some time in leading positions in the American Metal Company, too, so that family ties helped to establish close connections between the management in Frankfurt and New York (MGA/1: 17, 18, 35, 36). Other subsidiaries and joint ventures of Metallgesellschaft recruited their leading managers from Frankfurt, too.

Diversification and expansion abroad

While Aron Hirsch & Sohn and Beer, Sondheimer & Co. basically restricted themselves to the trade in copper, lead and zinc, Metallgesellschaft expanded further into aluminium, nickel and pyrites on a large scale. 'Product diversification' was part of Metallgesellschaft's response to the threat of elimination. In connection with the development of its technological services, Metallgesellschaft was able to become Rio Tinto's sales agency in 1903 (Harvey 1981: 81; MGA/1: 43, 57, 58). Much of the business in aluminum and nickel can be ascribed to the dense network of business contacts established by Zacharias Hochschild (Auerbach: 194). When the international ore market evolved at the turn of the century, Metallgesellschaft, Aron Hirsch & Sohn and Beer, Sondheimer & Co. also branched out into ore trading. Unfortunately, there is no ready explanation of why Metallgesellschaft diversified more than its competitors. Principally, the other companies would have been able to apply the same means, but why they refrained from doing so or why they were less successful cannot be explained.

Internationality became a prerequisite for German metal trading companies when Europe became increasingly dependent on foreign ores and metals. Consequently, the German metal traders had to organise their business internationally. Reaching out to all important centres of the non-ferrous metal business, the metal traders could principally choose between two different methods of organisation: either to appoint agents and representatives or to internalise their function through branch offices or investments in legally independent companies. The American example is informative in this respect. In 1887, Metallgesellschaft founded the American Metal Company in New York. Aron Hirsch & Sohn followed ten years later when they participated in the formation of the firm of L. Vogelstein & Co. on the basis of a 35 per cent investment. Similar to Metallgesellschaft, Aron Hirsch & Sohn favoured shareholdings in legally independent foreign companies instead of creating branch offices (Zielenziger 1930: 202). Beer, Sondheimer & Co. not only lagged far behind, but they also chose a different organisational framework. In 1906, they established their New York branch office.

While Metallgesellschaft did not completely dispense with agents and representatives, it was nevertheless very active in creating trade subsidiaries: Compañia Minerales y Metales, Mexico (Mexico) (1889); Australian Metal Company Ltd., Melbourne/London (Australia) (1897); and Compagnie des Minerais, Liège (Belgium) (1900). The latter was organised in reaction to the increasing importance of the international non-ferrous ore business. It shows that Metallgesellschaft was not only able to spot new opportunities, but it also managed to provide them with an organisational framework at an early stage in their development. Consequently, Metallgesellschaft gained an advantage over its competitors (MGA/1: 70). It is interesting to note that Wilhelm Merton appears to have been rather proud of the organisational abilities of Metallgesellschaft (MGA/2: 6).

Contrary to Metallgesellschaft, Beer, Sondheimer and Aron Hirsch & Sohn seem to have been much more in favour of agencies and representations. In Australia, for example, where Metallgesellschaft established the Australian Metal Company, its competitors preferred to appoint indigenous companies as their agents. Aron Hirsch & Sohn used Francis H. Snow of Adelaide as their agent and Beer, Sondheimer & Co. engaged the firm of Elder Smith & Co. for the same purpose (APC 1919: 66).

The only example of Beer, Sondheimer & Co. founding a foreign company proved to be a failure. In 1897 they established their ore trading company, the Société Anonyme Minière at Liège, Belgium. Like Metallgesellschaft's Cie. des Minerais it was designed not only to trade in ores, but also to own and exploit mines. Unlike its counterpart, S.A. Minière accumulated losses only a few years after its foundation so that it was finally dissolved in 1910 (Devos 1986: 285, 287). This experience might explain the reluctance of Beer, Sondheimer & Co. to create legally independent trade subsidiaries. Instead, at the outbreak of the First World War, they had representatives in Paris, London, New York, Philadelphia, Adelaide, Haiphon, Calcutta, Mexico, Santiago de Chile, St Petersburg, Constantinople, etc. and in various German locations (StA/1: 3, 4).

Attempting to explain the organisational differences regarding the metal traders' international expansion, Wilhelm Merton offers some insights into the choice of Metallgesellschaft. In a controversy with a well-known German scholar (Robert Liefmann) over Metallgesellschaft's motivation to establish foreign joint-stock companies, he claimed that only his company possessed the degree of autonomy necessary to encompass both the commercial and also the industrial activities from the outset.[5] According to Wilhelm Merton, poor means of communication and transportation inhibited the establishment of branch offices because under such conditions they could not be sufficiently monitored from the Frankfurt headquarters. In order to create distinct responsibilities and autonomy Metallgesellschaft chose the establishment of legally independent joint-stock companies (MGA/2: 8; MGA/3: 39a). A decentralised organisation of its international business was implemented by Metallgesellschaft, while Aron Hirsch & Sohn and Beer, Sondheimer & Co. favoured a more centralised organisation.

Whether Wilhelm Merton chose the organisational framework of foreign subsidiaries because autonomy was an essential prerequisite for successful operations under the existing conditions of communication and transportation can be questioned in two ways. First, on one occasion Wilhelm Merton is known to have complained forcefully about the Australian Metal Company's managers not following his advice and his instructions, even though Metallgesellschaft owned the majority of its shares (MGA/5: 13, 16).[6] This stands in contrast to his claim that independent development of Metallgesellschaft's foreign subsidiaries was his aim. He was aware of the potential for conflict included in his views and tried to reconcile them. By means of interlocking shareholdings and market-sharing agreements, Metallgesellschaft aimed at enforcing the cohesion of its legally independent subsidiaries (MGA/3: 39a). For example, there was an agreement between Metallgesellschaft and Henry R. Merton & Co., its British sister company, on the one side and American Metal Co. on the other according to which the latter never acted in Europe (MGA/6; APC 1919: 72, 73).[7] Moreover, the foreign subsidiaries' managers were usually delegated from the Frankfurt headquarters. Wilhelm Merton's aforementioned complaint about the Australian Metal Company failing to follow his advice and instructions is informative in another respect. It can illustrate the general problem of the theory of multinational enterprise to distinguish between portfolio and direct investment purely on the basis of percentage of equity ownership. The same applies to Aron Hirsch & Sohn who were understood to control the firm of L. Vogelstein & Co. even though they only held the minority of shares in this company.

Second, Beer, Sondheimer & Co. established a branch office in New York so that there was not much freedom of decision making for the local managers because they remained employees of the Frankfurt headquarters (APC 1919: 88; Kabisch 1982: 240). It is exactly because of this that Wilhelm Merton kept a high degree of control over branch offices (MGA/5: 14). Nevertheless, it also diversified into non-trading as both the American Metal Co. and L. Vogelstein & Co. did (Wilkins 1989: 270–273). This observation contradicts Wilhelm Merton's previous argument. Consequently, it can be suggested that personal preferences were very influential in the decision about how to organise the international business. Wilhelm Merton himself remarked that he personally disliked branch offices (MGA/3: 39, 39a). A wider implication of this observation is the support it lends to the view that a dynamic factor of entrepreneurship should be introduced into the theory of multinational enterprise.

Regardless of individual factors of influence the creation of independent trade subsidiaries did not lack rationale. On the one hand, the advantage of foreign trade subsidiaries over agents and representatives was the higher standing they generated for the mother company in the respective host countries. On the other hand, they enabled the mother company to deal with third parties directly (Rieger 1992: 97, 101). These reasons for horizontal integration can be interpreted in the light of transaction cost theory putting emphasis on the internalisation of reputation.[8]

Vertical integration

When considering the German metal traders' strategy to avoid elimination, two types of vertical integration are evident: full-scale vertical integration through investment and quasi-vertical integration by means of long-term contracts. The latter is considered an intermediate mode of production since it neither operates in the market place nor within the hierarchy.

As early as 1820, Aron Hirsch & Sohn acquired their first copper-manufacturing works at Werne (Germany), soon being supplemented by another at Ilsenburg (Germany). In 1863, they diversified into the manufacturing of brass by means of an acquisition next to Eberswalde (Germany) which developed into one of the most modern and largest of its kind (Zielenziger 1930: 201; Auerbach 1965: 190). Aron Hirsch & Sohn not only integrated forwards, but they also established smelting facilities. Apart from Germany, Belgium was chosen as a productive location in order to found the zinc-smelting company, the Compagnie Métallurgique franco-belge de Mortagne in 1905 (Schaefer 1918: 124; Waechter 1913: 175). Moreover, Aron Hirsch & Sohn owned the majority of the shares of the British Swansea Vale Smelter Co. (APC 1919: 201; Cocks and Walters 1968: 17, 23).[9]

Soon after its foundation Metallgesellschaft made its most important investment in production facilities by founding Usine de Désargentation at Hoboken (Belgium) in 1887.[10] After only seven years it had developed into the most important European lead-smelting plant. Its non-ferrous output was entirely marketed by Metallgesellschaft thereby achieving the prominent position in the international lead business it had lacked hitherto (MGA/4). Other important direct investments were made into the production of non-ferrous metals in domestic locations. There were, for example: Metallhütte AG, Duisburg (Germany); Bergwerks- und Hütten AG Berzelius, Bensberg (Germany); Oberschlesische Zinkhütte AG, Kattowitz (Silesia); Norddeutsche Affinerie, Hamburg (Germany). Wilhelm Merton claimed in retrospect that the need to integrate backwards stemmed from his observation that the independent metal trade ran the risk of being bypassed (MGA/3: 31a).[11] In other words, transaction cost theory can be used as an argument for vertical integration of the German non-ferrous metal traders. All stages of production of non-ferrous metals are characterised by economies of scale and high-asset specificity, which results in small number conditions (Hennart 1991: 90). As producers and consumers increasingly dealt directly with each other, small number conditions caused rising transaction costs for independent metal traders. The latter were therefore inclined to integrate backwards in order not to be opportunistically upheld by producers.

Apart from this theoretical explanation a factor specific to Jewish entrepreneurs deserves consideration. The founder of the firm of Aron Hirsch

& Sohn, Aron Hirsch, also wanted to become an industrialist as well as being a wholesaler (Zielenziger 1930: 201). Many Jews went into production simply because they were allowed to at the beginning of the nineteenth century after having been restricted to trading for many years. So again, very individual reasons might have influenced the decision-making process.

Strikingly enough, Metallgesellschaft almost entirely refrained from forward integration. Initially Metallgesellschaft possessed a small copper-processing works at Oberursel, which were abandoned in 1882 in favour of a minority shareholding in Rheinisch Westfälische Kupferwerke, Olpe (Germany). In 1892, Metallgesellschaft also took a minority shareholding in Heddernheimer Kupferwerke (Germany) (MGA/1: 17, 27, 30). Looking at the date when Aron Hirsch & Sohn integrated forwards, the explanation could be that Metallgesellschaft concentrated its financial resources on backward integration because at the time of its foundation Europe as a whole was already in need of raw material. Contrary to this, Aron Hirsch & Sohn integrated forwards when Europe was still an important producer of non-ferrous ores and metals itself so that the metal trading company had to be less concerned about its supply and could devote its financial means to processing as well. Moreover, the previously mentioned tendency towards elimination of the independent metal trade had not yet gained importance. Finally, it should also be considered that forward integration always necessitates market-making investments, which backward integration does not.

The above explanation is backed by the observation that as far as vertical integration is concerned, Beer, Sondheimer & Co. resembled Metallgesellschaft rather than Aron Hirsch & Sohn as both were founded in the same era. Unfortunately the data concerning Beer, Sondheimer & Co. are very incomplete so that it is thought that this company integrated backwards into the production of zinc and lead by means of its 50 per cent shareholding in the German Metallwerke Unterweser AG, Nordenham and in the Belgian Société Anonyme La Nouvelle Montagne (StA/2; Schaefer 1918: 128; Waechter 1913: 175). Moreover, Beer, Sondheimer & Co. had financial interests in at least two other Belgian zinc smelters (Compagnie des Métaux Overpelt-Lommel; Societé de Prayon) believed to be direct investments of the German metal trader (Schaefer 1918: 116, 128; Waecheter 1913: 175; Devos 1986: 280–285).

In their desire to control the output of as many smelters and refineries as possible the German metal traders also made extensive use of long-term contracts of supply/delivery. As these were regularly supplemented by loans, advances or minority investments as well as by managerial and technological assistance or by interlocking directorships relations developed between the metal traders and their legally independent suppliers and consumers that were very much different from market relations (quasi-vertical integration). The latter relied on the metal traders' efficient and far-reaching sales organisation and on their competence to find customers for their output because this task did not only call for technological know-how, but it also necessitated a profound knowledge of the market and the needs specific to each consumer (Devos 1986: 61; MGA/1: 14, 39). Here lay the basis of the German metal traders' success in fullfilling both requirements.

The relationship between Beer, Sondheimer & Co. and the German Chemical Works Weickel AG, Worms may serve as an example. Despite the metal traders' minority shareholding in the firm of Weickel it was understood to be dependent on the former on account of other means of influence applied (supply of raw material and sale of output through Beer, Sondheimer & Co., loan) (StA/2). The company history of Metallgesellschaft speaks of 'special' or 'friendly' relations in similar circumstances. In 1893, for example, Metallgesellschaft participated in the foundation of Société Anonyme des Zincs de la Campine, Budel (Netherlands) by taking a minority shareholding as well as by sending one of its directors onto the new company's Conseil d'Administration. Moreover, it granted a loan to the zinc smelter on the basis of which Metallgesellschaft was allowed to sell the latter's entire output (MGA/1: 32, 33).[12] It goes without saying that all of Metallgesellschaft's industrial subsidiaries relied for their procurement of raw material and the sale of their output on Metallgesellschaft. From Metallgesellschaft's point of view it was their *raison d'être* to stimulate its ore- and metal-trading business. Unfortunately, there are no data which could be used to compare the profitability of the commercial and industrial business of the German metal trading companies. Concerning Metallgesellschaft, however, trading yielded the major share of profits and remained its core business (MGA/1: 68, 111). Still, it should not be overlooked that the commercial business was considerably supported by industrial activities and technological services resulting in an increased market share – either directly or indirectly through valuable relations to producers and consumers of non-ferrous ores and metals. It can only be assumed that the same applied to Aron Hirsch & Sohn as well as to Beer, Sondheimer & Co.

Long-term contracts gained greatest significance between the German metal traders and the mining companies.[13] This is not to say that they were not important at the smelting and refining stages. Yet, there the metal traders not only relied on long-term contracts, but made direct investments, too. Contrary to this there is no example of full-scale vertical integration into mining by the German metal traders. Metallgesellschaft only acquired a minority shareholding in the Mexican mining venture, Compañía Minera de Peñoles. This, however, was rather by coincidence than the result of a strategy of backward integration into mining.[14] Even though Peñoles developed successfully, Metallgesellschaft remained averse to risk as far as mining ventures were concerned. Rather, it preferred to reduce the risk associated with mining ventures by taking part in the foundation of Société Auxiliaire des Mines in Paris in 1905. Via its shareholding in this company Metallgesellschaft participated in various mining projects which in most cases, however, did not develop successfully (MGA/1: 95, 96).

Why was there this conspicuous bias towards long-term contracts of supply/delivery at the expense of full-scale integration in the case of mining? There are several factors contributing to an explanation. Most importantly, these long-term contracts proved to be an efficient means by which the metal traders could virtually control the mines' production without heavy capital commitment. How far reaching was this control is illustrated by the fact that Belgian zinc smelters were considered to have been 'at the mercy' of the German metal traders, having almost monopolised the supply of zinc ores before 1914 (PRO/3).[15] They could afford to abstain from large investments into mining because they were able to control much of the international ore market on the basis of long-term contracts. In combination with financial, technological and/or managerial assistance and interlocking directorates, long-term contracts of supply/delivery proved to tie the mining companies closely enough to the metal traders so that the latter could rely on these contractual agreements as the basis of their ore trade, reducing uncertainty satisfactorily.

Moreover, there was a non-rational reason preventing the German metal traders from integration into mining. Metallgesellschaft's managers are said to have been instinctively afraid of the risk associated with underground ventures because they never seemed to be assessable enough (MGA/1: 65–7). This timidity probably resulted from a lack of expertise in mining. Additionally, the German metal traders might have shunned heavy capital commitments in mining companies because they were not usually situated in the German sphere of political influence.

Contrary to this, backward integration into smelting and refining presents a very different case. Here, the German metal traders were able to develop highly valued technological expertise. In 1889, Metallgesellschaft established its Technological Department intended to prepare the metal trading company for the necessary step into production by gathering metallurgical know-how. In 1897, it merged into Metallurgische Gesellschaft, founded by Metallgesellschaft. This company applied itself intensively to the development and marketing of patented inventions and processes (MGA/1: 21, 50). Consequently, the metal trader gained technological know-how which facilitated backward integration into the production of non-ferrous metals. Almost all of Metallgesellschaft's industrial undertakings – whether portfolio or direct investments – received technological assistance of one kind or another.[16] It is known that the Belgian zinc and lead smelter, Nouvelle Montagne, relied on Beer, Sondheimer & Co. not only for its supply of raw material, but also for its technological reorganisation on the basis of the former's 50 per cent shareholding (Schaefer 1918: 120). Moreover, Beer, Sondheimer & Co. used its American branch in order to engage in the introduction of the new flotation process all over the world. Since 1910, its American branch was the representative of the company, holding the respective patents (Wilkins 1989: 273).

The foundation of Metallurgische Gesellschaft is informative in another respect as Metallgesellschaft grouped its industrial shareholdings in this separate company. Its competitors followed several years later: Aron Hirsch &

Sohn established their Hirsch Kupfer- und Messingwerke AG in 1906. Beer, Sondheimer & Co. vested their industrial interests in Tellus AG für Bergbau- und Hüttenindustrie in the same year (Auerbach 1965: 190, 195, 199). The German metal traders' diversification into non-trading received its organisational underpinning by means of these foundations.

However, Metallgesellschaft, Aron Hirsch & Sohn and Beer, Sondheimer & Co. differed in so far as Metallgesellschaft took the lead. This does not only apply to the fact that it was first to separate its industrial business from its commercial activities organisationally. Metallgesellschaft was also most advanced concerning the sophistication of its organisation. In addition to Metallurgische Gesellschaft, it created holding and financing companies, Berg-Metallbank AG in 1906 and Schweizerische Gesellschaft für Metallwerte in 1910. The underlying motivation for these functionally defined administrative structures can be summarised in three main objectives: division of labour; distribution of risk; and enlistment of outside capital (MGA/2: 25; United States Federal Trade Commission 1916: 365).[17] For Schweizerische Gesellschaft für Metallwerte, tax burdens were less heavy in Switzerland than in Germany (MGA/1: 80).

Finally, from the organisational point of view it is interesting to note that Metallgesellschaft created a system of financial links among its subsidiaries resulting in a dense web of interrelations between the different parts of its organisation by which their cohesion was supported. Usine de Désargentation, for example, participated in the acquisition of the German zinc smelter Call in combination with Metallgesellschaft and Norddeutsche Affinerie. The Ore Trading Co. was jointly founded by Metallgesellschaft, American Metal Co. and Henry R. Merton (MGA/1: 88, 110). Metallgesellschaft, however, emerged at the centre of all the business activities so that during the First World War it was dubbed 'Octopus' in order to illustrate its tight relations to companies all over the world. Metallgesellschaft was the head of the octopus and its subsidiaries the tentacles (MGA/7).

Competition and co-operation

The German metal traders' dominance in the international non-ferrous ore and metal business was not only based on their vertical integration and extensive use of long-term contracts of delivery/supply. They managed also to instrumentalise the producers' inclination to form cartels and syndicates. In this way Metallgesellschaft, Aron Hirsch & Sohn and Beer, Sondheimer & Co. intensified their degree of control of the international non-ferrous metal market. However, they also colluded among themselves for this purpose.

Each of the German metal traders had established a firm foothold in Australia at the turn of the century. After they had not only established their own trading base, but had also taken minority investments in Australian mining and metallurgical companies, competition between them became fierce (MGA/5: 3; APC 1919: 66). Metallgesellschaft owned one-third of the

Tasmanian Smelting Co., which did not develop into a successful investment (MGA/3: 24, 25). Aron Hirsch & Sohn owned one-third of Mount Morgan Company, one of the largest Australian copper-producing companies. Moreover, they were interested in the Electrolytic Smelting & Refining Co. (United States Federal Trade Commission 1916: 369).

In order to combine their forces as well as to avoid competition, a joint-account agreement was signed by Metallgesellschaft and Beer, Sondheimer & Co. concerning the purchase and exploitation of Australian zinc ores in 1905 (MGA/8).[18] Aron Hirsch & Sohn were soon included in this agreement on the basis of which the three German metal traders acted as a 'buying combination'. Their co-operation enabled the German metal traders to contract for huge amounts of ores on a long-term basis which no single company would have been able to handle. In 1914, most of the Australian mining companies had contracted with one of the German metal traders. Consequently, Metallgesellschaft, Aron Hirsch & Sohn and Beer, Sondheimer & Co. virtually controlled the Australian zinc ore market at the outbreak of the First World War (MGA/5: 4; APC 1919: 66; PRO/3).[19]

Of course, the question arises as to why the Germans, of all the metal trading companies, were so predominant. Surprisingly enough, there does not seem to have been much concern about this before the outbreak of hostilities (Cocks and Walters 1968: 19). Metallgesellschaft, Aron Hirsch & Sohn and Beer, Sondheimer & Co. not only virtually monopolised the supply of Australian zinc ores in their hands, but at the same time, they were also in charge of most of the raw material of the European zinc smelters, which spared them searching for a market for Australian ores. It was this combination of supply and demand in their hands which effected their dominant position.

Trying to explain why so many producers of non-ferrous ores and metals entrusted the sale of their output and/or the supply of their raw material to Metallgesellschaft, Aron Hirsch & Sohn and Beer, Sondheimer & Co. requires a twofold answer. On the one hand, the German metal traders became owners of smelting and refining companies which then appointed them their sales agents. On the other hand, the metal traders had competitive advantages because of their knowledge of the market, their long-established channels of distribution and their technological expertise. Metallgesellschaft, Aron Hirsch & Sohn and Beer, Sondheimer & Co. managed to make themselves valuable and sometimes even indispensable to many mining, smelting and refining companies. Moreover, they created administrative structures which enabled them to conduct their business appropriately. In short, on the one hand, Metallgesellschaft, Aron Hirsch & Sohn and Beer, Sondheimer & Co. had created dependencies on the basis of financial investments and long-term contracts. On the other hand, they could offer valuable services.

A combination of these factors also contributed greatly to the German metal traders' position *vis-à-vis* the producers of non-ferrous metals during the period of cartelisation. On earlier occasions, the cartels had refused to include the metal traders in international agreements. Until 1909, however,

Metallgesellschaft, Aron Hirsch & Sohn and Beer, Sondheimer & Co. had developed into important zinc producers themselves so that they could be no longer excluded from the International Zinc Syndicate that was to be formed if it were to operate effectively (Devos 1986: 85). Even more important for the metal traders was the fact that they were appointed its exclusive selling agents. It can be assumed that the metal traders were able to achieve this position because of their sophisticated sales organisation, which could easily handle the cartel's output (Devos 1986: 85). Moreover, they could play another card as they were in control of the Australian zinc ore supply upon which some of the cartel members depended for their alimentation.

Considering the importance of international cartels' sales agencies, it is not surprising that there seems to have been some kind of competition for them. Being appointed sales agents of international cartels meant a huge increase in trade in the respective metals for the German metal traders. In the case of the International Zinc Syndicate the agreement covered 80 per cent of the European market, which was now served by Metallgesellschaft, Aron Hirsch & Sohn and Beer, Sondheimer & Co. exclusively. Thus, international cartelisation was instrumentalised by them in order to secure for them a share of the market even bigger than that gained by vertical integration and long-term contracts of supply/delivery. Thereby, the metal traders managed to turn the potential threat to their business posed by international cartels/syndicates to their own advantage.

Metallgesellschaft was able to become the sole selling agent of the International Lead Convention, too. Aron Hirsch & Sohn and Beer, Sondheimer & Co. were only admitted to the cartel as producers. It can be assumed that it was Metallgesellschaft which was able to wring this concession from the producers instead of its competitors because it was the largest lead producer of the three German metal traders. Consequently, it probably possessed the strongest basis for negotiations.[20] A comparison between the case of zinc and lead suggests the conclusion that Metallgesellschaft, Aron Hirsch & Sohn and Beer, Sondheimer & Co. did not give up competition completely. It is possible that they continued to compete for the sale of metallic lead because there was no such joint-account agreement for lead ores as in the case of Australian zinc ores.

In 1910, Metallgesellschaft was instrumental in founding the French Aluminum Syndicate. It was appointed the exclusive agent of its sales company, L'Aluminium Français S.A. even though Aron Hirsch & Sohn had hoped to participate in the business (MGA/9). Competition continued to exist in some areas while the international zinc business was largely based upon a scheme of co-operation between Metallgesellschaft, Aron Hirsch & Sohn and Beer, Sondheimer & Co. Consequently, they were accused of controlling world prices for zinc which, however, can be questioned because the organisational structures of the International Zinc Syndicate did not provide officially, at least, for the metal traders' fixing prices.

Conclusion

Metallgesellschaft, Aron Hirsch & Sohn and Beer, Sondheimer & Co. enjoyed an outstanding position in the international non-ferrous metal trade prior to the First World War.

By means of their commercial organisation they managed to establish a firm foothold in all important centres of the international non-ferrous metal business. The three German metal traders differed in so far as Metallgesellschaft was most active in founding legally independent foreign trade subsidiaries while its competitors preferred representation through agents in most cases. In the end, reasons for this different organisational pattern come down to personal preferences.

Vertical integration was another way for the German metal traders to increase their impact on the market. Thereby they became less exposed to the producers of non-ferrous ores and metals among whom a growing tendency towards elimination of the independent traders prevailed. Metallgesellschaft, Aron Hirsch & Sohn and Beer, Sondheimer & Co. chose either to integrate on a full scale through direct investment or to engage in long-term contracts of supply/delivery. In the latter case various other means of influence were applied, too, resulting in quasi-vertical integration. It is especially interesting to note the importance of long-term contracts sufficiently reducing the metal traders' uncertainty concerning their procurement and sales.

Long-term contracts were especially prominent at the mining stage while the metal traders fully integrated into the production of non-ferrous metals at the same time as they applied contractual measures. With regard to mining, the metal traders failed to generate technological know-how and therefore remained afraid of large capital investments. Aiming at a reduction of uncertainty conveyed by market transactions Metallgesellschaft, Aron Hirsch & Sohn and Beer, Sondheimer & Co. consequently created stable relations to producers and consumers on the basis of long-term contracts. In order to further increase their durability, the metal traders supported these contractual agreements through minority investments, loans/advances and managerial assistance/interlocking directorates. In Australia, for example, the German metal traders were able virtually to control the zinc ore market purely on the basis of this kind of quasi-vertical integration.

Concerning the production of non-ferrous metals, a different situation emerged as the metal traders became important producers themselves – either by acquisition or by founding smelting and refining companies. At this stage of the production chain Metallgesellschaft, Aron Hirsch & Sohn and Beer, Sondheimer & Co. could fully capitalise on the metallurgical expertise they had built up as well as on their long-established commercial relations. Despite the successful development of the German metal traders' industrial undertakings, trading remained their core business. However, the support it received from their industrial basis should not be underestimated.

Collusion between Metallgesellschaft, Aron Hirsch & Sohn and Beer,

Sondheimer & Co. as well as with producers in the context of international cartelisation contributed to their international standing, too. The Australian zinc ore business as well as the sale of the International Zinc Syndicate's output were based on a scheme of co-operation, for example.

The question arises on which factors the German metal traders' success rested. On the one hand they possessed certain types of knowledge they could capitalise on. Owing to their sophisticated commercial organisation, Metallgesellschaft, Aron Hirsch & Sohn and Beer, Sondheimer & Co. acquired a profound knowledge of the market. Soon they also began to generate metallurgical expertise they were able to offer as a service to producers of non-ferrous metals. Moreover, they also possessed organisational capabilities enabling them to implement adequate administrative structures. This applies to the foundation of separate industrial companies, for example. On the other hand, as a result of vertical integration, the German metal traders were in control of various German and foreign smelters and refineries so that they became important producers of non-ferrous metals themselves. This control did not necessarily mean ownership of the production facilities, but long-term contracts of supply/delivery were decisive, too. Owing to a combination of these factors Metallgesellschaft, Aron Hirsch & Sohn and Beer, Sondheimer & Co. were able to exercise a very considerable degree of influence on the international non-ferrous metal market.

This case study of the German non-ferrous metal trade prior to the First World War has highlighted some of the current questions of the theory of multinational enterprise. First, the mere percentage of ownership is a poor indicator of the control of a company as it neglects other means as long-term contracts and interlocking directorates, for example. Multinationality should not only be exclusively defined on the basis of shareholdings. Second, the dynamic factor of entrepreneurship is exemplified. Organisational questions were especially subjected to the entrepreneurs' attitude. It would appear that Metallgesellschaft was able to survive longer than Aron Hirsch & Sohn and Beer, Sondheimer & Co. – which both liquidated during the early 1930s – because it was ahead of its competitors in organisational terms. This applies to Metallgesellschaft's geographical expansion as well as to the organisation of its industrial business. It was thanks to Wilhelm Merton alone that Metallgesellschaft received its elaborate administrative structure which proved to be adequate during the time under consideration.

Acknowledgements

I am much obliged to the participants of the Reading conference on trading companies in September 1997, most of all to Geoffrey Jones, for constructive criticism on an earlier draft of this chapter. I am also grateful to Stephan Pfisterer for his comments.

Notes

1 Unfortunately, there are no data that could quantify this statement. Yet, there seems to be no question about it as virtually every publication on the international non-ferrous metal business alludes to the dominance of Metallgesellschaft, Aron Hirsch & Sohn and Beer, Sondheimer & Co.

2 Other German metal traders of less importance were: M. Lissauer & Co., Cologne; N. Levy & Co., Berlin; Altheim, Speier & Co., Frankfurt/Main. Unfortunately, there is only very limited information on the German non-ferrous metal trade apart from Metallgesellschaft, Aron Hirsch & Sohn and Beer, Sondheimer & Co.

3 Ralph Merton was the father of Wilhelm Merton and owner of the firm of Ph.A. Cohen. The father of Leo Ellinger, Phillip Ellinger, had been a partner in the firm of Cohen. He was succeeded by his son after his death in 1875.

4 German company law distinguishes between easily transferable bearer shares (*Inhaberaktien*) and personal shares (*Namensaktien*).

5 Robert Liefmann criticised what was known as stock and bond capitalism. Taking Metallgesellschaft as a prime example he endeavoured to show that by means of majority shareholdings German companies were able to control foreign firms which were legally still independent. According to Liefmann this was the basis of the German companies' international success. In his response Wilhelm Merton tried to demonstrate that Metallgesellschaft's policy was motivated by its desire to create truly independent business organisations.

6 The occasion referred to above was the British and Australian public discussion about Metallgesellschaft's position in the international non-ferrous metal market at the outbreak of the First World War.

7 In 1860 a brother of Wilhelm Merton had founded Henry R. Merton & Co. in London of which Metallgesellschaft possessed the majority of shares only after 1912–13 (MGA/3: 9). Yet, the London company which in turn had a considerable interest in Metallgesellschaft never appeared to have been controlled by the latter so that it is not considered one of its foreign direct investments.

8 For a discussion of transaction cost theory see Hennart (1991).

9 Other contributions claim that Australian smelting and refining works, mines in Central and South America, works in France, Belgium, the United Kingdom and Siberia were included in the company's activities (Zielenziger 1930: 203; Auerbach 1965: 190). Yet, there is no distinction between portfolio and direct investment which would make it possible to decide in which of these cases Aron Hirsch & Sohn embarked on full-scale backward integration. Other sources are not precise either.

10 Hoboken was a 50 per cent joint venture with Degussa (Deutsche Gold und Silber Scheideanstalt).

11 Unfortunately, it cannot be said whether Metallgesellschaft's business was already affected by this tendency or whether it was anticipated by Wilhelm Merton. This would be informative in order to assess whether Metallgesellschaft's decision to integrate backwards was of a defensive or an offensive kind.

12 For example, the same applies to: Duisburger Kupferhütte (Germany), Norddeutsche Affinerie, Hamburg (Germany), Süddeutsche Metallindustrie GmbH, Nürnberg (Germany), S.A. G. Dumont & Frères, Liège (Belgium).

13 Just one example shall be mentioned briefly. In 1901 Metallgesellschaft struck an agreement with Société des Mines de Balia-Karaidin, Constantinople about the sale of its annual output of lead bullion. This contract was prolonged several times, finally until December 1913 (MGA/10).

14 In 1889, Metallgesellschaft had founded the Compañia de Minerales y Metales whose purpose was to negotiate ore contracts with Mexican mines. In this

context, Metallgesellschaft happened to acquire shares of Peñoles in 1896 after it had not been able to pay back an advance granted by Compañia de Minerales y Metales. Even though Metallgesellschaft never owned the majority of shares of Peñoles it was considered to control this company because most of its output was shipped to Metallgesellschaft's Usine de Désargentation (MGA/1: 32, 98). Therefore, Peñoles was virtually dependent on Metallgesellschaft.

15 Even if one concedes that the British Government's judgement might have been a little exaggerated due to the First World War, the German metal traders' influence on the supply of ores was nevertheless considerable.

16 This applies, for example, to: Usines de Désargentation, Hoboken (Belgium), S.A. des Zincs de la Campine, Budel (Netherlands), Cia. Minera de Peñoles, Peñoles (Mexico), Usine Mouchel S.A., Normandy (France), Heddernheimer Kupferwerke (Germany), Bergwerks- und Hütten AG Berzelius, Bensberg (Germany), Oberschlesische Zinkhütten AG, Kattowitz (Silesia), S.A. des Anciens Établissements Sopwith, Linares (Spain).

17 Wilhelm Merton also transferred his organisation principles to Britain and the US as he pressed Henry R. Merton and American Metal Co. to administer their industrial activities through equivalents of Metallurgische Gesellschaft, the Merton Metallurgical Co. Ltd. and the Metallurgical Co. of America (MGA/1. 20, 70, 71, 79).

18 An agreement concerning lead was also signed, but did not work successfully so that it was not extended.

19 MGA/11, h3, 20 contains an exhaustive list of Australian companies having contracted with the 'Trio'.

20 This fact can only be evaluated correctly if one considers that initially the international lead producers aimed at collusion in order to strengthen their position *vis-à-vis* the metal traders. Then they not only allowed them to participate, but they also handed their sales over to one of them.

References

Published texts

Adey, A. (1930) 'Die Organisation und die Funktion des deutschen Metallhandels', Ph D thesis 1925, Bergisch-Gladbach: Heider.

(APC) United States Alien Property Custodian (1919) *Alien Property Custodian Report. A Detailed Report by the Alien Property Custodian of all Proceedings Had By Him under the Trading With The Enemy Act During the Calendar Year 1918 and to the Close of Business on February 15, 1919*, Washington: Government Printing Office, reprint 1977.

Auerbach, S.M. (1965) 'Jews in the German metal trade', *Year Book of the Leo Baeck Institut*, 10: 188–203.

Cocks, E. J. and Walters, B. (1968) *A History of the Zinc Smelting Industry in Britain*, London: Harrap.

Devos, M. (1986) 'Kapitalverflechtungen in der Montanindustrie zwischen dem westlichen Deutschland und Belgien von etwa 1830 bis 1914', Ph D thesis, 1983, Bonn: Rheinische Friedrich-Wilhelms Universität.

Harvey, C. E. (1981) *The Rio Tinto Company. An Economic History of a Leading International Mining Concern 1873–1954*, Penzance: Alison Hodge.

Hennart, J.-F. (1991) 'The transaction cost theory of the multinational enterprise', in Pitelis, C. N. and Sugden, R. (eds) *The Nature of the Transnational Firm*, London: Routledge.

Hirsch, S. (1967) *Revolution in Messing*, Lamersdorf: Junker.

Kabisch, T. R. (1982) *Deutsches Kapital in den USA von der Reichsgründung bis zur Sequestrierung (1917) und Freigabe*, Stuttgart: Klett-Cotta.

Mosse, W. E. (1987) *Jews in the German Economy. The German–Jewish Economic Élite 1820–1935*, Oxford: Clarendon Press.

Prenzel, E.-M. (1972) 'Hochschild, Zacharias', in *Neue Deutsche Biographie*, vol. 9, Berlin: Duncker & Humblot.

Prinz, A. (1984) *Juden im deutschen Wirtschaftsleben. Soziale und wirtschaftliche Strukturen im Wandel 1850–1904*, Tübingen: Mohr.

Ratz, U. (1994) 'Merton, Richard', in *Neue Deutsche Biographie*, vol. 17, Berlin: Duncker & Humblot.

Rieger, H. (1992) 'Die Metallgesellschaft – ein Fall des Effektenkapitalismus. Wilhelm Merton als Kontrahent eines wissenschaftlichen', *Disputs Dokumente und Schriften aus dem Historischen Archiv der Metallgesellschaft*, 1: 87–113.

Schaefer, E. (1918) 'Die Zinkindustrie', in Landesstelle Belgien für Rohstofferhebung (ed.) *Die Hauptindustrien Belgiens*, vol. 1, München: Oldenburg.

United States Federal Trade Commission (1916) *Report on Cooperation in the American Export Trade*, Washington: Government Printing Office.

Waechter, F. (1913) 'Die Kartellbestrebungen der Blei- und Zinkhütten Europas', *Bergwirtschaftliche Mitteilungen*, 4: 153–209.

Wilkins, M. (1989) *The History of Foreign Investment in the United States to 1914*, Cambridge Mass.: Harvard University Press.

Zielenziger, K. (1930) *Juden in der deutschen Wirtschaft*, Berlin: Heine Bund.

Manuscript sources

MGA/1 Metallgesellschaft Archives, Sommer, J. (1931) Die Metallgesellschaft. Ihre Entwicklung, dargestellt für die Concern-Angehörigen, non-published manuscript, Frankfurt/Main.

MGA/2 Metallgesellschaft Archives, Merton, W. (1913) Erwiderung auf Robert Liefmann, Frankfurt: Privatdruck.

MGA/3 Metallgesellschaft Archives, Merton, W. (1907) Memorandum on the history of Metallgesellschaft.

MGA/4 Metallgesellschaft Archives, Minutes of the Board of Directors, 20/09/1892.

MGA/5 Metallgesellschaft Archives, Merton, W. (1915), Memorandum on the Australian situation.

MGA/6 Metallgesellschaft Archives, a16, Henry R. Merton & Co. to Metallgesellschaft and American Metal Co., no date.

MGA/7 Metallgesellschaft Archives, h3/20, Extract from *Financial News* 13/10/1915.

MGA/8 Metallgesellchaft Archives, w8, Metallgesellschaft to Beer, Sondheimer & Co., 3/08/1905.

MGA/9 Metallgesellschaft Archives, a2, Note of Z. Hochschild, 23/08/1909.

MGA/10 Metallgesellschaft Archives, b3, Contracts with Société Ottomane des Mines de Balia-Karaidin.

MGA/11 Metallgesellschaft Archives, h3, 20, Extract from *The Mining Journal*, 17/7/1915.

PRO/1 Public Record Office, MUN 4/2113, Secretary of State for the Colonies to Governor of Canada, 30/09/1918.

PRO/2 Public Record Office, BT 13/87, Report of the Departmental Committee appointed by the Board of Trade to consider the position of the non-ferrous metal trades after the war, London 1918.

PRO/3 Public Record Office, POWE 26/9, L. LePersonne to Sir Evans, 17/12/1917.

StA/1 Archiv für Stadtgeschichte Frankfurt/Main, Magistratsakten T119, Exposé by Beer, Sondheimer & Co. on the development and current situation of the company, 15/05/1930.

StA/2 Archiv für Stadtgeschichte Frankfurt/Main, Magistratsakten T119, Supplement of the Exposé by Beer, Sondheimer & Co., 23/05/1930.

5 Dutch multinational trading companies in the twentieth century

Keetie E. Sluyterman

The history of the Dutch multinational trading companies in the twentieth century is still a rather unexplored field, as most attention has been focused on the seventeenth-century merchants. It would be interesting to know at the start of this research how many trading companies existed during the twentieth century and how important they were in terms of assets, employees and turnover. When trying to answer these questions, the first problem that arises is one of definition. Which companies are covered by the English term 'trading companies'? Casson's definition: 'a firm that specialises in market-making intermediation may be defined as a trading firm' is of some help, but covers thousands of firms of very diverse nature and sizes varying from two-man retail traders to multinational companies with large numbers of staff. (Casson, Chapter 2, this volume). We can only start comparing like with like if we narrow down the number of companies to those engaged in roughly similar business activities. In this chapter I want to concentrate on multinational companies in the twentieth century, with the exclusion of those trading in one commodity only. This still leaves a group of fifty to one hundred companies and private firms, judging very roughly from the stock exchange handbooks (Van Oss' Effectenboek 1904–72).

There is, however, a second problem. Some trading companies diversified into other activities, notably production, to form what Casson termed a 'hybrid trading company'. It is not easy to distinguish between a multinational trading company integrating backwards into production and a producer integrating forwards into marketing its exports. According to Casson, this ambiguity over the terminology is not a sign of any ambiguity in the underlying theory but is in fact predicted by it. His conclusion is that where trading companies are concerned, it is a mistake to become transfixed on questions of terminology. It is more relevant to find out why some trading companies became hybrid and others remained pure multinational trading companies (Casson, Chapter 2, this volume). For this reason, in this chapter I shall disregard the question of the numbers and importance of Dutch trading companies and concentrate instead on their function as intermediaries in international trade.

The intermediation process involves several stages, including export, import and wholesaling. Multinational trading companies are often involved in several of these stages, though they may have different roles in different countries. In one part of their business they may be active as resellers (assuming ownership of the products) and in other parts act only as brokers (not owning the products they deal in). The classic function of the wholesaler is to collect goods from a large range of producers, stock them temporarily if necessary and redistribute the goods among a large range of retailers. Their aim is to increase the value of a good by bringing it nearer to the user. The trader earns money by providing such services as covering distances, breaking down large quantities into smaller ones and guaranteeing quality (Polak *et al*. 1966). If the trader also owns the goods, he is subject to price changes and therefore speculates. The core competence of the wholesaler lies in his knowledge of markets and products, and in his flexibility to change his product ranges and outlets. This flexibility is all the more precious in times of rapid economic change.

Characteristic of Dutch discussions on the role of the intermediaries and more specifically, the wholesalers, is the persistent doubt about whether there is a lasting place for the independent intermediary within the economic system. The future of the wholesaler has been repeatedly questioned. In the 1920s, the Dutch author Tobi came to the conclusion that the wholesaler would in due time be deprived of his function by large manufacturing companies on the one hand and retailers on the other (Tobi 1928: 94–112). Doubts on the future prospects of the independent intermediary or the wholesaler were again voiced in the 1960s and early 1980s (Abeln 1969; Van der Torn & Bunningh 1981). More or less the same conclusion was reached by Chandler on the American situation in his book *The Visible Hand* (Chandler 1977; 209–40). He argued that the wholesalers were supplanted by the mass retailers on the one hand and the manufacturers on the other. Such discussion about the disappearance of the wholesaler is interesting because it reflects expectations and theoretical logic much more than reality. In this chapter I intend to survey for the first time, the different roles the Dutch colonial trading companies have played during the twentieth century.

Colonial traders before the Second World War

At the end of the nineteenth century three developments contributed to the establishment of Dutch internationally active trading companies. A first source of trade increase was the rapid industrialisation of Germany combined with the Dutch liberalisation of the transit trade. The SHV (Steenkolen Handels Vereeniging) had its basis in trading German coal. The SHV was set up by eight Dutch wholesalers in coal in response to the formation of the Rheinisch-Westphälisches Kohlen Syndicat in 1896. In the following years they expanded their activities into retail trade, transhipment and Rhine shipping. SHV also participated in the foundation of several important Dutch industries. After the Second World War, SHV's involvement in the energy sector was enlarged to include the trade, transport and storage of oil and petrol retailing across Europe. In the 1960s SHV embarked on an entirely new field of operations: the self-service wholesale cash-and-carry stores under the name Makro. In both sectors, Energy and Makro stores, SHV expanded worldwide and achieved high growth rates. Thus it developed into by far the biggest trading company in the Netherlands measured in capital, turnover and staff in 1995, but it still remained a family-owned company (SHV 1996).

The second source of new trading opportunities arose from the expansion of the home agrarian sector, which reacted to the late nineteenth-century crisis by switching from staple foods to higher-value meat products, vegetables and horticultural products. As a result farming became highly dependent on importing grain, feed and fertiliser and exporting its produce. These developments were encouraged by the establishment of co-operative selling and purchasing organisations (Knibbe 1993; 217–21). A few of these organisations developed into international traders, as was the case with Het Centraal Bureau (the future Cebeco-Handelsraad) and the Friesche Coöperatieve Zuivel Export Vereeniging (Frico) (Sluyterman 1993; 20). Cebeco-Handelsraad is a co-operative society, set up in 1899 to counteract the monopolisation of the import trade in potassium fertilisers. During the interwar years Cebeco developed into the most important Dutch importer and distributor of fertilisers and animal feed. After the Second World War Cebeco increased its activities in the cultivation and worldwide export of seeds. Apart from its own activities, Cebeco supported co-operative societies in the agribusiness at large in the Netherlands and abroad. Measured in turnover and the number of people employed, in 1995 Cebeco was among the top ten Dutch trading companies (Van Sluijvenberg 1949; De Boer 1976).

Last but not least, the economic exploitation of the Dutch Indies from the 1870s onwards generated very large trade flows between Europe and colonial Indonesia. Old colonial houses experienced a new elan, while new trading companies, large and small, were founded in the Netherlands as well as in the Indies. Now well known companies, such as Internatio, Borsumij and Hagemeyer, capitalised on the opportunities offered in colonial Indonesia.

I will now focus on the first group of companies, the colonial traders. These resemble the British ones and have some links with the Japanese experience and therefore seem best suited for international comparison (Jones, 1996; Yonekawa and Yoshihara 1987, Yonekawa 1990).

Up until 1870 the Dutch government and the colonial authorities had a dominating influence on the economic development of the Dutch Indies, but after that date private enterprise was allowed to exploit plantations and mineral resources. This led to an explosion of activities, first in Java and later also in the Outer Provinces. In its wake, some older colonial trading houses, such as H.G.Th. Crone, Van Heekeren & Co. and A. van Hoboken, expanded and new companies were set up. On the other hand, the Nederlandsche Handel-Maatschappij (Netherlands Trading Company), set up by the Dutch government with a monopoly in 1824 to revive the days of old East India

Company, gradually withdrew from trading and concentrated on banking. Basically two kinds of colonial traders were active: those taking raw material out of the colony – the commodity traders, and those bringing manufacturing products into it – the merchants or distributive traders. The first group often became involved with the agrarian sector. In the case of Handelsvereeniging 'Amsterdam' (HVA), the running of plantations eventually became the core business. Some traders combined both activities, as was the case with Internatio and Borsumij; others did not.

Internatio (Internationale Crediet- en Handelsvereeniging 'Rotterdam') was founded in 1863 to create an overseas outlet for the Dutch textile industry. After several years, the company restricted its activities to Java and added commodity trade to the handling of consumer goods. The growing commodity trade was in a modest way supported by investment in plantations. In due time the company assumed several agencies for shipping and insurance companies (Mees 1938). The roots of Borsumij (Borneo Sumatra Handel Maatschappij) lay in the firm J.W. Schlimmer, which started in 1883 as a 'management buyout'. When the Nederlandsche Handel-Maatschappij decided to leave the commodity trade and concentrate on banking, their manager in Borneo, J.W. Schlimmer, took over the commodity trade in that area from his former employer. The firm was incorporated in 1894 to increase the financial means and developed a wide range of activities ranging from import, export, commission trade, banking and agencies. However, it was not directly involved in plantations. Borsumij took on shipping for some time, but that was mostly a strategy to challenge the dominating position of the Koninklijke Paketvaart Maatschappij and to force a reduction of shipping freights (Zwaag 1991; 226–229 and Campo 1992; 348–358; Minutes of the Board of Supervisory Directors Borsumij). A latecomer to the scene such as Hagemeyer restricted its activities to distributive trade. Hagemeyer started as a family firm, founded by two brothers Hagemeijer in 1900. For many years it was a modest firm, importing a wide range of consumer goods into colonial Indonesia. The main clients were the Chinese retail shops (Hagemeyer Archives 1 and 2). Apart from these three companies, whose names have become familiar because of their longevity, there were many more Dutch trading firms active in colonial Indonesia, differing in size and span.

The First World War interrupted activities and the flow of trade changed. Shipping lines were affected by the countries at war. Even for a neutral country such as the Netherlands, the effects were considerable. The traders were eager to look for new ways of handling their trade. Some opened branches in the US and in Japan. The 1920 crisis brought about a big shake-up not only for industry and the banks but for trade as well. Many companies that had expanded freely in previous years were forced to write off part of their capital during the first years of the 1920s to cover their losses. (Van Oss' Effectenboek 1920–27).

The 1920 crisis greatly affected Hagemeyer. The firm was incorporated at the beginning of 1920. The large amount of share capital reflected the inflated value of possessions and stock, but soon had to be reduced drastically. It is clear that too many products were ordered in Europe and then shipped to colonial Indonesia, arriving there by the time the boom was over. Obviously the warning signals did not reach Amsterdam quickly enough. The company lost enormous sums on the devaluation of stocks. Subsequently, the headquarters in Amsterdam formulated stricter rules about keeping stock. They also decided to follow the changes in stock more closely. The branches overseas had to send monthly reports to the Netherlands. The basic information was sent by telegram, while the more detailed information went by mail. The Amsterdam headquarters also gave detailed instructions on how to administrate goods, how to value them, how to insure them and what to do in case of damage or in cases where the specification of a product was not in accordance with the order. There was a close contact between the headquarters in Amsterdam and the branches in the Dutch Indies. What Amsterdam had to offer was finance, administrative knowledge and contact with the European manufacturers, while the branches in the Dutch Indies had access to the local market via their network of Chinese shopkeepers. Hagemeyer combined the trade in consumer goods under their own label with exclusive rights to sell some brand products, such as Kienzle watches, Dobbelman soap, Camel cigarettes and Whisky Vat 69. These were termed 'monopoly products'. In the inter-war period Anton Hagemeyer went at least twice to the Dutch Indies himself to oversee his business. During the 1930s Hagemeyer sometimes imported Japanese products under the Hagemeyer label. An office was set up in Kobe for the Japanese import trade. The handling of the yen currency was left by Amsterdam to the discretion of the management in colonial Indonesia, mainly because headquarters lacked up-to-date information and also because there was no trade in yen in the Netherlands (Hagemeyer Archives, 2).

While some trading companies managed or even owned plantations, the possession of manufacturing activities was rare. Internatio set up a paper mill together with a Dutch paper manufacturer in 1923. In the 1930s Internatio participated in two textile ventures with Dutch textile manufacturers. The company owned a phosphate factory and participated in a sugar factory and a brick and tiles factory. These initiatives to set up industrial activities in the Dutch Indies were greatly encouraged by the colonial authorities at that time. The smaller Borsumij had a stake in a few companies on a more modest scale and even Hagemeyer invested a little money in the shares of industrial companies for a very short period. Though Internatio and Borsumij had some success with their factories, the participation of Hagemeyer was short-lived and without profits (De Jong 1995).

War and decolonisation

When the Netherlands became involved in the Second World War in 1940, the colonial trading companies lost contact with their overseas branches. Fortunately, some trading companies had transferred the base of the company out of the Netherlands. The headquarters in the Netherlands were mostly out of work. For a while they sold stocks that could no longer be sent overseas. Thereafter they did a bit of local trade, but mostly prepared for the future after the end of the war. The branches overseas, on the other hand, were very busy until the Japanese conquered the Dutch Indies in 1942. Between 1940 and 1942 a lively trade existed between colonial Indonesia and the United States, where many trading companies had their branches. After the Japanese conquest of the Dutch Indies, trading activities quickly diminished and virtually ceased to exist by the end of the war. All Dutch staff were put into the Japanese camps and many of them died during the occupation.

After the war, the world had changed and it proved impossible for the Netherlands to regain their former position as a colonial power. It took several years of colonial warfare before Indonesia became independent in 1949 (Booth 1996; 401–403). The Dutch traders resumed their activities as soon as the Japanese occupation was over, trusting the situation would return to 'normal' in due time. Singapore was the first place from which the old trading activities could begin. Slowly the business in Indonesia was rebuilt to a certain extent. While trading activities were the first to pick up, rebuilding manufacturing activities and repairing plantations were more complicated and took longer. Though the traders were aware that they should diversify their activities in order to lessen their dependence on Indonesia, at the same time they were full of optimism about their opportunities to continue to work in the former colony. This optimism was mainly based on the feeling that their managerial capabilities and know-how were necessary to bring prosperity to the Indonesian economy. Internatio strengthened its position as a wholesaler by setting up a retail organisation all over Indonesia. Hagemeyer took up business in New Guinea (West Irian) in 1950, supported by a one-year monopoly position granted by the Dutch government.

Rehabilitation of existing plants and infrastructure enabled Indonesia to grow quite rapidly in the immediate post-independence year. Yet, objection towards the remaining Dutch presence increased. It was felt that political independence should be supported by economic independence, because Dutch-owned interest might undermine the economic position of the struggling young Republic (Booth 1996; 412). The operations of Dutch trading companies were curtailed by import restrictions, restrictions on profit transfer and preferential treatment of indigenous importers. In 1957 all Dutch capital was nationalised and all Dutch employees were ousted. Internatio, Borsumij and Hagemeyer left their enterprises in the hands of local management hoping for a better relationship in the future. When in 1963 West Irian became part of the Indonesian Republic, Hagemeyer was ousted from one of its operational fields for the second time.

Directly after the end of the Second World War and despite their obvious wish to continue business in the country in which they had worked for so many years, the overseas traders started to look for other areas in which to operate. First, new branches were opened in relatively nearby regions such as

Malaya and Australia. Often to extend the business, existing trading firms in these countries were taken over. Most of the new activities were in trade during these years. In the 1950s the field of action was extended a bit further. It seemed at the time a logical choice to transfer their knowledge of trade and tropical products to other developing and/or tropical countries. Africa and South America were selected. Twice, in 1945 and 1953, Internatio explored the possibilities of starting activities in South America, but both times without success (Stout 1963; 55).

The Dutch colonial traders were general merchants, active in both commodity trade and universal distributive trade. This type of trader seemed no longer in demand, at least in Anglophone Africa, as the long established United Africa Company (UAC), a subsidiary of Unilever, discovered. During the 1950s UAC changed from general merchant and distributive agency, running the undifferentiated general store, into a specialised importer, servicer and owner of European-type departmental stores. Reasons for this change of policy were local competition, declining profit margins, governmental pressure and the attraction of new more specialised ventures. The other part of the business, the commodity trade in West Africa, was wound up during the 1950s. Increasing competition, state policy and a change in company strategy were behind this decision to end a long-established activity (Fieldhouse: 1994 411–27).

It is not surprising then that the Dutch traders had difficulty in making their new ventures into Africa into an attractive alternative for trading in Indonesia, though occasionally profits were certainly made. One after the other the African countries entered the phase of decolonisation. For the companies this brought controls on imports and the repatriation of profits and capital, non-convertible currencies at overvalued exchange rates and varying forms of indigenisation. Merchant companies already long used to work in Africa transferred the weight of their activities from one country to another, from trade into industrial enterprises in Africa and ultimately from Africa to Europe (Fieldhouse 1994: 674–76). The Dutch new entrants experienced more or less the same. Internatio went to Kenya, Tanzania and Uganda in 1953 and left again in 1960, sadder and wiser (Stout 1963: 54). Hagemeyer started earlier, in 1951, and stayed on much longer. During the 1950s investment in Africa was gradually increased, reaching a peak of 22 per cent of total investment in subsidiaries in 1962. This rise was caused by two acquisitions. In 1959 the trading company J. F. Sick & Co., with branches in Ghana, Nigeria and Cameroon, was taken over. In 1962, the takeover of L. E. Tels & Co., a former trader in the Dutch Indies that had concentrated on the Congo since 1948, followed. After 1962 Hagemeyer decreased its investments in Africa. By the end of the 1960s no more than 2 per cent was invested there. Some of the operations in Africa, however, lingered on until 1990. Borsumij went to the Congo in 1952. To extend its African business Borsumij closed an agreement with the Twentsche Overzee Handelmaatschappij in 1955. This Dutch company had been operating in Africa since 1920. The operations in Africa lingered on until 1985, but long before that date new investments were rare (*Annual Reports,* Hagemeyer 1936–1995, *Borsumij 1940–94*).

The lure of industry

The nationalisation of their properties in Indonesia had forced the former Dutch colonial trading companies to diversify their activities further. Their experiences outside Indonesia had so far been mixed. Some of the smaller traders merged to improve their situation. For instance, Geo Wehry merged with Borsumij in 1961. As the European economy was doing increasingly well, many trading companies turned to Europe and especially the Netherlands. They took over local traders and wholesalers. Maintz & Co, who in Indonesia had specialised in the development of public utilities, took over a Dutch company active in technical services, which represented several important foreign companies in the Netherlands (Van Oss' Effectenboek 1964). Some of the traders went into manufacturing industry to diversify their activities and spread their risks. The traders did presume that their managerial capabilities could equally well be used to run an industrial company as a trading company. Internatio concentrated strongly on Europe and moved gradually into manufacturing. Often the manufacturing activities were included in the takeover of smaller, specialised trading companies, as was the case with one wholesaler in pharmaceuticals. In 1968 the turnover and numbers of employees doubled when Internatio took over two Dutch companies in the field of electrical and electro-technical fittings. Two years later, Internatio merged with the Rotterdam company, Müller, which was of about an equal size and active in mineral trading, transport and harbour facilities. Thus was created a conglomerate of very diverse activities. In 1970 more than 80 per cent of investments were concentrated in Western Europe. The remaining activities in Asia were divested in 1967. The firm's strategy was based on two assumptions: one was the diversification of activities and the other the decentralisation of the organisation. The various subsidiaries were supposed to run themselves. The consequence was that synergy between the subsidiaries was hard to achieve (*Annual Reports Internatio* 1957–69, *Annual Reports Internatio-Müller* 1970–96).

Hagemeyer also diversified its activities with gusto. It took over several manufacturing companies in the Netherlands from 1965 onwards, including leatherware, kitchenware, cosmetics and electro-technical products. Some of the companies could be bought cheaply because they needed to be reorganised. At the same time investments were transferred towards Europe. While in 1962 only 21 per cent of invested capital was located in Europe, in 1970 this was 73 per cent (*Annual Reports Hagemeyer*). Borsumij was not much interested in manufacturing, but also transferred its activities towards Europe. In 1970 it had invested 66 per cent of its capital in Europe (*Annual Reports Borsumij*).

In the 1960s the combination of trade with industry was generally accepted as the right way forward. Illustrative of this way of thinking is the report G. H. J. Abeln wrote for the Association of Dutch Wholesalers on the future of Dutch international trading companies. He argued that the big modern companies needed stability and continuity and therefore had to integrate production and marketing. Within the system there was no longer a place for the adventuresome, risk-taking merchant, because the modern leader of the company had to possess analytical insight and the ability to synthesise. Advanced research in marketing and marketing techniques was very necessary. Furthermore, the trading companies needed to integrate backwards into production and turn themselves into American-style conglomerates (Abeln 1969). Implicit in Abeln's view was the continuation of stable economic growth on which rational managers could build with systematic and analytic strategies. This supposition turned out to be the weak spot in his reasoning. The 1970s demonstrated that the world economy could still be very turbulent.

During the 1970s it became clear that the Dutch traders, instead of spreading risks had increased their exposure. Nor did they succeed in achieving expansion in their industrial activities. While the period of The 1960s had been one of rapid growth, during the 1970s and 1980s the three leading trading companies stagnated, measured in numbers of staff. The experience of Hagemeyer in managing its industrial companies is a good example. During the second half of the 1960s the combination of trade and industry seemed to work well. Some of the companies in straitened circumstances could be turned around. This early success confirmed to the managers that their chosen strategy was successful. Also the shareholders praised the managers for their forward-looking policy. The profits, however, did not last. During the first half of the 1970s the manufacturing companies had to be reorganised several times. From 1975 onwards the wisdom of combining trade and industry was questioned. Despite a decade of reorganisation, Hagemeyer could not succeed in making its industrial companies profitable. In the end, all were sold or closed down.

Why did Hagemeyer fail? Why did the apparent advantages of integrating production and marketing, also outlined by Casson, fail to materialise? (Casson, Chapter 2, Table 2.3, this volume) In the first place, Hagemeyer, being an outsider and lacking technical expertise, might well have bought the wrong companies. Certainly it bought several labour-intensive industries, which had the most trouble weathering the recession of the 1970s. Those better acquainted with the industry might well have seen this problem coming, while Hagemeyer was insufficiently aware of it. In the second place, the scale and scope of the production and marketing did not match. The wholesale and industrial companies worked mostly independently from each other, thus lessening the potential gains from their belonging to the same holding. Last, the management of industrial companies requires different skills and attitudes from managing a trading company. The example of Japan, of course, shows that a combination of the two is not impossible. According to

Dutch wisdom, however, the two are hard to combine, because the leader of a capital and research-intensive industry has to think long term, while traders are inclined to think in the short term and take advantage of sudden opportunities. A Borsumij manager commented in 1983 that Borsumij did not want to involve itself in production, because traders think about the next six months and not about the next ten years (Huys 1983). At the 1981 annual general meeting, the managing director of Hagemeyer was asked to explain his vision of the future, especially with regard to Europe. He found this a hard question. His vision was simply 'making money wherever possible'. He added that the prospects in the Far East looked better than in Europe (minutes, Annual meeting of Shareholders, 31 May 1981). Having experienced that working in Europe was a mixed blessing, the former colonial traders turned their attention once again to other areas and back to their core business.

Back to core business

While the diversification into industrial activities had brought at best mixed results, the return to the intermediary trade offered better prospects. There were two good reasons to suppose there would be future room for trading companies. During the 1970s part of the manufacturing industry was transferred to the developing countries. This implied that products had to be transported over longer distances, creating new opportunities for intermediation. Also the life cycle of the products shortened, making it more important for the manufacturers to introduce their products quickly to get the most benefit out of them. Here the trading companies with good international covering of the important consumer markets could play an essential role (Salomons 1975; 31–35).

Not all trade seemed to promise equally good prospects. The commodity trade was known for its strongly fluctuating results. During a large part of the 1970s the commodity trade had supported the Dutch trading companies with high profits and high turnover, this way compensating the meagre results elsewhere, but in 1980 and 1981 the commodity trade created heavy losses. Therefore, Internatio-Müller restricted its commodity trade drastically, Borsumij ended this activity completely and Hagemeyer seriously considered doing the same, but postponed the decision until 1985.

With no commodity trade and no manufacturing activities, Borsumij became exclusively an import agent and wholesaler of a wide range of consumer goods in Europe imported from the Far East. This was more or less the reverse of what happened in the inter-war period, when European manufactured products were sent to colonial Indonesia. Textiles and footwear were supplied by the group's own purchasing offices for sale under its own or other people's brand names. Outside consumer goods Borsumij also traded in office equipment and, to give an example of the wide range of products, in fork-lift trucks. In some important product categories, Borsumij acted as an agent for competing lines. As the subsidiaries, being the group's profit centres, were supposed to act with a maximum of independence, headquarters were small. A handful of professional staff advisors provided the board and the subsidiary companies with support in accounting and information technology and counsel concerning staff, financial and legal matters. The primary function of the board was to take over profitable companies and divest loss-making activities. Companies themselves seemed to have become the most important merchandise. In 1992 Borsumij acquired Ceteco (Curaçao Trading Company). This company was also an old colonial trader, but it operated in the 'West-Indies', that is in Curaçao (*Annual Report Ceteco 1965*). From there it had extended its activities to South America. Borsumij hoped to create synergy between the two companies through combining its own purchasing power in the Far East with the outlets of Ceteco in South America (*Beleggers Belangen* 1992). In 1993 the takeover of another, though much smaller company, R. S. Stokvis & Zonen, followed. The idea behind this takeover was to strengthen the sector office and industrial products and to lessen the dependence on consumer goods (comprising 81 per cent of total sales in 1992). In 1995 Borsumij's final hour had come. Now it was Borsumij's turn to be taken over. A rumour of insider share trading discredited some of the board managers and in this uncertain situation Hagemeyer's offer to take over the company was accepted.

How had Hagemeyer fared in the meantime? After the prolonged liquidation of most of its manufacturing activities and the losses on commodity trading Hagemeyer was in urgent need of risk capital to create future opportunities by acquiring new companies at the beginning of the 1980s. One may see it as the irony of history that new share capital was found in Indonesia. In 1983 First Pacific became the majority shareholder (51 per cent) with the creation of new shares. It was decided that Hagemeyer should concentrate on import and distributive trade worldwide. After discarding all industrial activities, Hagemeyer relied entirely on its former strength, the agencies and the narrow relationship with the principals. In the principal–agent relationship there are two pitfalls. The agent is always threatened by the risk that the principal will decide to take over a market once the trader has succeeded in creating interesting sales. On the other hand, the principal runs the risk that the agent is not really interested in promoting his products. For instance, he may only have accepted the representation to cut out a possible competitor. Therefore in 1986 Hagemeyer decided it had to diminish its dependency on agency representation business by means of establishing a proprietary branded-products business. Together with the pursuance of autonomous growth, an aggressive acquisition programme was implemented. Contrary to the 1960s acquisition policy, this time good management, profitability and continuity were considered necessary preconditions for takeovers. This policy was formulated after a short adventure with Sears Roebuck. Sears was interested in the acquisition of a European outlet and created for that purpose the subsidiary Sears World Trade that acquired a 20 per cent participation in Hagemeyer in 1985. However, nine months later Sears Roebuck decided to wind down Sears World Trade and sell its participation in Hagemeyer. Since then, Hagemeyer has grown through successive takeovers. The proprietary-branded business did not grow substantially, but the number of principals was greatly increased, which served the same purpose of making Hagemeyer less dependent on a few large principals.

In 1991 First Pacific, the majority shareholder of Hagemeyer, announced that it had built up a 43 per cent participation in Internatio-Müller and that a merger between Hagemeyer and Internatio-Müller was suggested. The managers of Internatio-Müller were greatly opposed to the plans, but they were facing a difficult situation. During the 1980s the company had experienced no growth at all; sales decreased from 3.8 million guilders in 1980 to 2.9 million in 1990, while the number of people employed diminished during the same period from 15,000 to 12,000. All through this period, the management was busy restructuring the activities, buying promising new ventures and selling parts of the business that seemed to have no future or did not fit in with the other subsidiaries. The company was active in three diverse fields: trading, transport (ship broker, cargo-transport, distribution, storage) and technology (electro-technical fittings). One of the gems of the company was Interpharm, a Dutch wholesaler in pharmaceuticals. Hagemeyer was especially interested in this part of the business (Kosterman 1991). Though 1991 would turn out as a loss-making year, the management of Internatio-Müller was opposed to a takeover by Hagemeyer. They came with a new business plan to improve performance by concentrating on trading and technical services, while gradually retreating out of transport. The financiers gave the management the benefit of the doubt and the opportunity to implement their new strategy. So far, the new strategy has not led to substantial growth, but profits have increased and share prices have risen.

Hagemeyer withdrew to look out for another major takeover opportunity, which came in 1995 with Borsumij. In the growth strategy of Hagemeyer the acquisition of Borsumij was an important step forward and especially welcome was Borsumij's recently acquired foothold in South America. Combining the two companies was relatively easy because the two used the same policy of small headquarters with relatively independent subsidiaries. One may wonder what added value the headquarters did offer their subsidiaries, all the more as those companies regularly seemed to change hands. Hagemeyer and Borsumij both found their strength in import, marketing and distribution of consumer products and both used a multi-principal policy. Investment in modern logistics and distribution systems served to create added value for the principals. Fortified by Borsumij, the former colonial trading house Hagemeyer counts itself among the world's biggest trading companies, active in forty countries with more than 20,000 employees. In Table 5.1 in the Appendix to this chapter, the sales of Internatio-Müller, Borsumij and Hagemeyer from 1970 onwards are compared. The table highlights the phenomenal growth of Hagemeyer in recent years.

Compared to the Japanese trading companies, however, the size of Hagemeyer is still modest. The 1995 Fortune 500-list of the biggest companies (measured in revenues) outside the US is dominated by Japanese companies, while Hagemeyer is too small to figure. The only Dutch trading company on the list is SHV, which ranks sixteenth among the trading companies and 207th on the Global 500 Rank. Measured in turnover, SHV was in 1995 about five times the size of Hagemeyer (Fortune 500 list 1995; Financieele Dagblad 1996). For Hagemeyer the international competitors most comparable in size and range of activities were East Asiatic (Denmark), Diethelm (Germany), Inchcape (Britain) and Jardine Matheson (ultimately Britain).

Conclusion

The Dutch multinational trading companies were active as brokers and resellers. They also diversified their activities in several ways during different periods. Before 1940 the colonial traders went into plantations, shipping, insurance and related services as well as into manufacturing overseas. They used their managerial capabilities in a broad and unspecialised way. After the Second World War the Dutch traders in Indonesia tried to rebuild and to a certain extent adapt their business to the new circumstances within an independent Indonesia. In the meantime, some of the companies enlarged their field of operation by going into a wider range of countries and buying many local trading houses. They also turned to manufacturing activities, mostly at home. The latter activities were mostly abandoned during the 1980s.

The traders returned to their core business, the intermediary and wholesale trade, despite repeated predictions that the role of independent intermediary would become superfluous. Their present growth demonstrates that there is a lasting place for intermediaries. Their specific strength lies in their flexibility, their knowledge of products and markets and their use of modern technology. Recently, Casson has suggested that network structures, because of their flexibility, are better suited for periods of rapid economic change than managerial hierarchies. Therefore the large integrated industrial companies tended to decentralise during the 1980s (Casson 1997). The reverse side of the same process is that trading companies are invited to play a larger part in the intermediary activities. As traders are on the whole more flexible than manufacturing companies, one might expect them to cope better with periods of high economic volatility.

In Chapter 2, Casson introduced the trader as speculator and gambler. Speculating on price changes was indeed inherent in the traders' operations, but in my view it was not the main goal of many Dutch twentieth-century traders. They strove continuously to find new value-adding services in the ever-shifting chain between producers, retailers and consumers across the world. Of course, chances for speculative profits were not spurned, but as a rule they were not the main aim. Obviously, the aspect of speculation was stronger in commodity trade than in the trade of manufacturing goods. Maybe for that reason the three former Dutch colonial traders confined their activities more and more to the trade in manufacturing goods. As far as they owned the goods they traded in, the companies were subject to price fluctuations. Sometimes they lost, sometimes they won, but their regular income derived from the more mundane and less glamorous business of providing services and being paid for it.

Acknowledgments

I would like to thank Geoffrey Jones, Joost Jonker and Judith Wale for their valuable suggestions to improve on the first draft.

References

Main references

Abeln, G. H. J. (1969) *Het Nederlandse internationale handelshuis en de groei; Prae-Advies voor het Verbond van de Nederlandse Groothandel.*
Annual Reports Borsumij (1902–94).
Annual Report Ceteco (1965).
Annual Reports Hagemeyer (1936–96).
Annual Reports Internatio (1957–69).
Annual Reports Internatio-Müller (1970–96).
Beleggers Belangen (1992) no. 30, 24 July.
Booth, A. (1996) 'Growth and stagnation in an era of nation-building: Indonesian economic performance from 1950 to 1965', in Lindblad, J. Th. (ed.) *Historical Foundations of a National Economy in Indonesia, 1890s–1990s*, Amsterdam: North Holland.
Campo, J. N. F. M. à (1992) *Koninklijke Paketvaart Maatschappij. Stoomvaart en staatsvorming in de Indonesische archipel 1888–1914*, Hilversum: Verloren.
Casson, M. (1997) 'Entrepreneurial networks in international business', paper for the International Business History Conference Glasgow, July.
Chandler A. D., Jr (1977) *The Visible Hand*, Cambridge, Mass.: Bellknap
de Boer, I. J. (ed.) (1976) *Boer en markt. Ontwikkeling van de Nederlandse land- en tuinbouw en de Cebeco-Handelsraad-organisatie in de periode 1949–1974*, Rotterdam: Cebeco-Handelsraad.
de Jong, P. (1995) 'Handel en wandel in de kolonie; drie handelshuizen in Nederlands Indië', MA-thesis Leiden University.
Fieldhouse, D. K. (1994) *Merchant Capital and Economic Decolonization. The United Africa Company, 1929–1987*, Oxford: Clarendon Press.
Financieele Dagblad (1996) *De omzetcijfers van 1995.*
Huys, A. (1983) 'Borsumij Wehry: na diep dal en consolidatie nu expansie', *Mangement Totaal*, November/December.
Jones, G. (1996) 'Diversification strategies and corporate governance in trading companies: Anglo-Japanese comparisons since the late nineteenth century', *Business and Economic History*, 25 (2): 103–18.
Knibbe, M. (1993) *Agriculture in the Netherlands, 1851–1950, Production and Institutional Change*, Amsterdam: NEHA.

Kosterman, R. (1991) 'Laatste kans Internatio, ABN AMRO verhoogt de druk', *FEM*, 17 August.

Mees, A. C. (1938) *NV Internationale Crediet- en Handels-Vereeniging 'Rotterdam'. Gedenkboek uitgegeven bij het vijf- en zeventig jarig bestaan of 28 Augustus 1938*, Rotterdam.

Polak, N. J., van de Woestijne, W.J. and Homan, S.C. (1966) *De functie van de groothandel*, Rotterdam.

Salomons, J. (1975) *De koopman als slangenbezweerder; een verkenning van nieuw mogelijkheden voor de handelsonderneming in een veranderende wereld*, Deventer.

SHV (Steenkolen Handels Vereeniging) (1996) 'Jubileebook' (no title, no page numbers), Utrecht: SHV Holdings NV. See also *Logboek SHV 1899–1956* (1956) Utrecht SHV.

Sluyterman, K .E. (1993) 'De Nederlandse internationale groothandel', in *Groot-en tussenhandel. Een geschiedenis en bronnenoverzicht*, Amsterdam: NEHA.

Stout, H. (1963) 'Van de Toko uit Rotterdam en van wat daarna kwam', in Baudet, H. (ed.) *Handelswereld en wereldhandel. Honderd jaren Internatio*, Rotterdam: Internatio.

Tobi, E. J. (1928) *Uitschakeling van den groothandel in industrieele producten*, Roermond.

Van der Torn & Buningh, management consultants (1981) *De groothandel in de jaren '80*, Utrecht.

Van Oss' Effectenboek, 1904–1972.

Van Sluijvenberg, J. H. (1949) *Het Centraal Bureau. Een coöperatief krachtveld in de Nederlandse Landbouw 1899–1949*, Rotterdam.

Yonekawa, S. (ed.) (1990) *General Trading Companies: A Comparative and Historical Study*, Tokyo: United Nations University Press.

Yonekawa, S. and Yoshikara, H. (eds) (1987) *Business History of General Trading Companies*, Tokyo: University of Tokyo Press.

Zwaag, J. van der (1991) *Verloren tropische zaken. De opkomst en ondergang van de Nederlandse handel- & cultuurmaatschappijen in het voormalige Nederlands-Indië*, no place, De Feniks Pers.

Hagemeyer archives

1   Annual accounts, 1902–40
2   Instructions for the Indonesian branches, 1909–42
3   Minutes of the annual meeting of the shareholders, 1967 onwards
4   Minutes of the board of supervisory directors Borsumij, 1898–1950

Appendix: Comparison of three Dutch colonial trading companies

Table 5.1 Assets of three Dutch colonial trading companies, 1914–95 (millions of guilders)

year	Internatio	Borsumij	Hagemeyer
1914	23	7	1
1939	70	40	5
1960	134	83	15
1970	753	119	325
1980	1,503	539	648
1990	1,408	912	1,006
1995	1,138	–	3,563

Source: van Oss' Effectenboek, Annual reports, 1914–95.

Table 5.2 Turnover of three Dutch colonial trading companies, 1970–95 (millions of guilders)

year	Internatio	Borsumij	Hagemeyer
1970	2,400	300	758
1975	2,929	592	1,074
1980	3,838	1,414	2,060
1985	2,691	1,466	1,127
1990	2,949	2,139	2,509
1995	2,997	–	5,722

Source: Annual Reports, 1970–95

Table 5.3 Number of employees of three Dutch colonial trading companies, 1970–95

year	Internatio	Borsumij	Hagemeyer
1970	15,000	2,031	6,600
1975	17,600	2,093	6,580
1980	15,300	3,229	5,246
1985	10,500	2,098	2,194
1990	11,823	2,943	4,165
1995	7,862	–	12,118

Source: Annual Reports, 1970–95

6   British trading companies in South America after 1914

Robert Greenhill and Rory Miller

Since 1960 the British trading companies in Latin America have attracted a
fair amount of scholarly attention, taking the analysis beyond the largely
narrative histories of individual firms which had appeared before then.[1] Until
the 1980s the normal context for this research was the debate over informal
imperialism and dependency. The principal sources were merchant archives
which had become available in London and, to a lesser extent, Latin American
documents such as notarial registers and tax schedules. Historians published
studies of particular houses (Mathew 1981), the British merchant community
in a particular country or port (Reber 1979; Mayo 1987; Cavieres 1988), and
the overall influence and impact of British firms (Greenhill 1977a). Analysis of
the merchants from this perspective culminated in a short but sharp exchange
over the extent to which their influence on Latin American economic development had been positive or malign (Ridings 1985; Marichal 1986; Platt
1986).

At just this point the subject was transformed by the injection of more
orthodox business history perspectives. In their preoccupation with questions
of power and influence, Latin American specialists had paid relatively little
attention to other central questions. True, they had identified the 1870s, when
the transatlantic cable was inaugurated, as a crucial turning point which had
forced the major British trading houses to reorganise and take advantage of
their specialist skills, knowledge, and access to the City of London (Miller
1993: 97–105). However, very few historians had ventured beyond 1914, the
traditional terminal date for studies of economic imperialism, and issues such
as business strategy, management and organisation had remained marginal.

The impetus to the change of focus came from three directions. First,
Stanley Chapman's concept of investment groups based upon trading houses
encouraged a better understanding of the relationships between British
merchants in Latin America and the extensive array of companies floated on
the London Stock Exchange (Chapman 1985). Second, Mira Wilkins' idea of
the free-standing company as the primary conduit for British overseas investment took Chapman's formulations further. Wilkins identified merchants as
one possible core for clusters of free-standing firms, and, like Chapman, drew
attention specifically to the British houses operating in South America

(Wilkins 1988; Wilkins & Schröter forthcoming). Third, research on British multinational manufacturing firms and free-standing companies began to incorporate theoretical insights from economics, in particular the question of transaction costs and the problems of principal–agent relationships (Hennart 1994; Nicholas 1991). The concepts of investment groups and free-standing companies have informed the more recent research on merchant firms by British historians specialising in Latin America (Greenhill 1995; Jones 1997; Miller forthcoming).

In his analysis of British direct investment before 1914, Charles Jones makes the point that Latin America is a crucial arena in which to test recent reappraisals of the subject (Jones 1997: 23). The same is true of other significant debates regarding British business and economic performance. On the current evidence Britain's commercial and financial decline was arguably more abrupt in Latin America than anywhere else, and the fate of the merchants appears symbolic of it.[2] In 1914 British merchant houses still possessed an important role in several South American countries. By the 1970s, however, some had gone into liquidation, while the others had been absorbed into larger conglomerates, or else sold their interests to local investors. However, this process has not been analysed in detail, for few historians have studied any of the individual trading companies beyond the traditional watershed of 1914.

This chapter is very much an attempt to map a new area of research. The starting point is the weight of evidence which suggests that British trading houses in South America immediately before 1914 were exhibiting considerable dynamism and energy, yet by the mid-1960s those which had survived were suffering irreversible decline. What happened in the intervening half-century? It is clear that no British trading house in Latin America succeeded in replicating the experience of their counterparts in the east, such as Shell Transport and Trading, Jardine Matheson, or Harrison & Crosfield, all of which became fully fledged multinational firms with different specialities. Such a transition was not impossible in Latin America. The North American company of W. R. Grace & Co. had its roots in the overseas trade of Peru and Chile. Local groups like Matarazzo in Brazil, Edwards in Chile, or Bunge y Born in Argentina also developed wide-ranging activities in a business environment where British trading houses proved vulnerable (Clayton 1985; James 1993; Martins 1973; Schvarzer 1989). On the face of it, there were several British candidates for such a role on both the east and west coasts of Latin America in 1914, but none succeeded. How is this to be explained?

The trading companies before 1914

The nineteenth century represented the high water mark for British trading companies in the international economy. Throughout the world British merchants handled goods and provided business services for a wide variety of clients. Young businessmen would leave the United Kingdom with little capital but armed with introductions to contacts in overseas ports and cities, and links to industrial firms at home. Once they reached their destinations they would set up a partnership importing and distributing mainly British manufactures. Given the partners' lack of capital, goods were normally handled on a consignment and commission basis rather than bought outright, which also diminished the merchants' risks as they held no inventories. These incipient trading firms worked, in Casson's terminology in Chapter 2, as intermediators for many clients for whom they synthesised market information. The origins of Balfour Williamson, Duncan Fox, and many other British trading houses in Latin America and elsewhere conformed pretty much to this model (Hunt 1951).

The partners soon found that importing alone would not afford them a decent living because purchasing power in Latin America was generally low. A single ship bringing a consignment of textiles or hardware could overstock a market. Small merchants thus turned to exporting local produce, again normally on a commission basis, in order to increase business and make better use of shipping. Some traders quickly developed a triangular or even multilateral trading pattern. Edward Johnston, for example, loaded coffee from Brazil to New York or Baltimore where he picked up grain and timber for shipment to Liverpool. There, once more, he collected manufactures for the return leg to Brazil (Bacha & Greenhill 1992: 148–55). As the merchants accumulated wealth they moved from trading simply on a commission basis to working on their own account. This allowed them to make greater profits, but with a heavier risk.

Commodity trading drew many British merchants into local production for export. The investment of surplus profits into an estate, the transfer of mine ownership in settlement of a debt, or a joint venture with local capitalists all resulted in a deeper penetration into the export business.[3] Later in the century commodity trading also led to involvement in domestic manufacturing. Knowles & Foster in Brazil and the British houses in Chile, for instance, invested substantially in flour milling (Graham 1966; Mazzei 1990: 29–30). As well as owning sheep farms in Chile and Peru, Duncan Fox established two cotton textile mills in Lima, taking advantage of their dominance in cotton ginning and exporting in Peru. By the early 1930s they had developed manufacturing interests in Chile in polishes and edible oils (*Peru Today*: January 1910; Davies 1966: 64; FO/1).

British merchants also found they had to provide essential business services to complement their trading activities. Latin American economies rarely had sufficient capacity in shipping, insurance and finance to satisfy a merchant's needs. To avoid transaction costs and ensure quality control, merchants had to embark upon vertical integration (Casson, Chapter 2). Partners invested in shipping or chartered it, and, once regular steamship lines had been established, became agents for British and European shipowners. A similar strategy developed with regard to insurance, crucial to the security of shipments, where merchants represented a plethora of British companies in Latin

American ports. To ensure that sufficient finance was available, merchants also took on agencies for banks. Hence, by the last quarter of the nineteenth century British trading houses abroad had developed widely diverse businesses which penetrated almost every aspect of the economies in which they found themselves.

What were the main factors in their success? Undoubtedly, they exploited the improving communications of the nineteenth century: regular steamship services from the 1860s, the telegraph from the 1870s and a universally recognised postal system. For most British manufacturers, given the scale of the market in Latin America, it made sense to employ an intermediary to look after a firm's business interests abroad, despite the problems associated with principal–agent relations. Merchants could exploit their local knowledge, specialist skills and experience of markets for their clients. At the same time, the vertically integrated nature of the trading house's operations provided an all-in service from farm or factory-gate. After the 1880s the penetration of railways into the interior allowed merchants to expand their network of suppliers and customers. Moreover, as new business opportunities appeared, the growth of British capital markets and overseas investment permitted the merchants to raise finance for the development of ventures they had initiated privately, offloading the risks and costs on to the public while retaining the profitable trading and management agencies for themselves (Greenhill & Miller 1988; Miller forthcoming).

Within this general model, however, some variations are visible. Latin America was not homogeneous and British trading houses adapted to local conditions. A distinction may thus be drawn between British houses operating on the east coast, which appear to have become more specialist, and those on the west coast, which exhibited a much more diversified set of business relationships. Balfour Williamson and Antony Gibbs & Sons, for example, worked in both Peru and Chile, as well as other parts of the Pacific Basin (North America and Australia, respectively). Although there was some specialisation in guano and nitrate, the west coast houses had a far less easily discernible business core and operated in a very wide range of activities. The relatively small economies of these republics probably forced them to undertake all kinds of business in order to make ends meet. On the east coast the much more substantial economies of Argentina and Brazil offered different opportunities. Firms there seemed more reluctant to cross national boundaries, although houses in Buenos Aires frequently had close connections across the Plate in Montevideo and Wilson Sons & Co. did expand from Brazil into Argentina and Uruguay around 1890. Moreover, although some British traders in Brazil, like Norton Megaw, Quayle Davidson and Nicholsons, remained generalists, others specialised in a single commodity, as E. Johnston & Sons did for coffee, or in a narrow range of commercial undertakings. In Argentina, where railways and massive inflows of investment from the 1880s had opened up all sorts of business possibilities, the largest British trading companies had tended to develop into specialised importers, in particular of machinery and capital goods or branded consumer products, playing a relatively limited role in the export trades.[4]

The problems of British houses after 1914

Opinions about the drive and enterprise of the British merchants around the time of the First World War have varied enormously. Those observers who were concerned primarily with the contribution they made to British exports tended to be critical of their lack of effort, a view that is evident in two official inquiries, the Worthington Mission of 1898 and the d'Abernon Mission of 1929 (UK House of Commons 1899; UK Department of Overseas Trade 1930). Yet this contrasts with the perspective of US observers, who saw the British trading houses as a major threat to US attempts to expand trade with Latin America (Tulchin 1971: 33). Moreover, the merchants in Buenos Aires, the largest market in the region, defended themselves vehemently against charges of incompetence levelled at them in Great Britain in the 1920s, arguing that the real problems lay in the inability of British manufacturers to deliver quality goods that were in demand at a price and on credit terms that would permit sales (Goodwin 1981: 34; BCCAR/3). These divergent opinions have been reflected by later historians. Charles Jones, for example, has suggested that the traditional trading houses, 'this rickety and seemingly obsolescent system of business organisation', could not rise to the challenge of change in the late nineteenth century (Jones 1987: 101). Yet Stanley Chapman's view of merchant houses as incipient British multinational companies is much more positive (Chapman 1985).

In terms of developing new business activity the British merchants in Latin America probably reached their peak in the first decade of the twentieth century, reflecting the dynamism of Latin American economies overall. The total value of British trade with the region increased from £52 million in 1900 to £132 million in 1913 (Platt 1972: 316–23). Although both foreign competition and domestic production of manufactures were growing, Britain's loss of market share between the turn of the century and the First World War was not great compared with the inter-war period (Miller 1996: 129–30). Opportunities were present in every major aspect of the merchants' business: exports of produce; imports and distribution of merchandise; agencies; investments, whether direct or portfolio; and currency and stock trading. On the west coast Gibbs intensified their involvement in nitrate, while Balfour Williamson became major oil producers and traders between California, Peru and Chile, as well as increasing their investments both in nitrate and in flour milling (Hunt 1960). In Brazil major firms like Johnstons or Wilson Sons & Co. saw an enormous expansion of their activities, despite the competition from other traders.

This makes it all the more remarkable that none of the British houses proved able to survive as an independent and significant business into the last quarter of the twentieth century. That such a transition was not impossible is demonstrated by the Latin American and US examples already mentioned. In contrast, Antony Gibbs & Sons faded into merchant banking obscurity, Balfour Williamson was eventually absorbed into Lloyds Bank, and both Johnstons and Wilsons sold their Brazilian assets to local entrepreneurs. Eventually Lloyds Bank sold part of the assets acquired from Balfour Williamson to Lonrho in 1975 and Inchcape absorbed the remainder in 1981. Thus despite valiant attempts on the part of some British firms, as a group they all eventually proved unable to overcome the problems confronting them. Difficulties arose in all aspects of their business: commodity exports, merchandise imports, agencies, investments and currency trading.

After the First World War many Latin American commodity exports faced serious problems in world markets, and this was bound to have an impact on those British trading houses which had become dependent upon them (Bulmer-Thomas 1994: 156–74). Some products virtually collapsed, like nitrate, while in other cases, like sugar, flour, or meat, growing domestic markets absorbed earlier export surpluses. The growth of protection and the introduction of import quotas in the United States and Europe also affected Latin American suppliers. For the British merchants, however, the key issues regarding commodity exports during the inter-war period were price insta- bility and the growth of competition. Those who had traded on their own account, foreclosed on estates or diminished their liquidity through long-term assistance to producers suffered seriously from fluctuating commodity prices. Both the post-war depression and the price falls of the late 1920s brought problems for British merchants holding excessive stocks. In August 1920 Balfour Williamson had about £250,000 locked up in unsaleable cotton in Liverpool and Graham Rowe well over £1 million (BW/1). In this crisis J. Lionel Barber & Co., a trading firm of some significance on the west coast, collapsed. A decade later Graham Rowe, which had been established in 1822, went into liquidation, due largely to the financial difficulties which followed their foreclosure on Peruvian cotton estates in the 1920s (*West Coast Leader*, 19/1/1932).[5]

Not only were there problems in maintaining position in the older trades. From the 1920s new opportunities in the commodity trades were limited and competition was growing. The most rapidly expanding exports were now minerals and oil rather than agricultural products, but these were dominated by large multinational companies which had little need of the trading firms established in the region, except in smaller ports and markets. Meanwhile, the wider availability of commodity reports, exchange rate information, price movements and other such market knowledge reduced the barriers to entry for competitors in the older trades. Already from the 1880s, buyers from Europe and the United States had begun to send their own agents into the interior (Jones 1987: 106–9). As soon as the US coffee dealers, Arbuckles, entered Brazil they bypassed local intermediaries, the *comissarios* or commis- sion agents, and bought direct in local markets (Greenhill 1977b: 207). The US house of Anderson Clayton began to compete aggressively with the older houses in the Peruvian cotton trade during the inter-war period and then diversified into Brazilian coffee during the 1950s, going to the farm gate to secure supplies which it sold on to roasters in the United States (Anderson Clayton undated: 18; Yonekawa 1990: 19–21; Thorp & Bertram 1978: 318). Users sought control over their sources of supply in order to secure the right quality and to prevent cornering by merchants who might put an edge on early season prices. These developments inevitably squeezed profit margins and took business away from the old British trading houses.

For those firms which, unlike those on the west coast, had specialised in imports, the problems were different. The decline in Britain's international competitiveness, and in particular the difficulties that became obvious in the 1920s, both in selling staple exports and developing new ones, was a source of much concern (BCCAR 1923: 11; BCCAR 1924: 15; BCCAR 1925: 10). Moreover, changes in international business organisation, in particular the drive on the part of large firms to reduce transaction costs, also worked against the trading houses. To some extent this was a trend which had begun with the massive growth of British investment in the late nineteenth century, for companies like the major railways had always maintained their own purchasing offices and agents in Europe and the merchants had not shared directly in this trade. In contrast, the smaller free-standing firms such as mining, land and utility companies had frequently been the creation of merchants, who then profited from commissions on their transactions. Increasingly, though, the importing houses were threatened, in part because large local wholesalers began to obtain supplies directly from manufacturers, but also through the increasing dominance of multinational firms in primary production and manufacturing. Supplies for the oil and copper companies only rarely flowed through the merchant houses, and these firms also tended to take control of their own marketing and distribution within Latin America (Philip 1982; Miller 1982; Brown 1985). The growth of the oil trade, of course, undermined the specialist coal importers in South America like Corys or Wilsons as well. Large manufacturing companies like Unilever also expressed their dissatisfaction with the merchants who had previously handled their goods, and took control of their own advertising and marketing in the larger economies, although they might leave a certain amount of distribution in the hands of the local British traders (Unilever/5; Unilever/6).

The other aspects of the merchants' business which had seemed so promising in the upsurge before 1914 also became much more uncertain. The agency work for shipping and insurance companies might keep clerks employed and provide a steady income, but it would never be a major source of expansion, and the fire insurance business, in particular, was subject to increasing local competition (Jones 1977; Jones 1984). The growth of other agency business also suffered from the fact that new investment became much more scarce after the First World War, first because of the informal restrictions the Bank of England placed on flotations of companies concerned with Latin America, and then due to the collapse of Stock Exchange confidence in most of Latin America following the defaults of the early 1930s (Atkin 1970; Moggridge 1971).[6] There was new British investment in Latin America after the First World War, but the normal conduits were large multinational firms like Shell, Lever Brothers[7], and British American Tobacco (BAT), and this further marginalised the trading houses. The more speculative aspects of the merchant firms' business, trading in shares and currency, also suffered. Latin American stock markets did not expand quickly, especially as the state increased its share of business activity, and after the introduction of controls on currency trading during the depression of the early 1930s foreign exchange transactions normally became monopolised by central banks, eliminating a source of profits for the trading firms.

This catalogue of problems eventually resulted in a slow and lingering death for the British trading houses in Latin America. However, it is only in retrospect that their fate appears inevitable, and to assume that there was no way forward for them ignores or undervalues the way in which they attempted to respond to more difficult trading conditions. Firms like Gibbs and Balfour Williamson were still actively trying to escape from their difficulties in the 1960s. It is important, therefore, to look more closely at the strategies they adopted. This analysis will show some surprising signs of enterprise, but also some deeper problems which were never resolved satisfactorily.

The British merchants' response

As far as the export trades were concerned, the options were essentially withdrawal, specialisation, or retaliation in kind. One of the best examples of successful reprisals after the turn of the century can be found in the Brazilian coffee trade, but its antecedents lay in the late nineteenth century. E. Johnston & Co., which had been the leading Brazilian coffee exporter in 1872 but had dropped out of the top three a decade later after US and German houses entered the fray, adopted a retaliatory approach but determined to act more efficiently than their rivals. The house dealt directly with local *fazendeiros* through its own network of buyers who, using the railways, could now travel inland for spot or future purchases. Agents were placed in railheads on the Sorocabana and Mogiana Railways. This strategy, of course, required more working capital for advances to landowners, so Johnstons centralised banking facilities at Campinas for agents who worked the regional centres. Success depended also on more fixed capital invested in storage and milling capacity where coffee could be cleaned, sorted and graded (Bacha & Greenhill 1992: 178–89).

Government intervention in international commodity trading could also be turned to the merchants' advantage. Nineteenth-century precedents existed in the way in which Antony Gibbs & Sons had co-operated with the Peruvian government in the guano and nitrate trades, negotiating successive contracts to ship fertilisers to Europe and the United States in return for advances secured on the sales revenues (Mathew 1981; Greenhill & Miller

1973). During and after the First World War Gibbs worked with the Chilean government to operate an official export cartel in nitrate (Couyoumdjian 1974–5). Equally, foreign traders had no difficulty working with the Brazilian government once it began to intervene periodically in the coffee trade by means of valorisation programmes designed to hold stocks off the market and raise prices (Holloway 1975; Krasner 1973). In 1906 the German trading house of Theodor Wille successfully tendered to act as agents and shippers, but in 1921 Brazilian Warrant, an associate of Johnstons, secured the contract and this yielded massive windfall gains for the company. Indeed, Brazilian Warrant's earlier investment in warehouses was partly in response to the certainty that the Rio government would need to exploit increasing storage capacity whenever it intervened in the market (Greenhill 1995: 90–2).

The changes in trading patterns and increased competition, especially from German and US firms, intensified after the First World War. British firms trading in Latin America were particularly vulnerable to these developments given that there were no imperial sentiments to shield them at home. One solution was to give up those commodities where business prospects were poor and to concentrate on others where they continued to enjoy some comparative advantage. The strategy adopted was thus one of repositioning or selective withdrawal rather than total abandonment of the commodity trades. Those trading houses which made the adjustment found that they could survive beyond the 1920s.

Latin America's importance in the world cocoa trade, for example, was clearly on the wane from about 1910 when west African output eclipsed the traditional suppliers in Ecuador, Venezuela and Brazil (Clarence-Smith 1996: 102). The response of British merchant houses in Latin America was to retreat from the trade and leave what remained to German exporters or local shippers. Similarly, Antony Gibbs & Sons began an orderly withdrawal from the nitrate trade when it became clear that artificial substitutes developed during the First World War would continue to undersell Chilean production. Despite overtures from the Guggenheims to co-operate in exploiting nitrate using more modern technology, Gibbs preferred to relinquish their holdings where possible and invest their funds elsewhere (O' Brien 1989). Another west coast house, Locketts, sold some sugar estates in Peru and liquidated their interests in Chilean nitrate during the 1920s (Albert 1976: 240–1a; Jones 1997: 34).

By contrast, concentration on commodities with better long-term commercial prospects prolonged the life of some British trading houses. While the unstable supply and demand conditions for cocoa, nitrate, and even sugar, had moved against British merchants during the 1920s, in other trades, like coffee and meat-packing, demand was still buoyant and Latin America's role in world supply remained substantial. However, the trading houses often had to invest deliberately in value-adding facilities. The Argentine beef trade is a good example. British investment groups like the Drabbles had played a significant part in the rapid transformation of Argentina to become the leading exporter of chilled meat before 1914. After 1908 US multinationals built up a dominant position in the beef trade, but there was still room for the British-owned Vestey company to establish and expand an integrated operation which involved raising cattle on its own ranches, processing them in its own *frigoríficos*, and shipping the carcasses in its own refrigerated tonnage for sale in its own shops in the United Kingdom (Hanson 1938; Smith 1969). Liebigs, of course, had already established a business which linked their ownership of *estancias* in the Plate to the marketing of the Oxo and Fray Bentos brands in Europe; the latter, indeed, provided the main source of their profits in the 1920s (Crossley and Greenhill 1977: 320–34).[8]

Brazilian coffee offered similar business opportunities for Johnstons (Greenhill 1995). Recognising that the collection of coffee for export would not yield sufficient income, given the low margins induced by the presence of American and German shippers, Johnstons developed an integrated farm-gate-to-breakfast-table strategy. Either side of the First World War they invested in *fazendas* (estates), storage in the main market centres, and transport between railhead and warehouse. In addition, they introduced a warehouse and warrant system which enabled farmers to deposit coffee in return for a certificate detailing quantity and quality which could then be used as collateral at a bank. This in turn led to a primitive commodity exchange in coffee with the usual facilities for futures trading and hedging. Furthermore, Johnstons pioneered the marketing and brand-naming of Brazilian coffee in the United Kingdom. Before the First World War the firm produced the *Fazenda* label and during the 1930s it marketed *Cambuhy* coffee from its own estate of that name. While Johnstons' business remained around its traditional core, the firm now specialised in the essential services which complemented the coffee trade and added value to it as much as with the trade itself. One recent writer has suggested that under increasingly competitive conditions in Brazil 'the only way for the British firms to continue to maintain [their] privileged position . . . was that of beginning to invest more heavily in services and infrastructure' (Szmcrecsanyi 1992: 322). Under its new identity, Brazilian Warrant, Johnstons remained in business in Brazil until the 1950s, precisely by following this kind of strategy.

The trading houses also attempted to find solutions to the difficulties in the import trade, which were caused by a number of factors: the inability of British firms to supply the market, the growth of local industry and the expansion of the multinational manufacturing companies. With their vast experience of clearing goods through ports, internal marketing and local distribution, British traders could offer their skills and reputation to other countries' exporters. On the west coast British houses became the principal importers of US automobiles and trucks, Graham Rowe being particularly prominent (Mazzei 1990: 28).[9] After the collapse of Graham Rowe this side of their business was reconstructed by other trading houses, in particular Antony Gibbs & Sons, as Graham Agencies in Chile and the Peruvian Trading Co. and Peruvian Autos in Lima, which lasted into the 1960s (Gibbs/2; Gibbs/3). In the larger markets like Argentina and Brazil the principal US automobile manufacturers soon established their own sales subsidiaries and assembly plants, so this option was not available to British traders there. However, the growth of local industry and the rapid pace of urban construction offered plenty of opportunities for specialist machinery and engineering importers, a course followed by firms like Agar Cross and Evans Thornton in Buenos Aires, with heavy support from the British commercial banks (BOLSA/3; BoE/3). Local industries also demanded skilled internal distribution, a function which several trading houses in Chile and Wilson Sons & Co. and others in Brazil fulfilled for both domestic and multinational firms (CBI/1). Wilsons also developed a substantial business in the production, storage and distribution of salt in Brazil, as well as rice and linseed milling (Wilsons/2).

Investment in other business services and manufacturing was also an option. Wilsons had long possessed a stevedoring, warehousing, tugs, lighterage and ship-repair business in many Brazilian east-coast ports, as Gibbs did in Chile. Knowles and Foster invested in a São Paulo plant to produce agricultural machinery, and Ashworths manufactured textiles and shoes (Dean 1969: 24–6).[10] Vesteys became a major soap and glycerine manufacturer in Argentina and Brazil, competing with better-known multi-nationals (Unilever/1; Unilever/11; Unilever/10). Apart from boat-building, an extension of their ship repair business, Wilsons also manufactured such diverse articles as firebricks and dyestuffs. Later, in 1950, they established joint ventures with French and British companies for the manufacture of cellophane in Argentina and railway electrification equipment in Brazil, respectively (BoE/1; Wilsons/3; Wilsons/4; Wilsons/6; Wilsons/7). In Chile Graham Rowe, Duncan Fox, and Antony Gibbs all attempted to use their position in the key commodity trades to interest Lever Brothers and later Unilever in a joint venture in soap manufacturing in the 1920s and 1930s but were rebuffed (Unilever/2; Unilever/3; Unilever/4; Unilever/8; Unilever/9 Unilever/7). Before their collapse in 1931 Graham Rowe had, in fact, in the words of one of the Gibbs' partners, 'made rather a specialty of local factories of various kinds', either by starting new ventures themselves or buying into existing factories and reorganising them (Gibbs/1). At that time Gibbs had only just begun to consider this strategy, but within a few years their interests in Chile encompassed a nail factory and a cigarette plant, while Weir Scott manufactured glass, bottled water and various food-stuffs, including condensed milk (FO/2). During the 1940s Gibbs made a major investment in a Chilean soap firm as well as in paint manufacture (Gibbs/6). Duncan Fox's interests in Peruvian industry have already been noted. They also bought a British galvanising firm in Chile in 1946, and six years later made a major investment in a new bank in Lima (BSC/1; BOLSA/4). The trading firms also looked to expand geographically. After the Second World War Duncan Fox entered Argentina, and Gibbs Williamson, a joint venture between two of the oldest firms, moved into Brazil (BCCAR 1948: 23; Gibbs/1). One of the leading east-coast houses,

Wilson Sons & Co., also opened branches in Colombia and Venezuela in 1946–47 (Wilsons/5; Wilsons/6)

Organisation, staffing and management

Many of these strategies depended on the decision to invest more capital and this, in turn, created further problems of organisation and management. The old partnership status and the preference for liquidity rather than investment in fixed assets began to seem as anachronistic as the traditional supply of funds for British trading companies, past profits or short-term borrowing was inadequate. Capital shortage is a familiar theme in British economic history, as is the apparent slowness of family-owned firms to seek outside funding for fear of losing corporate control. Alfred Chandler has compared the willingness of American companies to exploit borrowed funds with the apparently irrational resistance of British firms to such a policy (Chandler 1990: 390). Certainly there are examples – W. R. Grace, Anderson Clayton and the Guggenheims – of US trading houses operating in Latin America enthusiastically embracing managerial capitalism.

While some British trading companies in Latin America, most of which retained a large measure of family control, were reluctant to replace their old financial structures, those which adopted a different strategy were better able to exploit new opportunities. With secular falls in commodity prices and increasing competition for business, there came a point when family-owned trading companies had to consider their options. Risk-averse partners could decide to scale down their operations while retaining family control, on the grounds that increasing commercial problems did not justify investing still more of their own relatively limited supplies of money. As late as the 1960s it remained the explicit policy of Gibbs & Co. not to invest any more of their funds in Chile so that the diversification which London encouraged the local directors to undertake would have to be achieved out of any locally held surpluses. The inherent danger was, however, that the whole business would eventually atrophy and the partners' income fall. The alternative was to seek capital for direct investment abroad on a scale beyond that which the family alone could supply. In this more adventurous approach the economies of scale resulting from concentration on a single commodity or the diversification involved in new ventures could maintain or even enhance profit levels. It was not an easy decision to make. The perils of incorporating – the disclosure of financial information, the distribution of dividends to shareholders, the fear of takeover and further dilution of control if performance was poor – were real enough.

The responses of British merchant houses thus varied enormously. Wilson, Sons & Co., which started trading as an agency house in Bahia in 1837, was incorporated as early as 1877 and reorganised as Ocean Coal & Wilsons in 1908 (Wilsons/1). Two years earlier, in 1906, a private limited company replaced the family partnership of E. Johnston & Co. and in 1911 the directors launched Brazilian Warrant on the London Stock Market to purchase the old limited company and finance a huge extension to its fixed assets in the coffee trade. By 1920, after successive flotations, the company was capitalised at £1.5 million, the former partners taking a large share of the equity but the public absorbing much of the preference stock (Greenhill 1995). This procedure raised capital while maintaining control within a limited circle of ordinary shareholders. A major west coast rival, Balfour Williamson, became a limited company in 1930 in order to protect its capital following the retirement of senior partners; Duncan Fox had also incorporated its Chilean subsidiary two years previously (Hunt 1960: 173–82; BOLSA/1). However, Antony Gibbs & Sons rejected the Guggenheims' overtures in the Chilean nitrate trade and, more critically, missed opportunities in the copper trade through their reluctance to be committed to fixed investment. The firm remained technologically stagnant, organisationally weak and reluctant to commit capital; it did not incorporate its Chilean subsidiary until 1948 (Gibbs/7). Such a variety of responses indicates that no single strategy was adopted.

The operation of large, capital-intensive undertakings, often in more than one republic, also presented managerial difficulties. The questions of British entrepreneurial decline and of business conservatism are a minefield for economic historians. But a considerable literature has arisen which suggests that essentially family-based firms in Britain found it hard to match the organisational expertise of, say, North American companies, which seemed more ready to recruit outside managers. Either Britain's family concerns refused to share power with outsiders, or a supply of trained and talented executives was unavailable.[11]

In fact, both these assertions need to be treated with some caution. Family relations allowed British-based partners to have more trust in their Latin American associates and, anyway, for most British trading companies ensuring an adequate supply of managerial talent was not a new problem. Every partnership had to face the issue whenever a gap occurred in the founding family's succession, forcing it either to choose among cousins and siblings or else promote a talented partner from outside the family. In the last quarter of the nineteenth century, for example, three generations of Johnstons could not supply sufficient managerial expertise because death or retirement robbed the firm of actual and potential partners while other members of the family declined to enter the business (Bacha & Greenhill 1992). In such circumstances, and in cases where existing family directors were not up to the job, outside talent had to be employed, especially overseas. How was this done, and how were the difficulties of principal–agent relations overcome?

In the nineteenth or early twentieth century, before British firms abroad considered using local executive talent, young men would be recruited because of their family or school background or because they were known to the directors. After interview, satisfactory candidates were sent to a branch overseas. No formal training was given in London but had to be acquired in a 'hands-on' fashion abroad. Those who proved successful in their managerial apprenticeships abroad could expect eventually to return home, before incorporation as partners, later as directors. Like British banks overseas, trading houses used socialisation and male-bonding strategies to imbue recruits with a corporate spirit of flexibility and trust (Jones 1993). When Edward Greene, who became chairman of Brazilian Warrant in the 1920s, arrived in Santos in 1891 he joined a group of expatriate businessmen in a *chacara* or country house with a shifting population as newcomers replaced men who left for marriage or another posting (Greenhill 1995: 96–8). English business and sporting clubs in the major cities were also important means of socialisation. Although, as Geoffrey Jones has remarked, this managerial system looks fragile compared to the formally trained hierarchies of American multinationals, it seemed to work with fewer crises than might be expected. An employee's loyalty and commitment to the firm would be rewarded by the prospect of lifetime employment and promotion in much the same way as Japanese firms have operated. Nor did there seem to be any shortage of expatriate trainees before the Second World War.

The trading houses faced other managerial problems besides the recruitment and retention of executives who were both alive to new opportunities yet sufficiently aware of the changing local environment to evaluate them critically. As companies integrated vertically and horizontally they had to develop a structural response to changes in their strategies. The issues were both qualitative and quantitative. For all trading companies there was almost certainly the major problem of inadequate financial controls and accounting practices retained from the old days of the original merchant house, weaknesses which proved increasingly troublesome as business expanded and posts were filled by outsiders. Balfour Williamson lost substantial sums through defalcations in the 1920s when the need for internal auditing procedures seems to have been ignored (Hunt 1960: 149–50). It is, perhaps, illustrative of the slack management of the trading houses, which controlled the British Chamber of Commerce in Buenos Aires, that this institution suffered two major defalcations in the 1920s (BCCAR/1; BCCAR/2). The high status normally accorded to the bookkeeper at Santos suggested that Brazilian Warrant recognised the possibility of similar problems, but the company found experienced accountants hard to recruit (Greenhill 1995: 100). Price Waterhouse established an office in Buenos Aires in 1913 (Jones 1995: 97–8) and company archives suggest that in Argentina many British firms recruited their book-keepers locally from them or from other firms like Deloittes. For the most part, though, British firms were reluctant to employ 'Anglos' born in Latin America, especially in senior positions, until well after the Second World War.

Some British trading houses were alert to the problems of managing a large staff and complex business, and adjusted their governance structures accordingly. As early as 1912 Charles Johnston II questioned the management capacity of his company, especially in Brazil, viewing with alarm:

the number of shows for which we are becoming responsible for running. [It is] becoming clear that the Santos branch combines too many businesses to be run by one man on present lines and we shall aim at a greater subdivision of the business.

By the 1920s Brazilian Warrant had created a structure on three levels which lasted largely unchanged until the 1950s. First, there were the company's wholly owned branches. The main Santos office, which reported directly to London, was divided into separate operating spheres, based less upon conventional business functions than upon its main commercial activities. At the heart lay the key coffee and exchange departments. Branches established elsewhere in Brazil as well as in New York and New Orleans received their instructions from Santos or London. Second, the wholly and partly owned operating companies in and around Santos reported directly to the general manager there. At the third level was the network of agents inland or at the main European ports like Antwerp and Hamburg who depended less on the corporate payroll and more on fees and commissions. Inevitably such a structure raised staff costs and Charles E. Johnston II admitted he was 'rather aghast at the enormous salaries and percentages we stand committed to'.

Other trading firms took much longer to form such an integrated and hierarchical organisation. In other respects, too, trading houses remained wedded to older methods of communication and decision making, with fortnightly letters passing between London and Latin America reporting market changes and discussing policy options. Their archives contain little evidence of strategic planning or sales and financial forecasting, even in the 1950s. Only rarely, much more infrequently than in the case of the major multinational companies, did senior executives from London travel to South America, and policies regarding the home leave of executives posted to the branches seem much less structured than in the case of the multinationals.[12] As the London headquarters became, in effect, holding companies for a range of different activities and investments but without clear business strategies, they became more dependent on the initiative of their local managers both to anticipate crises and develop new business.

This image of trading houses continuing to operate as holding organisations, even when they had replaced the original partnership with a limited company, is a significant one which requires more exploration. Many of the trading companies which lay at the core of the British investment groups which Chapman and Jones have recognised in Latin America seem to have done much less than Johnstons to develop management functions at headquarters or the organisational structures appropriate to a geographically diverse operation where information flow, the appropriate balance between integration and initiative, strategic planning and imaginative crisis management were the keys to long-term survival (Chapman 1985; Jones 1997). For the most part local branches retained their autonomy and resisted attempts to incorporate them into a more centralised structure controlled from London.

Increases in British taxation may also have contributed towards this trend by encouraging the parent firms to create distance between themselves and subsidiaries overseas (Hunt 1960: 85). Thus Balfour Williamson, which was one of the more dynamic firms in developing new opportunities, never pulled its interests together to become the international oil and foodstuffs trader which at one time seemed possible. In contrast to Brazilian Warrant, another of the more successful firms, Wilson Sons & Co., did not place all its Brazilian branches under one manager until 1953 (Hunt 1960: 111–13, 181–7; Wilsons/8).

The collapse, 1945–70

Relatively little is known about the fate of the British trading firms during the Second World War, but it seems that they gained from handling those Latin American exports which were in demand in Britain while attempting to overcome the difficulties of the import trade through local investments. After 1945 conditions became much more difficult for the traditional British trading houses, especially in Argentina, Brazil and Chile, the countries where they had remained significant. The import trade remained unpredictable due to official restrictions, quotas and changing foreign exchange regulations, as well as the fact that in the bilateral commercial system that still prevailed Latin American governments preferred to use scarce sterling for imports of oil, jute and rubber (BCCAR 1953). The rapid pace of industrialisation offered opportunities for machinery imports, investments in joint ventures and the expansion of internal distribution, but other serious problems remained in the shape of inflation (and the consequent exchange depreciation), economic instability, labour conflict and nationalism.[13] In addition to the problems of trade, the British government had taken the decision during the war to discourage new investment in Latin America, partly to protect sterling, partly because the Foreign Office believed that many fixed investments merely exacerbated nationalist tensions (BoE/2; FO/3; Miller 1993: 245). The major emphasis of British post-war financial and commercial policy lay in the Empire, further marginalising the trading firms in Latin America.

The critical period seems to have been the early 1950s, when Argentina, Brazil, and Chile all experienced major economic crises. The Latin American expert of the Federation of British Industries referred in March 1953, following Brazil's default on its commercial obligations, to:

> the deteriorating position of British firms having offices or houses in Brazil. The impossibility of maintaining any reasonable flow of imports into Brazil and the present restrictions on exports by Brazil are resulting in such offices and branches being unable to earn sufficient to cover their overheads. . . . Unless something is done quickly, it seems probable that the British Marketing Organisation in Brazil will be whittled away, as has already occurred in the Argentine.
>
> (CBI/2)

While Bank of England and other archives suggest that the trading firms continued to invest quite heavily in local economies immediately after the war, by the early 1950s some were entering negotiations to sell their assets to local entrepreneurs. Balfour Williamson sold their Peruvian milling interests in 1951, and Johnstons relinquished their interests in the coffee trade to Brazilian investors the following year (*Stock Exchange Yearbook 1952*: 3146; Greenhill 1995: 105). At the same time, with the coal trade in decline and commercial conditions deteriorating, Wilsons pulled out of all South American countries except Brazil, selling its short-lived but profitable operation in Venezuela to a local firm (Wilsons/1).

In this more difficult environment the questions of staffing and access to capital became all the more critical. However, the firms were now often under the control of those who had been recruited in the boom conditions of the 1910s and 1920s and who were reaching the end of their careers just as business conditions became more uncertain. In the case of Brazilian Warrant, for example, the cautious approach of an experienced but elderly management team in the late 1940s contrasted markedly with the more dynamic strategies of new rivals like Anderson Clayton. Robert A. Sandall was still with Brazilian Warrant in Santos after forty years of service, while Robert Barham had been general manager since 1934 (Bacha and Greenhill 1992: 246). In Chile Gibbs faced enormous problems in easing aside what they termed 'the elder statesmen' in order to make way for a younger chief executive (Gibbs/5). Moreover, the supply of emigrants from the United Kingdom had now largely dried up, and for those still willing to work overseas the trading firms were not an attractive prospect in comparison with companies like Shell, ICI, Unilever or BAT (Miller 1997). Gibbs did not solve their problems either in Chile or Peru. In 1961 three of the five directors in Santiago were over 60, and there was nobody to replace them as, in the words of one of the London partners, there had been 'an alarming exodus of young Englishmen from Gibbs & Co's staff' (Gibbs/8). Partners or directors nearing retirement were unlikely to attract new business, and even if they did, financing it was a problem. Yet firms like Gibbs were reluctant to dismiss or retire long-serving employees and if new business opportunities came along, finding capital remained an obstacle. It was for this reason that Balfour Williamson sought the shelter of the Lloyds Bank group in 1960, while Gibbs also began to reorganise its overseas houses in order to attract outside funds and reinvigorate the firm's business (Gibbs/10).

Behind these difficulties lay a deeper problem of morale and function. The prevailing mood was summarised by a Gibbs director touring the Chilean branches in 1961:

> The overall impression with which one leaves Chile is that Gibbs & Co. is slowly dying. It appears to lack direction and drive. There seems to be a complete absence of ideas for developing business. . . . The policy of the firm, if the word policy can be used, appears to be to allow the Directors

and Departments to develop their own business and their own interests. . . .

(Gibbs/11)[14]

In a changed world of import substitution, industrialisation and substantial, and, at times, unpredictable government intervention in markets, just what were these companies aiming to do? Few had any real answers. For a time Balfour Williamson was able to play a role as the investment finance arm of the Bank of London and South America, gaining agencies in return for its investments (Gibbs/9; Holley 1970: 216). Other companies, though, remained wedded to the idea that they should not tie up excessive amounts of capital in countries where it had become almost impossible to repatriate earnings on time, thus exposing British-based companies to substantial exchange losses. The alternative strategy, perhaps, was to commit oneself, as many of the manufacturing multinationals did, to retaining and building up market share in local industries, especially if particular niches could be found where firm-specific knowledge could be exploited, in the hope that conditions would improve. Perforce this had to be in industries which were unlikely to be subject to government controls or intervention, and it demanded skilled local executives able to perceive opportunities and to supply or purchase specific expertise, something which the trading houses did not now possess. Moreover, the London managers of the trading companies were normally unwilling to take risks with exchange fluctuations and would not contribute new capital, even for seed-corn finance, insisting instead that new investments be funded from the operating surplus earned in current transactions (Wilsons/8). This created a real problem for managers faced with increasing overheads due to rises in wages and welfare payments and other unpredictable government demands. The contrast with the success of other merchants of British extraction who were committed to the local economy, such as the Michells who successfully built up a wool business in southern Peru after the 1930s, is striking (Bustamante 1989).

Conclusion

British trading companies in Latin America faced a crisis in the 1870s when transport improvements diminished the advantages they possessed in access to credit and information. At that point many of them adapted successfully by specialising or diversifying into areas where the skills and experience of the firm allowed them to continue to enjoy advantages over newcomers or competitors. The expansion of the British capital market and growing interest in investment in Latin America permitted several important merchant houses to develop into investment groups with a range of interlocking interests in services and production. Despite the disruption caused by the First World War and the effective closure of the City of London to new investments in Latin America for long periods afterwards, there is considerable evidence from the

merchants' own archives and from other sources that expansion and diversification remained viable options during the 1920s, although crises in
commodity prices exacted a toll at the beginning and end of that decade.
Even as the movement towards import substitution intensified in Latin
America, the merchant houses still found ways of adapting, although there are
indications that problems of finance, organisation and staffing were becoming
more acute as the Second World War approached.

Many of the older foreign firms felt themselves under threat in Latin
America from the 1930s, especially once populist leaders like Perón and Vargas
assumed power. However, nationalist criticisms of foreign capital did not
normally target the trading houses in the way they did the public utilities or
the foreign banks. Their problems lay rather in increasing government intervention, which made trade more difficult. The introduction of price controls
on consumer goods affected many of the industrial activities like foodstuffs or
soap in which the trading companies had invested between the wars. Inflation
and exchange controls deterred new investment and made the sale of a business to local entrepreneurs more attractive. But the crucial period of decline
may perhaps even be dated as late as the early 1950s, when the British
government and the City finally turned away from Latin America, while the
key Latin American countries in which the trading houses had concentrated,
Argentina, Brazil, and Chile, became the most difficult in which to do business. The Bank of London and South America, whose branch banking
network was concentrated in exactly the same countries, faced similar problems: As one BOLSA executive wrote in 1953 comparing the ABC countries
to those of the northern Andes and Central America:

> All these factors point to the necessity of reconsidering urgently where
> we now stand and where we wish to go. . . . We must either go forward
> or backward; we cannot stay as we are because if we do we shall almost
> certainly decline in prestige or profits or both . . .
>
> (BOLSA/5)

At exactly the same time Wilson Sons & Co., having concentrated their interests in Brazil, were restructuring the company's management and reorganising
both their financial and personnel procedures in order to meet the challenges
of doing business there in the early 1950s (Wilsons/8). Overall, though, the
problem for most of the trading houses was that their organisation, staffing
and financial resources were now insufficient for a major reorientation of
strategy. None was now in a position to replicate the experience of the British
Far East houses or their US and local rivals.

It does not appear, therefore, that 1914 was the crucial watershed for the
trading houses, which much of the literature on Anglo-Latin American business would suggest. The decline in British trade with Latin America and the
decline of the British trading companies are distinct issues, which need to be
analysed separately. The succeeding forty years saw considerable efforts on the

part of the trading firms to diversify and overcome an increasingly difficult and unfamiliar environment. Nor does the critical period lie between the wars, despite the collapse of some old-established houses like Ashworths and Graham Rowe, but in the decade or two following the Second World War. Why, then, did the attempts at diversification which had marked the inter-war period run into the sands? To some extent the eventual demise of the trading companies as powerful and independent firms forms part of a larger story which involves the shift of British financial and commercial policy first towards the Empire, then Europe. The lack of interest British capital markets showed in Latin America after 1945 certainly weakened them. Those which entered joint ventures with British manufacturers may have suffered from the technological and managerial weaknesses of many medium-sized British industrial firms. However, there also seems to be *prima facie* evidence of entrepreneurial and managerial failure on the part of the trading firms themselves, as attitudes and structures formed in the early twentieth century proved insufficiently adaptable to new business environments in Latin America. One final point should be made. While, in retrospect, the histories of the individual houses appear to have converged towards the same end, it is clear too that each had its own individual problems, successes and failures. Exploration of these histories in greater depth will illuminate further the issues addressed here.

Notes

1   Part of the research on which this chapter is based was financed by the Nuffield Foundation (grant SOC 253 (238)). Thanks are due also to the following for permission to use material from their companies' and organisations' papers: Charles Lagrange of the Cámara de Comercio Argentino-Británica; John Booker of Lloyds Bank; Tony Cole, Jeannette Strickland and Gary Collins of Unilever. Helpful comments on earlier drafts were made by Charles Jones, Geoffrey Jones and Judith Wale, but they bear no responsibility for the outcome.
2   For earlier attempts at analysing and explaining British 'decline' in Latin America see Platt 1972: 305–13; Bethell 1989; Miller 1993; Cain & Hopkins 1993: 146–70; Miller 1996. Charles Jones offers some suggestive ideas on the extent of inertia and failure in merchant investment groups, see Jones 1997: 35–8.
3   A well-documented example is Gibbs' involvement in copper mining and the nitrate industry: see Mayo 1985; O'Brien 1982.
4   Although Britain was a major export market, British houses did not play a dominant role in either the wool or grain trade from Argentina.
5   An even more critical problem in 1931, not just for British business in Latin America but for the City of London more generally, was the insolvency of the Anglo-South American Bank due to its overexposure in the nitrate industry. On this important episode see Joslin 1963: 65–73; Jones 1993: 240–2.
6   For long periods during the 1920s the Bank of England restricted the capitalisation of new companies to a maximum of £1 million. Argentina was the one major country which did not default during the 1930s, but confidence in investments there was undermined by the financial problems of the major British-owned railway companies, which largely ceased to pay dividends and

interest and complained incessantly about their treatment by the Argentine government: see García Heras 1987.

7   Lever Brothers merged with Margarine Unie in September 1929 to form Unilever.

8   On Liebigs' migration from Belgium to London, see Jones 1987: 157.

9   See also the advertisements in the English-language business press of Lima and Valparaíso.

10   The Ashworth investment group collapsed in 1930, however (BOLSA/2).

11   The classic statement is Chandler 1980.

12   This comment is based on the evidence of the Gibbs, Unilever, Reckitt & Colman, and J. & P. Coats archives as well as the reports of visitors from Britain contained in the files of the British Chamber of Commerce in Buenos Aires. Wilsons' archives, however, suggest that in their case visits by London directors were customary, and this may be one explanation for the strength and diversification of the firm.

13   Labour unrest forced Harrods to pull out of Chile in 1952 and seriously affected Duncan Fox (*The Times*, 9 January 1952).

14   This reads like a textbook statement of the principal–agent problem.

References

Published texts

Albert, W. (1976) *The Peruvian Sugar Industry, 1880–1920*, Norwich: University of East Anglia.

Anderson Clayton e Cia Limitada (undated) *Brazilian Coffee*, Brazil.

Atkin, J. (1970), 'Official regulation of British overseas investment, 1914–1931', *Economic History Review*, 23: 559–88.

Bacha, E. and Greenhill, R.G. (1992) *150 Years of Coffee*, São Paulo: Marcellino Martins.

Bethell, L. (1989) 'Britain and Latin America in historical perspective', in Bulmer-Thomas, V. (ed.) *Britain and Latin America: A Changing Relationship*, Cambridge: Cambridge University Press.

British Chamber of Commerce in the Argentine Republic (1923) *Annual Report, 1922–23*, Buenos Aires.

—— (1924) *Annual Report, 1923–24*, Buenos Aires.

—— (1925) *Annual Report, 1924–25*, Buenos Aires.

—— (1948) *Monthly Report*, 28 (7).

—— (1953) *Report for the Year Ended 30 June 1953*, Buenos Aires.

Brown, J.C. (1985) 'Jersey Standard and the politics of Latin American oil production, 1911–1930', in Wirth, J. D. (ed.) *Latin American Oil Companies and the Politics of Energy*, Lincoln: Nebraska University Press.

Bulmer-Thomas, V. (1994) *The Economic History of Latin America since Independence*, Cambridge: Cambridge University Press.

Bustamente, F. (1989) 'Dinámica y acumulación de los grupos económicos regionales: el caso del mercado de fibra de alpaca en el sur andino, 1970–1989', *Apuntes*, 25: 61–79.

Cain, P. J. and Hopkins, A. G. (1993) *British Imperialism: Crisis and Deconstruction, 1914–1990*, London: Longman.

Cavieres Figueroa, E. (1988) *Comercio chileno y comerciantes ingleses, 1820–1880: un ciclo de historia económica*, Valparaíso: Universidad Católica.

Chandler, A. D. (1980) 'The growth of the transnational industrial firm in the United States and the United Kingdom: a comparative analysis', *Economic History Review*, 33: 396–410.

—— (1990) *Scale and Scope: The Dynamics of Industrial Capitalism*, Cambridge, Mass.: Harvard University Press.

Chapman, S. D. (1985) 'British-based investment groups before 1914', *Economic History Review*, 38: 230–51.

Clarence-Smith, W. G. (ed) (1996) *Cocoa Pioneer Fronts since 1800: The Role of Smallholders, Planters and Merchants*, London: MacMillan.

Clayton, L. A. (1985) *Grace: W. R. Grace & Co., The Formative Years, 1850–1930*, Ottawa, IL.: Jameson.

Couyoumdjian, R. (1974–75) 'El mercado de salitre durante la primera guerra mondial y la posguerra, 1914–1921: notas para su estudio', *Historia* (Santiago), 12: 13–55.

Crossley, J. C. and Greenhill, R. G. (1977) 'The River Plate beef trade', in Platt, D. C. M. (ed.) *Business Imperialism: An Inquiry into the British Experience in Latin America before 1930*, Oxford: Clarendon.

Davies, E. E. (1966) 'Short history of Duncan Fox & Co. Ltd., 1843–1956', unpublished.

Dean, W. (1969) *The Industrialization of São Paulo, 1880–1945*, College Station: Texas A&M UP.

García Heras, R. (1987) 'Hostage private companies under restraint: British railways and transport coordination in Argentina during the 1930s', *Journal of Latin American Studies*, 19: 41–67.

Goodwin, P. B. (1981) 'Anglo-Argentine commercial relations: a private sector view, 1922–1943', *Hispanic American Historical Review*, 61: 29–51.

Graham, R. (1966) 'A British industry in Brazil: Rio Flour Mills, 1886–1920', *Business History*, 8: 13–38.

Greenhill, R. G. (1977a) 'Merchants and the Latin American trades: an Introduction', in Platt, D. C. M. (ed.) *Business Imperialism: An Inquiry into the British Experience in Latin America before 1930*, Oxford: Clarendon.

—— (1977b) 'The Brazilian coffee trade', in Platt, D. C. M. (ed.) *Business Imperialism: An Inquiry into the British Experience in Latin America before 1930*, Oxford: Clarendon.

—— (1995) 'Investment group, free standing company, or multinational? Brazilian Warrant, 1909–52', *Business History*, 37 (1): 86–111.

Greenhill, R. G. and Miller, R. (1973) 'The Peruvian Government and the nitrate trade, 1873–1879', *Journal of Latin American Studies*, 5: 107–31.

—— (1988) 'Merchants, industrialists, and the origins of British multinational enterprise in Latin America, 1870–1950', unpublished conference paper.

Hanson, S. (1938) *Argentine Meat and the British Market: Chapters in the History of the Argentina Meat Industry*, Stanford: Stanford University Press.

Hennart, J.-F. (1994) 'International financial capital transfers: a transaction cost framework', *Business History*, 36 (1): 51–70.

Holley, H. A. (1970) 'Bolsa under Sir George Bolton', in Fry, R. (ed.) *A Banker's World: The Revival of the City, 1957–1970*, London: Hutchinson.

Holloway, T. H. (1975) *The Brazilian Coffee Valorization of 1906: Regional Politics and Economic Dependence*, Madison: State Historical Society.

Hunt, W. G. G. (1951) *Heirs of Great Adventure: Balfour Williamson 1851–1901*, London: Balfour Williamson.

—— (1960) *Heirs of Great Adventure: Balfour Williamson 1901–1951*, London: Balfour Williamson.

James, M. (1993) *Merchant Adventurer: The Story of W. R. Grace*, Wilmington: Scholarly Resources.

Jones, C. (1977) 'Insurance Companies', in Platt, D. C. M. (ed.) *Business Imperialism: An Inquiry into the British Experience in Latin America before 1930*, Oxford: Clarendon.

—— (1984) 'Competition and structural change in the Buenos Aires fire insurance market: the local Board of Agents, 1875–1921', in Westall, O. M. (ed.) *The Historian and the Business of Insurance*, Manchester: Manchester University Press.

—— (1987) *International Business in the Nineteenth Century: the Rise and Fall of a Cosmopolitan Bourgeoisie*, Brighton: Wheatsheaf.

—— (1997) 'Institutional forms of British foreign direct investment in South America', *Business History*, 39 (2): 21–41.

Jones, E. (1995) *True and Fair: A History of Price Waterhouse*, London: Hamish Hamilton.

Jones, G. (1993) *British Multinational Banking, 1830–1990*, Oxford: Clarendon.

Joslin, D. M. (1963) *A Century of Banking in Latin America: To Commemorate the Centenary in 1962 of the Bank of London and South America Ltd.*, London: Oxford University Press.

Krasner, S. D. (1973) 'Manipulating international commodity markets: Brazilian coffee policy, 1906 to 1962', *Public Policy*, 21: 493–523.

Marichal, C. (1986) 'Foreign Predominance among overseas traders in nineteenth-century Latin America: a comment', *Latin American Research Review*, 21 (3): 145–50.

Martins, J. de S. (1973) *Conde Matarazzo: o empresário e a empresa*, São Paulo: Hucitec.

Mathew, W. M. (1981) *The House of Gibbs and the Peruvian Guano Monopoly*, London: Royal Historical Society.

Mayo, J. (1979) 'Before the Nitrate Era: British Commission Houses and the Chilean Economy', *Journal of Latin American Studies*, 11: 283–302.

—— (1985) 'Commerce, credit and control in Chilean copper mining before 1880', in Culver, W. W. and Greaves, T. C. (eds) *Miners and Mining in the Americas*, Manchester, Manchester University Press.

—— (1987) *British Merchant Houses and Chilean Development, 1851–1886*, Boulder: Westview.

Mazzei de Grazia, L. (1990) *Sociedades comerciales e industriales y economía de Concepción, 1920–1939*, Concepción: Editorial Universitaria.

Miller, R. (1982) 'Small business in the Peruvian oil industry: Lobitos Oilfields Limited before 1934', *Business History Review*, 56: 400–23.

—— (1993) *Britain and Latin America in the Nineteenth and Twentieth Centuries*, London: Longman.

—— (1996) 'British trade with Latin America, 1870–1950', in Mathias, P. and Davis, J. A. (eds) *The Nature of Industrialization: Vol. 5: International Trade and British Economic Growth from the Eighteenth Century to the Present Day*, Oxford: Blackwell.

—— (1997) 'The British communities and the management of British firms in postwar Latin America', unpublished conference paper.

—— (forthcoming) 'British free-standing companies on the West Coast of South America', in Wilkins, M. and Schröter, H. G. (eds) *The Free-Standing Company in the World Economy, 1830–1996*, Oxford: Oxford University Press.

Moggridge, D. E. (1971) 'British controls on long-term capital movements, 1924–1931', in McCloskey, D. N. (ed.) *Essays on a Mature Economy: Britain after 1840*, London: Methuen.

Nicholas, S. (1991) 'The expansion of British multinational companies: testing for managerial failure', in Foreman-Peck, J. (ed.) *New Perspectives on the Late Victorian*

Economy: Essays in Quantitative Economic History, 1860–1914, Cambridge: Cambridge UP.

O'Brien, T. F. (1982) *The Nitrate Industry and Chile's Crucial Transition, 1870–1891*, New York: New York University Press.

—— (1989) '"Rich Beyond the Dreams of Avarice": the Guggenheims in Chile', *Business History Review*, 63: 122–59.

Philip, G. (1982) *Oil and Politics in Latin America: Nationalist Movements and State Companies*, Cambridge: Cambridge University Press.

Platt, D.C.M. (1972) *Latin America and British Trade, 1806–1914*, London: A. & C. Black.

—— (1986) 'Wicked foreign merchants and macho entrepreneurs: Shall we grow up now?', *Latin American Research Review*, 21 (3): 151–3.

Reber, V. B. (1979) *British Mercantile Houses in Buenos Aires, 1810–1880*, Cambridge: Harvard University Press.

Ridings, E. W. (1985) 'Foreign predominance among overseas traders in nineteenth-century Latin America', *Latin American Research Review*, 20 (2): 3–28.

Schvarzer, J. (1989) *Bunge y Born: crecimiento y diversificación de un grupo económico*, Buenos Aires: CISEA-GEL.

Smith, P. H. (1969) *Politics and Beef in Argentina: Patterns of Conflict and Change*, New York: Columbia University Press.

Szmcrecsanyi, T. (1992) 'German capital investment in the early industrialization of São Paulo', *Ciencia e Cultura*, 44: 320–25.

Thorp, R. and Bertram, G. (1978) *Peru, 1890–1977: Growth and Policy in an Open Economy*, New York: Columbia University Press.

Tulchin, J. S. (1971) *The Aftermath of War: World War I and US Policy toward Latin America*, New York: New York University Press.

United Kingdom, Department of Overseas Trade (1930) *Report of the British Economic Mission to Argentina, Brazil, and Uruguay*, London: HMSO.

United Kingdom, House of Commons (1899) 'Conditions and prospects of British trade in certain South American countries', *Parliamentary Papers*, 96: 449–613.

Wilkins, M. (1988) 'The free-standing company, 1870–1914: an important type of British foreign direct investment', *Economic History Review*, 41 (2): 259–82.

Wilkins, M. and Schröter, H. G. (eds.) (forthcoming) *The Free-Standing Company in the World Economy, 1830–1996*, Oxford: Oxford University Press.

Yonekawa, S. (1990) *General Trading Companies: A Comparative and Historical Study*, Tokyo: The United Nations University Press.

Manuscript sources

BCCAR/1 British Chamber of Commerce in the Argentine Republic (hereafter BCCAR), Council, Minute Book #1, 21/9/1921.

BCCAR/2 BCCAR, Council, Minute Book #2, 24/6/1926.

BCCAR/3 BCCAR, Executive Committee, Minute Book #3, 27/9/1927.

BoE/1 Bank of England, OV 102/168, 'Capital Remittances to Argentina'.

BoE/2 Bank of England, EC4/303, Eden to HM Representatives in Latin America, 12/8/1944.

BoE/3 Bank of England, EC 5/594, Memorandum, 11/1/1962.

BOLSA/1 Lloyds Bank plc, Bank of London and South America archive (hereafter Lloyds/BOLSA), book 4361, BOLSA Minute Book #12, 2/10/1928.

BOLSA/2 Lloyds/BOLSA, book 4361, BOLSA Minute Book #12, 18/2/1930 and 25/2/1930.

BOLSA/3 Lloyds/BOLSA, book 4362, BOLSA Minute Book #13, 15/9/1931.

BOLSA/4 Lloyds/BOLSA, book 4409, 'Peru: Report by the Hon. B. Pleydell-Bouverie, March 1952'.

BOLSA/5 Lloyds/BOLSA, file 4409, 'The Policy for the Future', 5/5/1953.

BSC/1 British Steel Corporation, John Summers & Sons archive, file 425/35/9, Accounts of Anglo-Argentine Iron Co. Ltd., 1946.

BW/1 Balfour Williamson, Archibald Williamson papers, letter book #6, Williamson to Milne, 23/8/1920.

CBI/1 Confederation of British Industries, Federation of British Industries archive (hereafter CBI/FBI), file 200/F/38/1, G. Lucock, 'Report on Brazil; Preliminary Report on Argentina, August 1923', p. 12.

CBI/2 CBI/FBI, file 200/F/D3/6/9, McKechnie to Kipping, 6/3/1953.

FO/1 Public Record Office, Foreign Office archives (hereafter FO), file FO 371/15787/A2128/23/51, Bentinck to Simon, 4/2/1932.

FO/2 FO 371/18697/A7521/1536/51, Cavendish-Bentinck to Hoare, 17/8/1935.

FO/3 FO 371/52078/AS945/11/51, Perowne to Hadow, 8/3/1946.

Gibbs/1 Antony Gibbs & Sons (hereafter AG&S), Guildhall Library London, file 16875/3, Dobree to Walter Gibbs, 12/9/1931.

Gibbs/2 AG&S, file 16875/3, G. E. Gibbs to Dobree, 2/3/1932.

Gibbs/3 AG&S, file 16875/3, G. E. Gibbs to Dobree, 30/3/1932.

Gibbs/4 AG&S, file 16870, Gibbs & Co., Minutes of Partners' Meetings, 5/4/1946.

Gibbs/5 AG&S, file 16898, Aldenham to Korn, 18/2/1947; Aldenham to Blair and Dobree, 2/3/1947.

Gibbs/6 AG&S, file 16898, Aldenham to Korn, 9/3/1947.

Gibbs/7 AG&S, file 16870, Gibbs & Co., Minutes of Partners' Meetings, 1947.

Gibbs/8 AG&S, file 16878, 'DCC's Agenda for Discussion with Mr Gibbons, 13/7/1961'.

Gibbs/9 AG&S, file 16878, DCC: Memorandum of Discussion with Mr Gerald Cooper of Williamson Balfour, 12/9/1961.

Gibbs/10 AG&S, file 16878, 'Memorandum of Agreement with Mr Gibbons, 3/10/1961'.

Gibbs/11 AG&S, file 16878, 'Gibbs & Co., Chile' [1961].

Johnston CEJ II, letter book (out letters) of Charles Edward Johnston in private possession.

Unilever/1 Unilever Archives, Port Sunlight, Overseas Committee (hereafter U/PS/OSC), 'Mr Roberts' Report on Argentina, April 1924'.

Unilever/2 U/PS/OSC, Agendas Book A, 8/12/1926.

Unilever/3 U/PS/OSC, Agendas Book C, 27/10/1927.

Unilever/4 U/PS/OSC, Agendas Book F, 3/1/1929.

Unilever/5 U/PS/OSC, unnumbered file, 'Report on Mr Chipperfield's Visit to Brazil, September/October 1930'.

Unilever/6 U/PS/OSC, OSF 3/3, 'Mr Sidney van den Bergh's Report on his Visit to Brazil, February 1933'.

Unilever/7 U/PS/OSC, Agendas Book L, 1/5/1933.

Unilever/8 U/PS/OSC, Agendas Book U, 28/1/1938.

Unilever/9 U/PS/OSC, Agendas Book Y, 12/6/1940.

Unilever/10 U/PS/OSC, OSF 3/17, 'Report of Mr J. L. Heyworth. Visit to Brazil, March 1947'.

Unilever/11 U/PS/OSC, OSF 1/21, 'Argentina: Report by Sir Geoffrey Heyworth and Mr J. L. Heyworth on their Visit, November/December 1949'.

Wilsons/1 Wilson Sons & Co. (hereafter Wilsons), file 20203, 'Wilson Sons and Co. and Ocean Coal and Wilsons: Short History'.

Wilsons/2 Wilsons, file 20186/8, Board Minutes, 1942–1947, passim.

Wilsons/3 Wilsons, file 20186/8, Board Minutes, 17/11/1942.

Wilsons/4 Wilsons, file 20186/8, Board Minutes, 24/9/1946.

Wilsons/5 Wilsons, file 20186/8, Board Minutes, 28/11/1946.

Wilsons/6 Wilsons, file 20186/8, Board Minutes, 16/12/1947.

Wilsons/7 Wilsons, file 20186/9, Board Minutes, 20/1/1950.

Wilsons/8 Wilsons, file 20186/9, Board Minutes, 26/5/1953: 'Memorandum on the Powers of the General Manager in Brazil'.

7 Trading companies in twentieth-century Sweden

Hans de Geer

Introduction

Scandinavia has been linked to the international trading network as long ago as the early Middle Ages. Viking raids to the east and the west can be seen as initiatives from Scandinavia to develop commercial and cultural links both with the Eastern Roman Empire, and partly in Western Europe, which began to take shape after the time of Charlemagne. The contacts were sometimes more violent than peaceful – more a matter of conquest than an exchange – even though both were often found side by side in the risky trading expeditions of those days.

Later, when the Scandinavian countries had begun to take shape, and more stable institutions had developed, often based on continental or English models in the wake of Christian missionaries, the Scandinavian market was dominated by the Hanseatic League, the federation of trading cities around the Baltic and North Seas, which stretched from Novgorod in the east to London in the west, from Bergen in the north to the English Channel coast in the south, and within which the dominant role was played by Lübeck. The Hanseatic network became established in the most important Swedish port cities, including Stockholm.

The Scandinavian role in this was on the economic periphery: raw materials, which were in demand in the more developed cities in the continental part of the network, were gathered from the extensive hinterland. Salt, spices and other precious commodities flowed back. Clear commercial control was exercised from the centre. The German influence, which was sometimes institutionalised, could constitute, be interpreted or depicted as a threat to national independence. But participation was also a learning process; within the framework of the network, both a commercial culture and a commercial maturity were established.

In the early sixteenth century, Swedish commerce freed itself from its strong dependence on Lübeck and the Hanseatic League. But international trade relationships were still in the hands of foreign merchants, who carried out their operations within the framework of a virtually mercantilist policy, which channelled the international flow of goods to certain port cities, and thereby increased state control and taxation opportunities. During the seventeenth century, German influence gave way to Dutch influence. Dependence on Amsterdam as a financial centre increased with the Swedish participation in the Thirty Year War, the outcome of which saw Sweden make a short 'guest appearance' as a European superpower.

The superpower role was expressed in colonial ambition, both in North America and on the west coast of Central Africa. In both cases the projects were short-lived. At the beginning of the 1730s, an East India Company was formed, which continued to trade until 1806. A bridge was built between the two distant markets. There was no question of specialisation by product or sector. Over time, the merchants involved gained more experience. More long-term and stable contacts were established, the networks were extended and the risks reduced. The character of the projects also changed from adventurous to routine (Frängsmyr 1990; Nováky 1990).

More important than exotic trade were the trading houses that were established during the eighteenth century to market Swedish iron in Western Europe. The great period for Swedish bar iron was during the eighteenth century and at the beginning of the nineteenth century. Production took place in rural ironworks, and was generally carried on in parallel with forestry and agriculture. Exports were channelled through the cities of Stockholm and Gothenburg, where all export iron was inspected and weighed; each ironworks had its set volume to export. Both the administration, which the regulatory system gave rise to, and the lack of market expertise on the part of the rural ironworks owners, created a need for middlemen. A new type of trading firm grew up in Stockholm and Gothenburg, which exported onto the international market. These firms put their stamp both on Swedish foreign trade in the late eighteenth century and on social life in the leading port cities. The trading houses were often run by foreign immigrants, from Britain, from Germany and from the Netherlands, frequently in partnership with Swedish interests. At the beginning of the nineteenth century, a number of Jewish families also became involved. This merchant aristocracy formed a separate and fairly homogeneous social group: the beginnings of a Swedish bourgeoisie (Samuelsson 1951; Kuuse 1996).

The trading firms normally did not specialise in their export trade, but iron was very much the dominant sector. Here, they developed two different roles. Certain trading firms functioned primarily as receivers of iron, which was delivered from the ironworks to the ports, while others specialised in international trade and often took over iron, irrespective of who had produced it, from the receivers. The largest trading firms often functioned in both roles.

When the market for Swedish iron became more difficult in the nineteenth century, it meant a decline for those trading firms which were not capable of changing their activities to other products. For a period in the middle of the century, as a result of the Crimean War, grain exports played a major role. Later, the output from the sawmill and the pulp industry took the lead.

In their import business, trading firms often specialised according to the place of origin of their founders. If the founder came from Germany, grain imports in general dominated, while colonial goods dominated in firms founded by Englishmen or Scots. Normally, the value of exports exceeded imports, with the result that the financial resources of the trading firms grew, and this gave scope for other investments.

The trading houses developed commercial activities alongside their purely trading operations. They frequently engaged in shipping, particularly in the form of shipping partnerships, but also often in manufacturing, e.g. in sugar or tobacco. Later, from the middle of the nineteenth century, the trading firms played a leading role as promoters of banks and railways, educational establishments and, in the industries which would come to dominate the industrial period, the timber industry, paper-making pulp and engineering.

They also came to function as financiers for the ironworks in whose production they dealt. This frequently resulted in them acting as the principal with regard to the ironworks, i.e. they took the initiative in the relationship and in many cases became owners of the works. By extension, several of the trading firms became merchant bankers and played a significant role from the end of the eighteenth century up to the latter part of the nineteenth, when a modern banking system and a modern stock exchange developed.

With industrialisation, the role of the traditional trading firm diminished. The development of communications made remote markets more accessible and reduced the risks involved in long-distance trade, which the trading firms had absorbed. There was still a gap between the domestic market and distant markets, between language areas and cultures, between buyers and sellers in new industries, which could be exploited through new business operations. A Johnson & Co. was one of these in Sweden. But it became more and more the case that national and international commerce was seen as an integral part of the activities of the producing companies. At the same time, import trade was developed by wholesalers, who emerged in the wake of retailers, and who took over a significant share of imports of colonial goods and of consumer goods.

The traditional trading firms were squeezed out as modern commerce developed, but in several cases there was room left for the modern form of trading firm to develop. Not many of the older trading firms managed to survive. Some new trading firms emerged during industrialisation or later; an investigation in the middle of the 1980s revealed a handful of companies, of which some had gone out of existence before the end of the decade. However, interest in trading firms underwent a marked revival from the 1970s as the 'Japanese miracle' focused attention on the *sogo shosha*.

The trading company: towards a definition

Commerce is greater than ever, but trading firms are fewer. This statement cries out for a definition: what is a trading firm in the modern sense? As has been argued in Chapter 2, theoretically a trading firm can be described as a market-making intermediator. The function of intermediation can be fulfilled either as a broker or a reseller, which implies differences in ownership of the goods, opportunity and risk. This is a distinction of functions, not a categorisation of firms: as will become apparent from the empirical evidence below, a trading firm might well act as a broker in some business and as a reseller in other business.

It is necessary to add other characteristics to the definition. Normally, a trading firm will concentrate largely on trading in goods. Trading in services or ideas also come into the picture, but must not dominate; a trading firm is not a consultancy. A trading firm – and even more so a trading house – must also have a certain breadth of operation. With this comes variety and flexibility, but it also makes heavy demands on product expertise and market knowledge. The trading firm that is discussed here operates in international trade and must be able to handle both exports and imports. It must also be able to carry out transactions where these concepts – export and import as seen from a specific viewpoint – have lost some of their meaning, namely where exchange is carried out between two foreign countries, i.e. cross-trading. The trading firm should have a certain degree of financial independence so that it can handle part of its financing from its own resources and absorb part of the risk involved in trading.

The trading firm should in principle remain independent and free in relation to production interests so that it can maximise its flexibility and its ability to close deals wherever they arise. According to Casson (Chapter 2, this volume), when a trading firm integrates upstream or downstream by investing in shipping or in production, it changes from being a pure trading firm into a hybrid one. This concept is not very clear-cut: hybrid trading firms 'can usually be described in some alternative way'. As Casson points out, this ambiguity calls for a deeper understanding of the various ways in which the trading companies become hybrid and function as such. Obviously, there is a great variety, but we can see some different patterns. In the typical imperial/colonial relationship we see trading companies headquartered in the imperial centre, going into production in the colonies in order to make production more rational or more reliable, or the produce more in keeping with the standards required by the home market. The presumption here is that the native country is more 'developed' than the colony. In other cases, as with the Swedish firms that will be discussed in this chapter, there might be a different balance. A trading company might invest in production capacity in its own native country and then act as a marketing organisation in the export markets in the more industrialised countries. A trading firm might also invest in production in the importing country, with a more or less advanced economy, in order to avoid political impediments to business, like protectionism in some cases (e.g. the USA), or in order to comply with other nationalistic industrial policies (as in Latin America or India in the 1970s). Maybe it is also worthwhile to note the difference between the case when the trading firm itself invests in production and the situation when the owners of the trading company invest in production facilities. The latter case might give the trading company more freedom of action, provided that the owners' different businesses are kept at arm's-length.

The specific expertise of trading firms often has more to do with the market than with the product. Their most important function is to act in distant markets, or in markets which, for other reasons, which may be political, cultural or linguistic, are difficult for producers to cultivate. Its clients are, in general, small companies which do not themselves have the opportunity to get to know the market, or large companies for whom the particular market involved is new or peripheral. With its network expertise, the trading firm may also be particularly suitable for handling situations where it is necessary to connect different transactions, such as in counter-trading of various types. Trading firms may also have a role as project co-ordinators, where several producing companies act jointly.

But it is a balancing act; forces in financial and industrial development constantly create pitfalls, which can probably only be avoided through alertness and flexibility on the part of the trading firm. There is always the classic dilemma of the agent, that as soon as business in a market begins to go very well, the client becomes interested in rescinding the agency agreement and marketing on his own account. Trading on an agency basis is the art of earning as much as possible from an acceptable level of business. For the producer companies, it is essential at the same time to have their own marketing organisation; direct contact with customers has an information value that is easily lost if it goes through a middleman. At the other end of the distribution chain, wholesalers are lying in wait, and the major retail chains, which, when they are powerful enough, prefer to dispense with the trading firm's services and do business directly with the producer. Technical developments – in terms of depth, complexity and multiplicity – are another threat. These tend to increase the requirement for specialist knowledge in marketing, which may become increasingly more difficult for the trading firm to cope with if it is to maintain the breadth of its activities. The trading firm can increase the market value of its own trading goods through repackaging and branding, but if this development is taken too far the result will be a wholesale business.

The trading firm is, by definition, a middleman in trade. Its operations are built on differences in availability, demand and price between different markets. This can create troublesome ideological stalemates in certain situations. But more important is the fact that this position is on the point of being undermined. Increasing internationalisation at all levels is tending to reduce barriers connected with distance, language and culture. Information technology developments have in more and more areas established international market places, where previously they were national or regional. The differences, which the trading firm relied on, are becoming smaller or more short-lived. The intensity of trade is rising, and it may be that it is in the ability to handle rather sophisticated information systems, which are also being developed into executive systems, that the decisive expertise of the trading firm will lie in the future.

Three Swedish trading firms

Three Swedish trading firms that are still in business will now be described. The discussion will focus mainly on A. Johnson & Co. The other two trading firms, Ekman & Co. and Elof Hansson International, are included mainly to provide a degree of comparison.[1]

Ekman & Co

The trading firm of Ekman & Co. was established in 1802 and is the oldest of the three. Its history begins even earlier than this. The Ekman family had been involved in the timber trade since the end of the seventeenth century. At the end of the eighteenth century, the family moved to Gothenburg and ran a successful business in the herring trade and herring processing. Herring oil from the west coast of Sweden was used to light the streets of London and Paris. At the beginning of the nineteenth century, the firm became involved in iron exports. At that time, Gothenburg was experiencing a period of very successful foreign trading as a result of the continental blockade, but after the fall of Napoleon, trade through Gothenburg declined. The trading firm of Ekman entered a period of reduced activity and lower turnover. From the 1840s, the firm was revitalised and expanded its iron exports, which continued to be its most important business for the rest of the century. The Ekman family played an important role in the rebirth of Swedish iron production, triggered by the introduction of the Lancashire Forge. When the cast-steel processes were introduced during the latter part of the century there was considerable pressure to adapt, and a large number of ironworks closed down. The older trading firms, which had built up relationships with the old ironworks, were facing a crisis. The solution was to diversify from iron into the forest-products industry. This mainly involved the production of paper-making pulp; the emerging industrial society required ever more paper. Ekman played an active role in the introduction of chemical pulp processes, and from the beginning of the twentieth century an increasing part of the business of the firm involved the export of pulp and paper.

The firm specialised to a very high degree at different times: the herring exporter of the eighteenth century became the iron exporter of the nineteenth, and the paper and pulp exporter of the twentieth. In the more distant past it was more diversified, with interests in a number of different operations. The leading members of the firm and the Ekman family played a major role in the foundation of the institutions of the industrial society, in railway building, the establishment of banks, the setting up of the university and the School of Economics and Business Administration in Gothenburg. They also played a significant part in the provision of welfare. The family had at times close connections to the Marvin Brethren, and several members of the family were involved in liberal politics at both local and national level.

The industrial connections which the firm of Ekman & Co.had developed, were particularly concentrated in the pulp industry, and had originally been initiated to safeguard supplies. These commitments resulted in the firm becoming overstretched during the crisis at the beginning of the 1920s, and it was decided to liquidate them all. At the same time, the firm was changed to a joint stock company. In the two decades following immediately after the Second World War, the firm entered into new ownership in the pulp industry, but this also ended badly; the company closed down the operation in 1964.

At about the same time, the family company was acquired by an investment company. Now Ekman moved in a new direction. The new management did not believe in such a specialised relationship with the paper and pulp industry, but started to diversify, particularly on the hitherto neglected import side. The international organisation was expanded, particularly in East Asia, and a significant level of imports of consumer goods resulted. Profitability in the business was, however, not strong.

In the middle of the 1980s, the company became closely linked to the vehicle producer, Volvo, which at that time was building up a diversified operation. Ekman, which continued as an independent company under the new owners, changed its strategy. Imports were now seen as an extraneous activity and were sold off. To strengthen the export side, where Ekman focused on pulp, another trading firm was purchased that was strong in exporting paper to markets outside Europe. But the merger was a disappointment. Ekman & Co, which was acquired in the mid-1990s by a consortium in which the Ekman family once again had a significant share, has built up a new trade in pulp in the 1990s through long-term contracts with international producers in North America and Russia.

Elof Hansson International

The Elof Hansson International company was founded in 1897 by Elof Hansson, a young Swede who was working in Hamburg. He came into contact with representatives of the Japanese firm, Mitsui & Co, who appointed Hansson to be their main supplier of cellulose. The company moved to Gothenburg in Sweden in 1914. There was an almost total concentration on pulp during the first decade.

Japan remained the most important market until the inter-war period, when Latin America, particularly Brazil and Chile, became more important. As a result of the blockade during the Second World War, Elof Hansson opened an office in New York, where his eldest son was based with the aim of supplying customers in Latin America with pulp from North American suppliers. Machinery and machine units for the paper industry became part of the firm's export range at the end of the 1920s, and on the import side after the Second

World War. They were at that time particularly involved in supplying the ship-building industry with steel plate and tools. Later, the firm moved into rolling stock for tram systems and railways. The import of consumer goods also took off after the Second World War, starting with textile products.

Elof Hansson is today purely a trading firm without production interests. The founder's sons entered the firm in the fifties, the youngest acting as Managing Director from 1972 until 1992. The shares in the company are owned by a trust, the Elof Hansson Trust. The firm operates in three product areas: forestry, engineering and consumer goods. The principal products are cellulose and paper, which represents approximately 70 per cent of the business, but the company is also involved in construction materials, machinery, forestry goods, steel, chemicals, textiles, home electronics and household electrical products. On the import side, the company is, to all intents and purposes, a wholesaler, since to a great extent it stores and repacks its own goods for distribution to the retail trade.

The distribution of the company in the 1990s is as follows. Asia and Australia account for approximately 40 per cent; Elof Hansson International was responsible in the mid-1980s for one quarter of Swedish trade with China. Next comes Sweden with 20 per cent, North and South America with approximately 15 per cent, Europe somewhat less, but the company has a growing market in Russia and Central and Eastern Europe. Trade with Africa amounts to over 10 per cent. The company has approximately twenty subsidiaries and agents in 100 countries.

A Johnson & Co. / Axel Johnson AB

The Axel Johnson Group is the largest of the three trading firms discussed here. The group currently consists of three concerns: Axel Johnson AB, with its principal operations in Sweden; Axel Johnson Inc., a diversified industrial group in the USA; and Axel Johnson International, which, from its base in Sweden, carries on international trade and carries the trading-firm tradition onwards.

A Johnson & Co. was founded in 1873 by Axel Johnson, who gained his experience of business as an employee of a fabric shop in Stockholm. He resolutely taught himself languages and gathered a small amount of capital by trading in the relatively new Stockholm Stock Exchange. He tried the colonial goods sector, with imports of French wines and cheeses, but soon concentrated his activities on trading with Swedish developing industries.

Trade involves utilising movements between supply and demand and taking advantage of imbalances between needs and satisfaction in time and space. The dynamics which Axel Johnson sought to utilise was the divergence between the old and the new generated by the early stages of industrialisation in Sweden. It was heavy industry for the export markets which developed first; the consumer goods industry and the domestic market came to prominence rather later.

The first to develop was the forestry industry. Previously the sawmill industry had taken off as a result of increased international demand. With the coming of steam power, large export sawmills could be located at good export harbours. Some decades later, at the end of the nineteenth century, the manufacture of pulp and paper became increasingly important. In parallel, the chemical industry developed, with products such as explosives (e.g. the Nobel enterprises) and safety matches, which gained a significant international market.

At the same time, the classical Swedish iron industry went through a critical transformation. The new opportunities created by the cast-steel processes exposed traditional, high-quality but expensive Swedish export iron to fierce competition. Some ironworks were able to utilise the new processes – Sandvikens Jernverk was a pioneer here – while other, older and capital-weak ironworks had to close down.

Others relocated their production into niche qualities and special steels, and found their salvation through the development of the shipbuilding and engineering industries with their particular demands on the quality and characteristics of the steel. The structural changes in the iron and steel industries also led to transformation in marketing; many of the old trading firms were forced out of business or had to reorganise into other business.

Axel Johnson found himself at the centre of events. Stockholm was, in competition with Gothenburg which for a time had the advantage, the import and export harbour for the many small and medium-sized ironworks in Bergslagen, where the bulk of the Swedish iron industry was located. The export routes to the Continent and to Britain ran through Stockholm, and through Stockholm also came the imports of coal, alloying agents, minerals and chemicals and of fire bricks for the blast furnaces. Stockholm's role in Swedish commerce was strengthened during the last quarter of the nineteenth century. Several of the new industries were located in Stockholm. It was the centre of political power, and the important institutions were concentrated there, not least those which were involved in the financial markets.

Axel Johnson began to take part in the trade between Stockholm and the iron industry of Bergslagen from the middle of the 1870s. There was a gap, which many tried to fill, since the old dominant trading firm of Tottie & Arfwedson had been forced into liquidation in 1867. The most important imports for A Johnson & Co. were hard coal and coke from Britain and from the Ruhr in Germany. Its customers were not only in the iron industry. The increasing traffic on the growing railway network demanded constantly increasing quantities of fuel. Alongside fossil fuel, the firm imported, among other things, fire bricks from Britain. On the export side, the most important product was pig iron, which was primarily sold to the British market. A short-lived ownership arrangement in the match industry led to the unsuccessful marketing of Swedish matches in Britain. The strong connection with the British market led the firm to establish an office in London for a few years at the end of the 1870s, but this was soon closed down.

As a tradesman, Axel Johnson became a major purchaser of transport services and during the 1880s he began to carry goods on his own account. From 1890 this activity increased, when the shipping company, Nordstjernan, was set up. During the 1890s the shipping company grew strongly, carrying freight in the North Sea and the Baltic. The major change to the shipping company came during the first decade of the twentieth century. In 1904 a trans-ocean line to the River Plate and other destinations on the South American coast was opened. In 1914, after the opening of the Panama Canal, Nordstjernan began scheduled services to the west coasts of both South America and North America.

Alongside the interest in shipping, which took an ever-greater part of Axel Johnson's interest and time, the business also developed in another direction. The connection with the Swedish iron industry led him into ownership of Avesta Jernverk, which had run into difficulties as a result of trade cycles, competition and a lack of innovation. After an initial and less successful arrangement at the beginning of the 1890s, Johnson accepted an offer to become the principal owner of the company in 1905. The reasons were to secure deliveries for exports and a market for imports, but also the acceptance of responsibility for an old business relationship, whilst the temptation to become an industrialist also played a part. Avesta was in practice run as a subsidiary of the trading firm.

Now the Johnson Group was comprised of three parts: the trading firm, the shipping company and the ironworks. This can be seen as a process of integration: the dependence of the trading firm on transport led to the estab-lishment of the shipping company. The trading firm guaranteed a certain amount of freight for the shipping company's vessels, and the expansion of the shipping company's routes created new business opportunities for the firm. The trading firm's market experience of the demands of iron production and the sale of iron made it a natural progression to integrate backwards into production, and the union of the marketing organisation and production generated a certain amount of security in planning on both sides. But at the same time it is obvious that something happened to the trading firm and the prerequisites for its flexibility. The links with its own transport and production companies created the conditions for developing certain types of business while, at the same time, severing access to others. Other ironworks will not automatically use a trading firm which owns its own ironworks, but will see it as a competitor in the same market. Through the link with Avesta, the trading firm began to compete with its own potential customers, which from the strict point of view of a trading company is an illogical and inappropriate situation. And there would be many more such links over time. A. Johnson & Co. had become a hybrid trading company.

With the establishment of Nordstjernan and the acquisition of Avesta, the trading firm became of secondary interest to founder Axel Johnson. The coal business, which was the most important at the beginning of the century, was regarded as necessary and good, but routine and boring; from time to time

Johnson considered abandoning this original bread-and-butter operation. This did not, however, mean that this entrepreneur was prepared to hand over control to someone else. He complained bitterly at times about the lack of good staff in the company: by good staff he meant someone who was prepared to put just as much energy and commitment into the business as he did himself, but at considerably lower benefit in the way of earnings or influence.

From the end of the 1890s, his elder sons Axel and Helge were trained in the firm. Axel, born in 1876, was made managing clerk in 1901, and could thereby formally represent the owner, and he was given some responsibility for transactions involving Avesta. Helge, born in 1878, was put in charge of the coal business. The decade during which the father and the two sons jointly ran the business of the firm was noted more for conflict than for collaboration. The pattern was the classic one: the entrepreneur who, in Schumpeter's words, was driven by his desire for his own kingdom, sees every attempt by his sons to create freedom of action for themselves within the system as a usurpation, and every deviation from a strictly expected pattern of action as disobedience. This was significant in several ways. It both prevented a smooth change between the generations, and created a management problem which was accentuated as the business diversified. No one, after all, is equally good at everything. But giving decision-making powers to sons is a threat since they potentially have the power of ownership, while decision-making powers given to an employed manager can be rescinded at the stroke of a pen.

Axel Johnson died after a brief illness in 1910. He had by then had a career which was remarkable in many respects. The youngster without means, who had been employed as a shop assistant in the middle of the 1860s, had created not only his own business and wealth, but had also gained a large family and an important social position. He had risen far socially. Axel Johnson had received political commissions, had been appointed Consul and later Consul General for Siam, received many decorations, and socialised with the Royal Family. This result reminds us that the purpose of private enterprise can rarely be defined only by the categories of business economics or organisational theory: it is very much a matter of the realisation of personal goals and aspirations.

The management of the family company was taken over by the eldest son, Axel, who after a couple of years won a position of sole power in the companies, and in return compensated his brothers and sisters financially. Axel Ax:son Johnson – generally known as the Consul General – succeeded his father to his position in Siam and remained at the head of the family firm for a long time. He died in 1958, and relinquished his grip on the family business only gradually during the 1950s.

The trading firm A Johnson & Co. was not the chief interest of the Consul General. The firm was a vehicle for business development, but to develop the firm was not a goal in itself. It carried on trade, but more and more of the content of its operations was dependent on developments in other parts of the Johnson company holdings, at the same time as the old import business of coal, coke and brick continued on a routine basis.

The Consul General's era was characterised by increasing diversification of the group and its business interests. This may also be seen as a continued integration, forwards in certain cases, backwards in others, and sometimes sideways. But this should not be over-interpreted in an effort, with the benefit of hindsight, to identify an intelligible rationale. In certain cases corporate acquisitions may have been motivated by very different reasons from those we imagine, and in some cases emotion may have had more to do with it than reason. Autocratic and dominating company management has no one to answer to, possibly apart from the banks. The Axel Johnson Group was at times much dependent on bank loans. Since the company was not joint stock, bank loans were the most important source of external capital.

The Consul General invested in mining deposits as early as 1911 to ensure the supply of raw materials to Avesta. The First World War increased the demand for iron, which caused him to buy further shares in ore deposits and blast furnaces. With these investments also came traditional agriculture and forestry. To ensure access to lime, which was required for iron production, a lime plant was bought in 1915. This later proved to be a way into the construction and building industries.

In the middle of the 1920s, interest turned to the oil industry. The Consul General had been an international pioneer of diesel-powered ships; at the beginning of the 1920s, he sold all of Nordstjernan's steamships to concentrate on diesel power. The oil purchases carried out for the shipping company provided essential experience. But it was motoring on land which emerged as a more important future sector, and which, in 1928, led Johnson's to build an oil refinery, the first of commercial size in Sweden. From the beginning, production at the refinery in Nynäshamn was directed towards heavier fuel oils and, above all, asphalt and lubricating oils, even though lighter qualities were also produced. A special sales company, Nynäs Petroleum, was formed for distribution in Sweden.

The oil interest converged towards and strengthened the interest in the building and construction industries. One of the country's oldest construction companies was bought as early as 1928. It specialised in asphalt surfacing, but developed into a multi-faceted building and construction company. Some years later, when Johnson's received a major order for road surfacing in Romania, a special company was set up, which over time also developed into a fully fledged building company.

The changes which followed the First World War involved major strains for the iron industry. When the Western world adjusted to peacetime conditions, the demand fell dramatically, and significant overcapacity led to many iron producers closing down their operations. The period was difficult also for Avesta, but the company survived by gradually changing to the production of stainless steel. During the 1930s, Johnson's integrated forwards, buying two engineering companies for whom stainless steel from Avesta come to play a major role. At the end of the 1930s and the beginning of the 1940s, further engineering companies were purchased, which included manufacturers of turbines and equipment for the processing industry, as well as ships and ship machinery.

Alongside both the shipping line and the interests in the oil industry – the expansion of a network of petrol stations in northern Sweden – a bus company, Linjebuss, was started, and this served wide areas in northern Sweden as well as taking Scandinavian tourists down to the Continent, which had opened up after the Second World War. An investment in a different direction proved to be highly profitable. An insurance company was started within the group in 1946; not least because the shipping company was a major purchaser of insurance. In parallel with these main thrusts, a large number of smaller companies were taken over or established, both in Sweden and abroad.

This diversification and focus on products within various parts of the Group affected the trading operations in a decisive way. A Johnson & Co. became a contact organisation for producing companies and international markets, both with regard to the purchase of materials for production and the marketing of products. This led to an expansion of the firm's network of international offices. Even in the time of the first Axel Johnson, the firm had been internationally orientated, and had made a short-lived attempt to establish in London during the 1870s. A new company was registered in Hull during the first year of the twentieth century, but this also closed down after a brief period. A more permanent international presence was preceded by the expansion of the network of subsidiary companies in Sweden.

The international operation was affected by events during the First World War. The outbreak of the war postponed the setting up of a planned office in St Petersburg. The blockades of the North Sea and the Atlantic created a need for the shipping company to be represented on the other side of the ocean. Once again Johnson's opened an office in London in 1916 and in New York in the following year. These two offices, which were rapidly transformed into subsidiary companies, were soon performing tasks within the framework of the firm. New subsidiaries were opened after the end of the war in Germany and in France.

In the 1930s, the shipping company opened representative offices in Brazil and Argentina. These were not part of or under the direction of the firm, but played a similar role within the framework of the diversified group. In the years immediately after the Second World War, plants in Argentina (which manufactured stainless steel, particularly cutlery), in Mexico and in South Africa were established. In 1956, an office was opened in Montreal in Canada.

The mission of the overseas offices was of a general character, but they primarily dealt with buying and selling stainless steel and its alloying agents for Avesta. As the group expanded and diversified, the breadth of the subsidiary companies' tasks also grew. The various national markets were different, and the staffing situation varied, so that subsidiary companies in different countries developed in their own individual way.

The main task was to represent the companies which were part of the Johnson Group in international markets. These producing companies were not to build their own market organisations abroad. Certain companies which were acquired already had distribution channels, and in such cases these were gradually co-ordinated. This process was not always problem-free: a barrier was put between the producing company and its market in the form of an independent sales and purchasing organisation. On the other hand, the firm could develop significant expertise in these markets, which would have been difficult for the producing companies to achieve, and there were important synergies to benefit from. All of the subsidiaries and the offices abroad were parts of the information structure of the firm and the group.

The Consul General died in 1958, and was followed in the important posts within the group by his eldest son, who was also called Axel Ax:son Johnson. The other son, Bo, had qualifications and experience in the oil business, and headed Nynäs Petroleum for a long period until, at the beginning of the eighties, he succeeded his brother as the head of the Johnson Group and paterfamilias.

The brothers Axel and Bo became partners in A Johnson & Co. as early as 1947. The threat of heavy inheritance taxes led to the making of dispositions which came into force on the death of the Consul General. The group consisted of a number of companies producing goods and services in Sweden, two transport companies and a trading operation which was, to an increasing extent, international and based abroad. The bulk of the shares in the Swedish Group companies were now held in a trust for the public good – the pattern was taken from the Ford Foundation in the USA – while the shares with substantial voting rights – a category which is common in Swedish companies – were transferred to a special family trust. The foreign business, which was particularly focused in the firm of A Johnson & Co., was taken over by Axel and Bo. The idea behind this organisation was that the brothers would have access to a source of high income through the foreign trade for the whole conglomerate. And it was an income source, which, in contrast to the producing companies, could easily be moved, in the event that Sweden was to move towards a socialist future. This was a financial disposition, which clearly indicated the distinctive role which trading activities in the firm were now considered to have. Private circumstances, however, meant that within a short period of the death of the Consul General, Axel became the sole owner of the firm. Over time the different ownership emphasised the divergence in interest between the producing companies and the trading company.

During the 1960s and 1970s, the firm's international network of subsidiary companies and branch offices expanded. New companies were set up in the neighbouring Nordic countries, in the Benelux countries and on the Iberian peninsula, in Central and Eastern Europe, in Latin America and in Asia. This reflected the globalisation of the firm's trade. It was essential for a trading company, with strong links with shipping to be locally based through a branch office. In certain cases, it was advantageous in view of legislation in the country to set up a local company with national co-ownership. In some cases it was necessary for political or other reasons to establish a producing company in the country. At its greatest extent, A Johnson & Co. was represented in over thirty countries. There were not many blank spots on the world map, although interest was least in black Africa and the Arab countries. The information network expanded.

In actual business, the representatives still had one major task: to sell special steels from Avesta. Their next duty was to market production and know-how from the engineering companies in the group, which could involve equipment for mass production in the cellulose, food-processing and chemical industries, or ships, or simpler objects such as stainless sinks and cutlery. They could also be involved in selling transport services. In export trade the trading firm and its subsidiaries normally acted as a brokers, while on the import side, they often acted as resellers, also in relation to the other companies in the group. Imports included purchasing materials required in the group's production, not least ores, minerals, chemicals and oil. At distant markets, as in the Soviet Union, or Eastern and Central Europe, the firm also took on brokering for external companies. These tasks gradually developed into a more independent, international trading operation, and the link to the actual needs of the producing companies gradually became weaker. In addition, each office or subsidiary would develop the opportunities offered in the local market. A certain amount of trade also developed between the foreign subsidiaries.

The expansion of the international presence was also a matter of the Johnson Group's image as a global company. In every market of even the least importance there should be a Johnson representative. The most significant were the USA and, a little paradoxically in the decades of the Cold War, the Soviet markets.

In the USA, the company Axel Johnson & Co., Inc., which was registered in 1923, maintained a presence which balanced on the boundary between profitability and unprofitability during the whole inter-war period. The office in New York tried to sell Avesta steel, which was not very easy, and everything else possible. The office also brokered the purchase of crude oil for the refinery in Nynäshamn. During the Second World War, shipping was to grow and generate income. But the principal task remained to sell what was produced in Sweden. This was not necessarily goods; it could also be ideas, patents or know-how. One of the group's engineering companies developed a propeller with adjustable blades, which was marketed in the USA. To increase the opportunities of obtaining Federal orders, manufacturing was farmed out to an American company, which was taken over by Johnson's in 1960. To make it possible to obtain orders from the US Navy, a board of trustees, consisting of American citizens, was appointed, which acted as a filter between the Swedish owner and the classified information, which an order from the Navy would bring. With this, the American operation also included production, and more was to follow. In 1967, a company in Florida was acquired which, at the beginning of the 1970s, bought the manufacturing rights for a wastewater separation technology developed by the group's own development company, the Axel Johnson Institute in Nynäshamn. It was supplemented during the following decades by other equipment for environmental use. In the 1980s, an additional company in a related business, based in Alabama, was purchased.

A department for oil purchases was set up at the office in New York. In collaboration with the firm's head office in Stockholm and the management of Nynäs Petroleum, this supplied the refinery in Sweden with crude oil, mainly from Venezuela. An agreement was signed with the Venezuelan authorities which gave Johnson's tax advantages as an 'insider trader'. At the beginning of the 1970s, an oil distribution company in New England, with an excellent customer network and access to terminals on the Atlantic coast, was bought.

Refining capacity was acquired. Johnson's were thus able to increase the quantities of their oil purchases, and partly through the terms offered by the Federal Government during the oil crises of the 1970s, the oil department generated a level of income which the company had never before experienced. After the second oil crisis at the end of the decade, the oil market changed rapidly. Refining and oil prospecting were closed down, the distribution company refocused on the distribution of other bulk goods, and was guided towards controlled market expansion rather than backwards integration. Oil remained important, but no longer so dominant as a generator of profits.

The well-filled cash reserves generated by the oil business were used for new corporate acquisitions. By the mid-1970s, Johnson's had bought a small steelworks in Indiana to circumvent American trade protection. The steelworks were not profitable in their new business environment and the company was sold in 1984. Involvement in the area of metallurgy continued in the refining of titanium and titanium alloys. Another activity, which was taken on through two company acquisitions in the 1980s, involved telecommunications.

Thus, under the umbrella of the trading company, an extensive, diversified industrial group was built up in the USA, with branches in Canada. The components of this group were reminiscent of the Johnson Group in Sweden: there were steelworks and oil companies, engineering firms, shipping and trading activities. The conditions for the American subsidiary to develop autonomously into an independent industrial group had been created. The trading operations became rooted in production; flexibility was sacrificed in the interests of manufacturing (de Geer 1995).

In the Soviet Union, a completely different logic applied. Johnson's had long been a favourite name with the Soviet authorities. Personal contact was of exceptional importance, and Axel Johnson was mentioned with the American businessman, Armand Hammer, as the most important Western businessmen. Johnson's excellent reputation was helped by the fact that the firm had been one of the very first of the regime's business partners in the West. As early as 1918, it purchased a load of flax and hemp, which, however, was arrested by a British warship in the Gulf of Finland, and never reached its destination. But trade with Russia was not extensive during the inter-war period or during the Second World War. Attempts to buy Russian oil for the refinery in Nynäshamn came to nothing, despite the Consul General's excellent personal contacts with the famous and magnificent ambassador to Stockholm, Alexandra Kollonaj. In the post-war period, trade began to take off, stimulated also by the politically motivated export credit agreement between Sweden and the Soviet Union.

The underlying logic in trade with the Soviet Union was a balance between exports and imports: the Soviet authorities had scant access to convertible and hard currencies. It was the import of Soviet oil products and later of crude oil which created the space for Johnson's to export ships and equipment for the cellulose and food-processing industries. An increasingly important part of the business was to act as brokers for products from other Swedish producers; by the end of the 1970s, this involved 70 per cent of Johnson's sales on the Soviet market. This did not involve counter-trade deals in their precise meaning, i.e. barter. Different transactions in different goods categories, imports and exports, were handled by different parts of the gigantic Soviet trade bureaucracy, and there was no direct link between the flow in one direction and the other. But nevertheless, there was a connection in terms of an agreed balance, stated as a cost framework, within which the parties undertook to accept an exchange.

Imports of fuel, both coal and oil, were not only a means of preparing the way for export transactions. In particular, oil imports developed during the 1970s into a highly-profitable business for Johnson's, and created – along with the American subsidiary's oil business – a platform for oil trading on a much larger scale on the international oil market.

The trade with the Soviet Union – where Johnson's business represented approximately one-third of Swedish trade – declined during the 1980s. This was caused by the fall in oil prices and some interruption in oil production, as well as to the relative growth in defence costs in the Soviet Union. The high level of Swedish interest rates also contributed to the problems: the Russians required ever-greater credit even on ever-smaller deals. Opportunities were reduced, and the planned modernisation of, for example, the cellulose and paper industries was postponed. Another reason for the decline in Johnson's oil trade with the Soviet Union has to do with information systems. When oil prices were quoted at the international markets, and the Russian authorities got access to better information through the Reuter screens, the huge profitability for Johnson's of the Russian oil trade vanished. A more integrated international market leaves less room for traditional trade that takes advantage of differences in price information.

For Johnson's, the Russian business to a certain extent was replaced by a significant trade with East Germany within the framework of similar business agreements. It was in trading with the countries of the Communist bloc that the firm's character of trading firm became most obvious. Flexibility was put to the test in the introduction of new sellers to the Russian market, and when it came to finding markets for the products which these countries offered for export. Not least, these cases involved the development of expertise in cross-trading. A large proportion of the goods, for example, the simpler electrical or electromagnetic material, was often difficult to dispose of in the firm's own domestic market or in the West in general, while in terms of price and quality it was often better suited to the demands of the Third World.

During the first part of the 1970s, the diversified conglomerate which formed the Johnson Group was at its peak. A varied and comprehensive industrial structure with significant capacity in steel, oil, shipbuilding and engineering, together with extensive shipping interests, transport companies, a growing industrial group in the USA, manufacturing in Britain, France, South America and South Africa, a network of subsidiaries in over thirty countries throughout the world, considerable trade in ore, metals and oil, and a strong position in trade with the Eastern bloc. The Johnson Group was an empire in Scandinavian terms; on the international market it was more difficult to keep up with the large companies in each industry. But it was precisely this attribute of the conglomerate, variety, the ability to change shape, to stand on many 'legs', which attracted the Consul General and which attracted his eldest son. There was something Renaissance-like about these businessmen: no transaction, no commitment was unthinkable for them. This is not to say they lacked a business moral; they certainly had a strong feeling about what to do and how to behave, but the kind of rational approach which depends on focusing, specialisation or reductionism does not seem to have appealed to them. Also, it was the way of the Renaissance man to be a collector: the Johnsons collected companies, operations and people, just as they did with cars, coins, books and stamps: nothing was too small, nothing was too large.

But this also created problems, which partly involved management and partly corporate structure. The management of the conglomerate was centralised, exceptionally strongly focused on the paterfamilias. This led to detailed control of an old-fashioned type: almost every decision, not only the great and strategic, had to be referred to the group CEO/owner, around whom gathered a few close collaborators with overall advisory tasks. The moment the leader could not carry out his function for any reason, the organisation was paralysed in its ability to take decisions. Just like other hierarchical organisations, which are not characterised by the impersonality of the classic bureaucracy, it can be difficult to see any logic for succession unless the sitting leader dies.

Through a stroke in 1975, Axel Ax:son Johnson found his capacity for work greatly reduced. The organisation lost tempo and effectiveness; there was no obvious successor who could take on the full responsibility of the leader. There were various attempts to divide functions, to create management groups, and to economise with the leader's reduced strength. He took up his responsibilities again after about six months, but with a tempo and energy rather less than before. This made matters even more difficult, since, during the following years, the pressure for change in commercial structures increased, not least in the traditional industries where Johnson's had its greatest production interests, such as steel, oil, shipbuilding and shipping.

The structural problem with a conglomerate of this type involved the connection between market, size and focus. When the market expanded and frontiers were negotiated away, it was not sufficient to be big in Sweden or Scandinavia, since the company was still significantly smaller than its competitors on the world market. If it were to become larger in any area from the global perspective, it would have to concentrate its capacity. If the company was privately owned, and so did not have the option of increasing its capital through the stock market, the difficulties were even greater; the industrial sectors in which Johnson's had its interests were capital-intensive, and it was impossible to remain in the front line of several such sectors at the same time.

The dramatic transformation came in the mid-eighties. Axel Ax:son Johnson retired and was succeeded in Nordstjernan, that is as Chairman of the Board of the holding company controlling the group's production companies, by his brother Bo, and in the trading company A. Johnson & Co. by his daughter, Antonia. Through this, there was no longer a union of leadership between the two functional parts of the conglomerate, and conflicts of interest between them became more obvious. On both sides there were professional managers appointed as CEOs, in A. Johnson & Co., one person who had served in the company for a long time and was keenly sensitive to the tradition, in Nordstjernan an outsider, who was hard-nosed and without sentiment. Now the old conglomerate was torn apart.

An analysis, which was carried out on the instructions of the new management of Nordstjernan, pointed to the building and property sector as the area in which the group, with its limited internal capital resources, could achieve a dominating position. At very high speed the majority of the 330 or so companies which formed the conglomerate were sold, much to the objection of the leadership of A. Johnson & Co. The trading company took over responsibility for the oil business in 1982, but sold it after a few years to foreign interests. At about the same time, the company was forced to give up its marketing for Avesta, and the same thing happened to all the other large agencies for the old Johnson Group. This left the company without the bulk of the business which it traditionally had. Now it had to find something new.

A. Johnson & Co., from 1985 called Axel Johnson AB, was now in a freer position than before. After a search which took almost a decade, the group identified a new role and direction in the creation of three independent concerns, all owned by Antonia Ax:son Johnson. The American activities at Axel Johnson, Inc. have developed in accordance with their own logic, with increasingly less to do with the sister Groups. Axel Johnson AB has orientated itself towards wholesalers and retailers of everyday goods. The new commitments have required a different business logic than that which suited the more diversified trading company in the past. Before, it was a matter of using market expertise and the contact network to take opportunities of concluding individual transactions. Now it is essential to cultivate an internal rationalisation and increase the rate of stock turnover; a matter of developing good routines rather than waiting for the good opportunities. Axel Johnson International was formed after a series of reorganisations, corporate acquisitions and sales. It retains the trading firm tradition, of a varied trade inside and outside Scandinavia. Through separating the international trading operations from the rest of the group's activities, flexibility has again been facilitated.

Conclusion

Using the three examples, it is possible to discuss in brief the development and role of trading companies in Sweden. The period of greatness of the trading firms in Sweden was the century before the industrial revolution. Since then, their position has been threatened, as exporters by the marketing organisations of large companies, and as importers by the increase in collaboration between wholesalers, and the growth of retail chains. But a smaller number of companies are still recognisable as trading firms and play a significant role in their field.

It is quite clear that the most important role of the Swedish trading firms is connected with Swedish production. Trading firms have emerged to sell Swedish iron, steel, paper and pulp, as well as engineering products, on the export markets. This has given them market expertise which has been utilised for imports both of intermediate goods for industry, and for industrial and consumer goods, in the more recent period not least from the markets of East Asia. In pulp, two of the companies discussed here have achieved such a position in the market that they are international rather than Swedish companies.

Ekman has been the most specialised: in herring, in iron, and in paper and pulp. A period of diversification in the 1960s and 1970s was unsuccessful. Elof Hansson has developed from a strong specialisation in the export business of pulp to a much more diversified trade. Since the 1920s, Johnson's has carried on a diversified business, particularly through its overseas subsidiaries, and this diversification has been accentuated during the post-war period by the concentration on the Russian and Eastern European markets. All three companies, but particularly Johnson's and Elof Hansson, have considerable experience in state trading countries and in counter-trade.

All three companies have histories going back over a century. Stability over time requires flexibility in the market. Of these companies, Elof Hansson is the one which is most free of production interests, – the 'purest' – and which, in this regard, has maximised its flexibility. During certain periods, Ekman has had interests in production, and has then lost a great deal both in terms of resources and mobility. The Johnson case shows much of the potential variety in the position of being a hybrid trading firm. A. Johnson & Co. has had the strongest links with production companies in its own group, and this has reduced flexibility considerably. The trading firm has in the long run changed into a permanent marketing organisation for certain manufacturing companies.

Stability is also a matter of financing. The role of the trading firms as financiers has declined with the emergence of a modern banking system, but taking advantage of the opportunities of the financial markets has become an essential competitive expertise for modern trading firms. Johnson's was one of the first Swedish companies to set up its own department for financing. As a result of the upswing in the oil trade, transactions had become so great that significant sums could be earned by giving special attention to this part of the business.

Ekman takes its traditions back to the great times of the trading firms, while Johnson's and Elof Hansson belong to the period of the emergence of industrialisation. All of them use their history to create confidence in their activities. To have been in the market for such a long time is an expression of the market's confidence, one of the most important arguments in the trading firm's armoury.

All three companies have had a marked family character and still carry the family name of the founder. This is also important for confidence. A name, an identifiable family, instils a sense of confidence. It is to a person, not to an impersonal bureaucracy, that one can entrust one's important business in distant and confusing markets; it might be an illusion, but it lives on and it works.

The relationship between people and company also has another side. This is not only that the trading activities benefit from the founder's reputation. For the founders and their heirs, the firm is often a prerequisite for social advancement. In a society organised by social class, there were social barriers and obstacles which the enterprising person without social standing found difficult to cross, but trade was a possible route. In early industrial society there were other gateways, but trade provided one where dividends could be significant even where the stakes were modest. The trading firm took the Ekman family to leading positions in its home city, and brought the Johnson family from obscurity to the highest levels of society. The Hansson family differs in its almost studied aversion to every form of social visibility, although this did not prevent the business creating for them similar opportunities to achieve a good life. Trading firms, so often family businesses, their strategy and incentives, must be seen also in a perspective that focuses the personal and entrepreneurial aspects.

Notes

1 On Ekmans, see Kuuse (1996). The description of Elof Hansson International is based on the published annual reports of the company. There is an unpublished manuscript on the history of the firm before 1970, by Jan Kuuse, part of which

is reflected in his book on Ekmans, but the company has denied publication as well as scholarly use of that manuscript. The analysis of A. Johnson & Co., from 1985 Alex Johnson AB, is based primarily on the author's history of that company (forthcoming). On the early history of the company, see Holtze (1973). On the shipping company and the Axel Johnson Group, see also Larsson and Saving (1990). On the North American company, A. Johnson & Co., Inc., see de Geer (1995).

References

de Geer, H. (1995) *A. Johnson & Co. Inc 1920–1995*, Stockholm: EHF.

Frängsmyr, T. (1990) *Ostindiska kompaniet*, 2nd edn, Göteburg, 2nd edn: n.a.

Holtze, B. (1973) *A. Johnson & Co. 1873–1890*, Stockholm: The Company.

Kuuse, J. (1996) *Ekamn. Ett handelshus 1802–1996*, Göteburg: Rundqvists Boktryckeri.

Larsson, S. and Saving, J. involved (1990) *Nordstjernan. The Inside Story*, Stockholm: The Company.

Nováky, G. (1990) *Handelskompanier och kompanihandel, Svenska Afrikakompaniet 1649–1663. En studie I feodal handel*. Uppsala: Studia Historica Upsaliensia, no. 159.

Samuelsson, K. (1951) *De stora köpmanshusen i Stockholm 1730–1815*, Stockholm: Esselte Aktiebolag.

8 The development of Swiss trading companies in the twentieth century

Sébastien Guex

Over the course of the twentieth century, Switzerland became one of the leading world centres of international trading. Swiss-owned trading companies, and foreign trading companies established in Switzerland, developed alongside the Swiss financial centre to produce an agglomeration of trading and financial markets and institutions in the country.

According to information given by the Swiss Commodities and Futures Association, for example, Switzerland was the 'second centre in Europe, after Great Britain, for the trade of raw materials' in 1985 (*Basler Zeitung* 27 March 1985). At this time, a statistical study of the leading international trading companies revealed that for each of twelve categories of products, extending from non-ferrous metals to grain, including petroleum, coffee and cotton, a Swiss company is included in half of all cases (Chalmin 1985: 164). When the count was repeated five years later, with a much wider range of products, a Swiss company was named in one-third of all cases (Chalmin and El Alaoui 1990). Moreover, according to different estimates for around 1980, between 30 per cent and 60 per cent of the trading transactions on the international grain market were then conducted in Switzerland (Green and Laurent 1985: 159; *Neue Zürcher Zeitung*, 10 January 1980; *La Suisse*, 17 October 1980). It is, therefore, unsurprising to discover that a specialist in the field has characterised Switzerland as the 'true centre of world trade' in grain, adding that Switzerland has the same function for several other products (Morgan 1980: 159–60). A final example is the 1981 study by the CNUCED, which stated that Switzerland had become a 'world centre for the trading of cotton and textiles' (CNUCED 1981: 67).

This 'success story' of the Swiss trading centre is even more remarkable when it is considered that it has been accomplished with neither colonial possessions nor any outlet to the sea. This double handicap was largely compensated for by a series of other advantages which will be examined in detail later in the chapter. For now, suffice it to say that the most important of these advantages were the relationship networks, established over several centuries, and Swiss political neutrality, especially military non-participation in the two world wars of the twentieth century. Of equal importance was the strength of the Swiss currency and the adoption of a tax system which looked favourably on companies. Other positive influences were the country's domestic political stability and the importance of Switzerland as a symbolic capital from which it profited on the international scene.

The state of knowledge on the history of the Swiss trading centre is poor, despite its considerable importance. A few studies exist that reveal the already substantial position some Swiss companies had acquired in international trade before the twentieth century (Veyrassat 1991). There has been, however, practically no research undertaken on the history of Swiss trading companies in the twentieth century.

One of the main reasons for this is the complete secrecy with which these companies carry out their activities. Even where it can be argued that secrecy is commonly preferable among the worldwide circle of traders, this aspect reached unequalled dimensions in Switzerland. In the 1990s, for example, only one of the fifteen main trading companies in Switzerland publishes any figures at all and these are limited to a few indicators such as sales figures. When in 1984, on the occasion of its fiftieth anniversary, the main association regrouping the Swiss trading companies asked each member to draw up a brief, one-page self-portrait, several failed to respond whilst others omitted their date of foundation (Bericht des Verbandes 1983–84, 11). Indeed, the motto of the Diethelm-Keller group is 'we don't give any information, either important or insignificant' (*Bilanz*, April 1982, 89). Moreover, during the three-hour interview that the Company Secretary of André & Cie granted to the author of this article in July 1997, it was not even possible to obtain the firm's exact number of employees: 'Between 1,000 and 4,000, it depends on the way you count' . . . was the most precise answer which he was prepared to give. (Interview with Yves Cuendet, Company Secretary of André & Cie 4 July 1997.)

André's strategy has proved so successful that even the Wirtschaftsarchiv of Basle, the main institution in Switzerland concerned with the history of Swiss companies and founded at the beginning of the century, has no mention of the firm. This, despite the fact that the institution has amassed files on 10,000 firms and that André has, for many years, been one of Switzerland's largest companies in all categories.

These circumstances rendered it impossible to base research on the traditional methods used for historical studies of firms, such as accounts and annual reports, not to mention archives. The main sources of information were, on the one hand, the press and, on the other hand, commemorative company brochures, written under the aegis of the trading companies themselves. The effects of this are clearly visible in the results and the account which follows can, therefore, only offer a cursory glance, incomplete and approximate, of the evolution of Swiss trading companies in the twentieth century. Indeed the information, especially concerning the figures on which it is based, must be treated with great caution. It is also important to bear in mind that the account is worth more in terms of the questions it raises than of the answers it gives.

An important point remains to be specified, in that, thus far the term 'Swiss trading companies' has been used without a precise definition. However, it is necessary to distinguish between three entities. First, companies which are wholly or mainly owned by Swiss capital. These will from now on be referred to as 'Swiss companies'. Second, there are companies that have been established and have their head office in Switzerland and are therefore legally Swiss, but are controlled by foreign capital. Henceforth, these will be referred to as 'companies established in Switzerland'. Finally, many foreign trading companies have installed branches or subsidiaries in Switzerland and, despite their sometimes considerable role, it is not possible to include them in this chapter, at least for the main part.

The chapter is divided into five sections. The first outlines the general development of Swiss trading companies or companies established in Switzerland in the twentieth century. The second section deals more specifically with Swiss companies, by revealing some of their specific features. The third section profiles the evolution of four leading firms. The fourth section considers the question of companies established in Switzerland and reveals two elements that explain why such companies became established in Switzerland, giving a brief sketch of the most important factors of the companies. The final section attempts to identify the most important factors that contributed towards making Switzerland a centre of international trade.

The evolution of trading companies in Switzerland in the twentieth century

Of the forty or so operational Swiss trading companies counted at the beginning of the 1980s, foundation dates could be established in thirty cases. This proportion is high enough to be significant and the findings are presented in Figure 8.1.

The first point of interest shown in Figure 8.1 is that almost half (fourteen out of thirty) of the Swiss companies which continued to exist up to the beginning of the 1980s are old, or even very old companies, of at least eighty years of age.

Second, the relatively regular foundation of trading companies during the second half of the nineteenth century suggests that this was a rather favourable period for their activities. In contrast, only three of the Swiss companies still existing in the 1980s were founded between 1900 and the end of the Second World War. From the evidence, it is probable that the first half of the twentieth century, which experienced two world wars and deep economic and political crises, was the most difficult period for Swiss trading companies. On the other hand, the period that followed the Second World War saw a very strong increase in the formation of new companies (twelve out of thirty from 1945–64). Thus the evidence seems to indicate a new, vigorous growth for Swiss trading companies at this time after what had been a long period of inactivity.

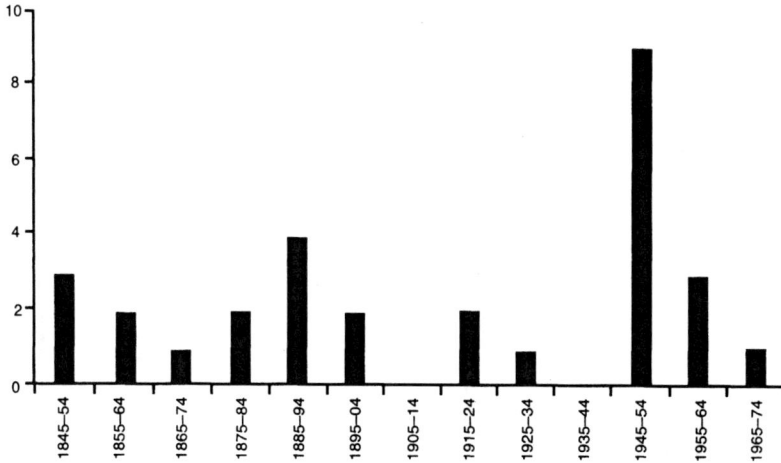

Figure 8.1 Founding of Swiss trading companies by decade (1845–1974)

Sources: Bericht des Verbandes 1983–84; Confederation of Swiss Firms for World and Transit Trade (1990), List of Members, Company Portraits.

Note: One company was founded before 1845, in 1788 and has been included in the decade 1845–54.

Even if it is extremely thin, the available data enables further analysis. Information about the turnover of the main Swiss trading companies or the trading companies established in Switzerland for the period between 1928 and 1936, for 1953 and for the years from 1983 onwards, is shown in Figure 8.2. The figures concerning the years 1928–36 and 1953 are relatively reliable, even if they are probably a little underestimated. This statement is based on the fact that the figures were taken from internal surveys conducted under the aegis of the association of trading companies itself, which guaranteed absolute secrecy to the companies.[1] The figures concerning the years from 1983 on, however, may well be less accurate since these were estimates made by a Swiss economic magazine, conducted in a rudimentary way so that they remain very rough. In fact, there are many grounds to suspect that these figures underestimate considerably the extent of business done by the trading companies and these estimates should, therefore, be considered as minimal values, more useful in giving a general picture rather than providing total accuracy.

Figure 8.2 illustrates the high level of development the trading companies had already reached by the end of the 1920s. Indeed, the total of their turnovers was equal to 11.9 per cent of the Swiss gross national product in 1928. Moreover, the person in charge of the survey indicated above was clearly astonished at the findings.

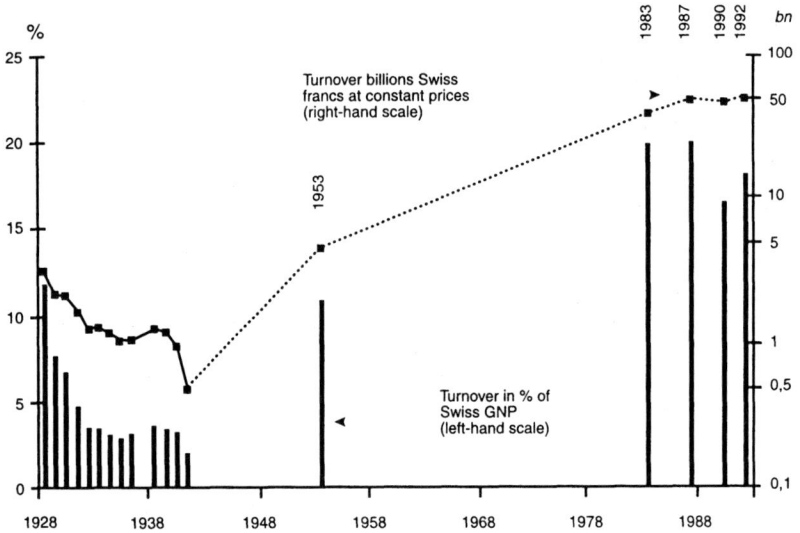

Figure 8.2 Turnover of the main Swiss and Swiss-based trading companies, 1928–92
(in constant Swiss francs of 1980)

> The turnover of the trading companies largely exceeds anything we had
> imagined, even among persons in the know, and the examination of the
> turnover [. . .] of each one of the companies, which unfortunately has to
> remain confidential, clearly confirms the importance of these companies
> that work in secrecy
>
> (Mangold 1935: 15).

The period marked by the First World War, therefore, does not appear to
have brought major difficulties to this sector, and the 1920s even seem to have
been very successful.[2] These findings appear to agree with the evidence of the
evolution of two other sectors between 1914 and 1929; that is, the generally
rather satisfactory development of Switzerland's foreign trade, and especially
the extraordinary expansion of Swiss banks and insurance companies (Vogel
1966: 157–87; Guex 1997).

It is clear that the trading companies suffered greatly from the world
economic crisis of the 1930s. In 1935 – the lowest point during the crisis –
the total amount of their turnover, in constant Swiss francs, accounted for
only one-third of that of 1928. Moreover, the drop was much more marked
than that of the gross national product. Whereas the sum of the trading
companies' turnover reached an amount representing 11.9 per cent of
Switzerland's gross national product, in 1928 it wavered at around 3 per cent
in the middle of the 1930s, a drop of 75 per cent. Thus, it can be seen that the

trade sector suffered more damage from the crisis than the majority of the other sectors of the Swiss economy.

The extent of the drop can largely be explained by a series of international factors, of which the most important was the decrease of world trade coupled with the rapid extension of protectionism. There was, however, also an internal reason of a political nature. From the beginning of the 1930s the Swiss government signed clearing agreements with a growing number of countries because of the shortage of currencies affecting the latter, notably, in July of 1934 when a very important treaty was signed with Germany, Switzerland's main economic partner.

These agreements established the global volume of trade and payments between Switzerland and each of the signatory countries, and then fixed the proportion of this volume assigned to the different sectors of the Swiss economy, such as industry, banks, insurance companies, tourism, etc. The important associations each of these sectors had provided themselves with, therefore, became crucial, with the help of various manoeuvres and the use of pressure, in order to obtain the largest possible proportion granted by the Swiss Government. The trading sector, however, did not have any association at its disposal and so found itself at a disadvantage in the defence of its interests on a political level. In fact the trading sector found itself the outcast of the clearing agreements Switzerland had concluded, especially the one signed with Germany. Here, the share of the global volume of trade and payments that was assigned to the trading sector was insignificant. Thus the already substantial difficulties experienced by the trading companies were increased. In fact, only some months after the conclusion of the German–Swiss clearing agreement, the latter founded an association which succeeded in obtaining a slightly better position for trading activities in the later treaties (Mangold 1935: 7; Bericht des Verbandes 1935, 8–16).

Figure 8.2 indicates that an upward movement seemed to begin in 1936, but it was halted by the outbreak of the Second World War. In 1939 and 1940, the decline still remained limited. The association of Swiss trading companies pointed out in 1940 that ' . . . the companies which had already had a solid foothold abroad managed to escape the drop . . . ' (Bericht des Verbandes 1940, 5). However, from 1941 on, with the entry into the war of the United States and Japan and the extension of the mutual blockade conducted by the Allies and the Axis powers, the decline was brutally accentuated. Indeed, according to one of the very rare Swiss authors to take an interest in the Swiss trading sector, the activities were 'practically paralysed' (Bammatter 1958: 42). Moreover, from a reading of the annual reports of the association of the Swiss trading companies, it is clear that several firms only managed to find an anchor by turning towards the country's supply operations (Bericht des Verbandes 1941, 5–20; 1943, 5–7).

It is evident, however, that the end of the war opened a period of rapid expansion in the Swiss trade sector. The sector benefited especially from the advantage caused by the fact that Switzerland was one of the few countries to

come out of the war disposing of an intact and highly coveted currency and
an unweakened financial vigour. In the report of the association of Swiss
trading companies for 1947, it was stated that ' ... the post-war period
brought new opportunities and caused [...] a considerable increase in the
activity [...] of Swiss international trading' (Bericht des Verbandes 1947, 9).

Figure 8.2 reflects this growth: it can be seen that in 1953 the combined
turnover of the main Swiss trading companies and the trading companies
established in Switzerland had quadrupled compared to that of the middle of
the 1930s. Expressed as a percentage of the Swiss gross national product, it
regained in a few years the high level it had reached in 1928.

At this point certain questions require consideration. First, what was the
pattern of global expansion of the Swiss trading sector after 1953, and second,
what were the stages of acceleration and of slowing down, and why did they
take place? Unfortunately, these questions cannot be answered here. In fact,
indications of the general development of business found from time to time
in the reports of the association of Swiss trading companies disappear
completely. No estimate of the main companies' global turnover can be established before 1983. Furthermore, the estimations for 1983 and the following
years are very approximate and, without doubt, strongly underestimated.

The only statement that is not too hazardous to make at the current state
of knowledge is that the growth of the trading sector continued at a steady
rate after 1953 until the 1990s, and was faster than the average growth of

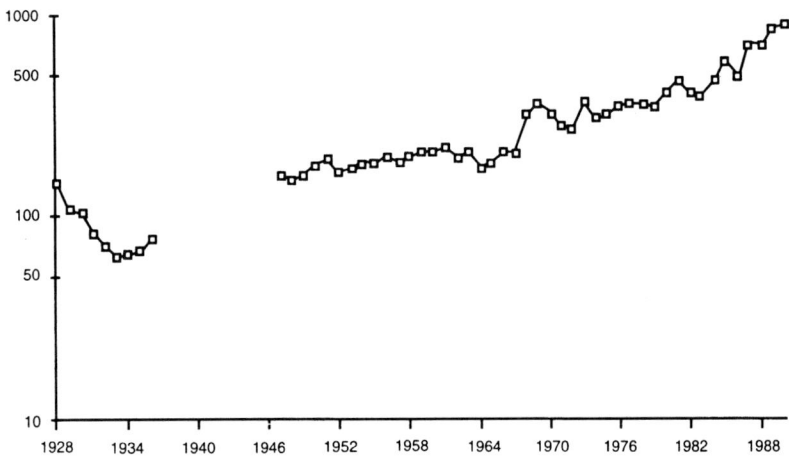

Figure 8.3 Annual revenues of trading activity to the Swiss balance of payments on
current account 1928–90 (in million constant Swiss francs of 1980;
logarithmic scale)

Switzerland's economy. Figure 8.2 confirms this. Since 1983 the sum of the turnover of the main Swiss trading companies and trading companies established in Switzerland is at a level close to 20 per cent of the country's gross national product whilst this level was still at 11 per cent in 1953.

The second set of data which is available barely enables us to go further (see Figure 8.3). It concerns annual revenues provided by the trading sector to the Swiss balance of payments on current account. Unfortunately, these figures are approximate estimations and partly arbitrary, so that it would be extremely unwise to draw exact conclusions from them with regard to the evolution of Swiss trading companies and trading companies established in Switzerland. However, they do offer a rough confirmation of the analysis presented above. That is, a very marked drop during the economic crisis of the 1930s with a strong growth rate during the immediate post-Second World War period, which allowed the trading companies to rapidly regain the level reached by the end of the 1920s. In the entire post-war period there is a remarkably steady growth, which seems to accelerate after the end of the 1970s. However, the question must remain that this acceleration might be the result of changes in the method of collecting and calculating the data.

Characteristics of Swiss trading companies

Before drawing a profile of the four largest Swiss trading companies it will be useful to identify some of the features that Swiss trading companies have in common. In the first place a very significant number of family firms are to be found among the Swiss trading companies. Not only does the majority of capital remain the property of a few founder families and/or related families, but also control of the companies remains in the hands of these same families. The survey conducted in the middle of the 1930s has already demonstrated this aspect (Mangold 1935: 8–9). In 1990 at least eight (of which all of the largest) of the fourteen main Swiss companies were family firms. This phenomenon, which also seems to be found among the trading companies in other countries, requires further analysis.

There are certainly several explanations which could be examined here. However, one point appears to be of crucial importance. In the activities of international trade, the technical knowledge of each company's main traders, combined with what one might call their relational capital,[3] along with their loyalty, form together a key element to success in the competitive struggle. The degree of loyalty that these traders exhibit towards their company thus plays a decisive role. At the end of the First World War, for example, the Basle company UTC avoided bankruptcy – the threat of which was provoked by the seizure of their property by British authorities – mainly thanks to the loyalty of its principal traders. When analysing this period, the specialist on the firm's history noted that UTC still disposed 'of its most important asset, the hard core of its experienced associates [. . .]. They represented a value, the company would in no case want to abandon . . . ' (Wanner 1959: 426).

And here lies the crux of the matter. On the one hand, the existence of family ties among the owners, who very often occupied leading functions in the trading business, diminished the risks of the company being torn apart or being deserted. On the other hand, the family's importance in the organisation of the firm created what Yonekawa termed 'pseudo-family consciousness' (Yonekawa 1990: 25) within the company – that is if it is not accompanied by a paternalism which is too inflexible – and reinforces the cohesion and the loyalty of the traders. 'The strength' of the André group, according to the magazine *Bilanz* in 1990, was to consider 'the employees as members of a big family' (*Bilanz*, October 1990, 172). The Lausanne company itself pointed out that it 'gives a lot of importance to a faithful staff [. . .] which has a sense of [. . .] loyalty' (André & Cie 1977: 3).

In this respect, two other features need to be mentioned briefly. First, it appears that most companies introduced a system in which their top traders participated in the company's profits. This system, as a specialist put it, gave 'a real feeling of being part of the family' (Waszkis 1987: 182). Second, the role religion played needs to be ascertained. Unfortunately, information on this subject is unavailable for the large majority of Swiss trading companies, but in two of the large companies discussed below – André and UTC – family ties were doubled by powerful religious bonds. This religious dimension included several aspects which require closer examination, but without doubt it contributed to cementing the relations of loyalty.

In Chapter 2, Casson has emphasised the frequent diversification strategies employed by trading companies. It is, therefore, interesting to note the similarities which existed in the field of diversification strategy by which most Swiss companies rapidly transformed themselves into hybrid trading companies. Looking first at geographical diversification, the majority of Swiss companies tried very early on to diversify their international networks, and this appears to have been a significant factor in their success. Alternatively, as is shown below, UTC proved with hindsight to have been a company which remained too closely linked to Ghana and Nigeria.

The problem of diversification in terms of activities remains complex. Nevertheless, it is possible to make one or two, albeit unconfirmed, observations. It would appear that up until about the time of the Second World War, measures of diversification taken by Swiss trading companies essentially concerned two types of activities. First of an industrial type, the closest – upstream and downstream – in the line of negotiated products. For example, the facilities for the treatment of cotton and coffee for Volkart; facilities for the treatment of cacao and oil works for UTC; grain silos as well as milling and oil works for André. Second, the activities of services closely linked to trading itself, for example, the representation of insurance companies, sea-borne transportation or tourism.

After the Second World War the measures of diversification seem to have grown in extent. Despite this, however, they remained prudent and of the same type as the ones described above. It was not until approximately the

1970s that a real change took place. The origins of this change were probably due to the fact that, to a certain extent, international trading ran out of steam stimulated by the beginning, in 1973, of a long phase of the slowing down of economic growth, coupled with the existence of abundant financial reserves, accumulated thanks to three very successful decades. At this time the Swiss trading companies plunged into a strategy of accelerated diversification. Volkart began trading in new products, André, Diethelm-Keller and UTC invested in industrial production, André and Volkart engaged in financial activities, André and Diethelm turned to engineering/consulting, and UTC to the retail trade. Whilst it is too early to take stock of these policies, certain patterns based on their successes and failures seem to emerge in which industrial activities independent of trading remain weak, trading maintains a central position and financial activities become increasingly decisive.

Profiles of the main Swiss trading companies

The André Group

At the beginning of the 1990s the André Group was the largest Swiss trading company, a position it had occupied for several decades. Moreover, it was one of the five companies which dominated the international trade in grain – wheat, corn, soya beans – and its many by-products. André's exact importance is, however, difficult to determine. Some ranked the company as the smallest of the five in the second half of the 1980s with a turnover of almost 10 billion Swiss francs and roughly a 10 per cent share of the world grain trade whilst others estimated the turnover to be closer to 20 billion, and believed André to be the second largest company after the American company Cargill (Chalmin 1985: 207; *Tribune de Lausanne*, 15 June 1984; *L'Hebdo*, 26 July 1984, 11; *Bilanz*, October 1990, 166–77). There are, however, grounds for believing that the second turnover figure was closer to the truth. For example, in 1997 the parent company established in Lausanne had subsidiaries and branches in more than seventy countries and employed 1,000 people in its trading activities alone (*Milling & Baking News*, 15 April 1997, pp. 28–34). Furthermore, the company itself has noted that it is 'today one of the biggest international trading companies in the world' (André Group 1997: 6).

André has remained a family business, with the major part of its capital in the hands of the founder family and a few related families. (The following information is based on: André & Cie SA 1977; *Bilanz*, July 1978, 26–30 and October 1990, 166–77; *Solidaire*, November 1982, 3–14; interview with Yves Cuendet, company secretary of André, 4 July 1997.) The successive generations of André – today's is the fourth generation – have always carried out the main managing functions of the group. Moreover, they have always been members of a Protestant sect, 'Les Frères étroits darbystes'. This sect is very elitist in its attitude and status and earnestly cultivates family values and economic success (Gisel 1995: 347 and 1435). Without doubt the company is deeply influenced by this culture to the extent that at the beginning of the 1980s the employees' meetings of the parent company started the day with a common prayer.

Founded in 1877, the André company was one of the main importers of grain in Switzerland by 1914. Yet it was the First World War and the 1920s that enabled André to risk establishing itself firmly on the international market. In fact, at the end of the 1920s André was already part of the limited group of companies that dominated the worldwide grain trade (Green and Laurent 1985: 32).

No doubt, two factors contributed to this impressive expansion. On the one hand, during the war and in the immediate post-war period, André played an important role in Switzerland's grain supplies, which compelled the company to establish – probably with the support of the Swiss authorities – a dense trading network in Europe. On the other hand, the strength of the Swiss franc at the end of the war represented a considerable advantage in a Europe devastated by war as well as by the intense, monetary crisis that lasted until the middle of the 1920s. Given such a sound basis André no longer limited its operations to importation but embarked on international trade, strengthened its network in Europe and extended it to other continents. In 1927 the Lausanne firm settled in Argentina, one of the main grain exporters at the time, where it quickly assumed a leading position. In 1937 André again expanded its network to include the United States by founding a formally independent company, although controlled by the parent company, which soon established a place for itself at the Grain Stock Market in Chicago.

Apparently, André did not suffer greatly from the effects of the Second World War since the company concentrated on supplying Switzerland, where it played a crucial role. This led André to found, without doubt by profiting once more from the Swiss government's support, Suisse-Atlantique. André continued to invest in this company which was successfully expanded so that today it charters about fifty ships, of which roughly twelve – a total of 700,000 freight tonnes – are owned outright by the company. The reasons behind this strategy seem to have changed over time. In the beginning it was mainly a question of being able to improve control over the quality of the transported grain. However, as discussed in Chapter 2, this volume, the diversification into sea-borne transportation seems to have been aimed increasingly at stabilising the benefits to the company. During the Second World War, André's business activities in Argentina were highly successful. So much so that the company was not only encouraged to expand its Argentinian operations to other sectors – livestock breeding, milling, oil-works, spinning, manufacturing machine tools – but also to set up similar operations in Brazil.

In the post-Second World War period the Lausanne company embarked on further expansion. At this time many countries, though eager to trade, were constrained by limited means of payment. André responded by adopting complicated operations which combined payments in kind, financial arrangements and the granting of credit. In 1951 a special department (FINCO), was created within the company in order to oversee these financial operations. During the following decades André, under the aegis of the FINCO department, came to specialise in this field, and the company turned increasingly towards financial, engineering and consultancy activities, especially from the mid-1980s. At the same time, and especially from the 1970s, André moved away from the less profitable industrial activities which it had developed in the immediate post-war period. This new orientation was reflected in the internal composition of the company's revenues. In the middle of the 1990s it appears that 40 per cent of the company revenue came from traditional trading, 40 per cent from the FINCO department plus financial investments, and the rest, in descending order, from sea-borne transportation, industrial activities and the importation of grain to Switzerland.

One final point of interest is that André apparently played a significant role in the circumvention of the trade embargo against the former Rhodesia (now Zimbabwe), declared by the United Nations at the end of the 1960s, Switzerland not being a member of the latter (Bertolami 1983: 22–4). A similar situation recurred in 1980 when the US government declared a grain boycott against the USSR. André immediately took advantage of the situation by capturing a part of the market left vacant by the American companies. This move allowed André to win several solid and long-lasting positions in the Russian market.

The Diethelm-Keller Group

The Diethelm-Keller Group was, at the beginning of the 1990s, the second most important Swiss trading company with an estimated turnover of about four billion Swiss francs. The origins of the group go back to the last third of the nineteenth century, when Wilhelm Diethelm, a Swiss resident in Singapore, took over a commercial house there, whilst Keller, who was also Swiss, settled in Manila and did likewise. (The information that follows is based on: Schweizer-Iten 1980; Eggenberger 1987; *Bilanz*, April 1989, 163–70; *Le Nouveau Quotidien*, 25 April 1993.) The two companies became closely linked after the marriage between the daughter and son of the two companies' founders in 1914. At this time, the two firms had their headquarters in Zurich but their businesses were firmly rooted in South East Asia, with branches in Singapore, in the Philippines, in Vietnam and in Thailand. Their main activity consisted of importing various products into these countries, especially textiles, purchased from Switzerland and Britain. Other lines included coal, petroleum – as representatives of Royal Dutch Shell – Nestlé's condensed milk and sugar. The firms were also involved, to a lesser extent, in the export of certain local products and the representation of several foreign and Swiss insurance companies. Moreover, they played an important role in the regional sea-borne transportation and, last but not least, they were engaged in tourism.

Although the First World War caused a certain stagnation of business, the inter-war years permitted regular growth. In fact, the group became established in Malaysia and in Hong Kong, expanded its sales network in the earlier mentioned countries, especially in Thailand, and founded purchasing offices in both France and Britain. The group also began to import new products into South East Asia: machinery (BBC, Sulzer), cars (Peugeot, Austin), chemical and pharmaceutical products (IG Farben, Illford, Ciba), etc. as well as moving into new activities, notably the purchase of an important aluminium plant in Singapore.

The outbreak of the Second World War resulted in a significant decrease of business for the company due to the Japanese occupation of large zones of South East Asia. The post-war period, however, proved very positive. Diethelm-Keller profits increased, particularly as a result of the considerably weakened Japanese trading companies, which had been very influential in the inter-war period. At this point the group developed a resolute strategy of geographical and business diversification, which proved successful. At the end of the 1980s the parent house controlled more than forty companies based in about fifteen countries. The centre of gravity remained South East Asia, but the group was also present in Europe and, to a lesser extent, in the United States and Australia. Even though trading definitely remained the centre of business, with an increased range of imported and distributed products, Diethelm-Keller was also very active in the manufacturing sector – furniture, cosmetics, dyes, telescopes, cleaning appliances, etc. – and in tourism. From the end of the 1970s, the group also developed engineering/consulting activities and financial services.

The Union Trading Company International Group (UTC)[4]

The company took its name in 1921, although its origins go back to 1859. (The following information is based on 'The Story of the Basel Trading Company Limited 1859–1935' *Supplement to the West African Review*, November 1935, 1–15; Wanner 1959, 1960 and 1984; UTC International AG 1988). The business was founded as a type of subsidiary of the 'Basler Mission', which was a mission established in British India and in what is today Ghana at the beginning of the nineteenth century, in order to spread the word of God. The mission's founders were a small group of families who belonged to the great Protestant bourgeoisie of Basle and the central objective of the new company was to support the missionaries' evangelical efforts. The distribution of the profits among the shareholders was, therefore, limited, with the main part handed over to the Basler Mission and/or reinvested in the country. The company remained under the influence of its religious origins up until 1909 when the business was reorganised so that commercial logic superseded religious influence. It was, however, several decades before the religious aspect disappeared completely and is important to note that UTC is still controlled by the same founder families today.

In Ghana, UTC quickly became both one of the main importers and distributors of manufactured products, and also exporters of local products (rubber and palm oil). More important still: cacao farming, apparently introduced to the country by the Basle firm, expanded greatly from the end of the nineteenth century. By 1910 Ghana was the largest producer of cacao in the world and a considerable proportion of it was exported by UTC. In India, the results were less spectacular. The company failed to make inroads into the trading business and its diversification into industrial activities – spinning and especially brick making – whilst thriving, were in no way as successful as the African undertakings. Indeed, in 1910 the volume of business in India is estimated to have been hardly more than a quarter of that in Ghana (loan prospectus issued by the Missions-Handlungs-Gesellschaft, 7 February 1912, Wirtschaftsarchiv Basle).

The First World War delivered an extremely hard blow to the Basle company. Accused by the British colonial authorities of being favourable to Germany, all of its firms and property in Ghana and in India were confiscated, UTC was on the brink of bankruptcy. Whilst the company's activities in India were never restored, it did recuperate a part of its possessions in Ghana thanks to the continual interventions of the Swiss government. Thus, in 1921, the company was once more active and, because the majority of the local staff had remained loyal to UTC, the company quickly returned to successful business in Ghana. From this success UTC went on to found subsidiaries in London, Hamburg and New York, and also became established in Nigeria.

This last expansion was decisive, and the importation of manufactured goods to Nigeria grew considerably from the end of the Second World War. Moreover, the business literally 'took off' from 1973 when the price of petroleum quadrupled, earning massively increased revenues for this large African country. Between 1973 and 1982 the yearly sales of UTC in Nigeria increased from 150 million in constant francs to 1.5 billion (*Dokumentation-Erklärung von Bern*, no. 5, 1986, 3; *Basler Zeitung*, 23 March 1995).

This windfall induced the Basle company to embark on an unrestrained policy of diversification: in production, retail trade, real estate and various kinds of services, etc. The outcome was that in 1985, the parent company controlled roughly eighty companies which carried out between them 40 different activities (*Neue Zürcher Zeitung*, 21 August 1996). It is also worth noting that in 1977 UTC bought the majority of shares in Jelmoli which was a large chain of stores in Switzerland.

However, the middle of the 1980s, brought a phase of stagnation, and even a decline. Following the collapse of both the local currency and the petroleum revenues, the business broke down in Nigeria. UTC management encountered many difficulties in integrating several of their new activities, especially in the case of Jelmoli. A process of reorganisation was therefore undertaken at the beginning of the 1990s, which appears to be ongoing, as the sale of Jelmoli in 1996 demonstrates. It remains to be seen whether this reorganisation strategy will regain a leading position for trading activities within UTC. That these activities have become marginalised over the last ten years is witnessed by the fact that they now represent only between 10–20 per cent of the total turnover (*Finanz und Wirtschaft*, 24 June 1995; *Basler Zeitung*, 14 August 1996). The outlook, then, for UTC trading activities does not look hopeful, though, given the eventful history of the Basle company, firm predictions would be unwise.

The Volkart Group

The Volkart Brothers company was founded in 1851 in Winterthur by two brothers, who were both members of local patrician circles, and with the objective of trading between British India and continental Europe. (The following information is taken from: *Schweizer Kaufmännisches Zentralblatt*, 28 June 1935; *Tages-Anzeiger*, 26 November 1980; CNUCED 1981; *Bilanz*, April 1984, 132–5 and October 1987, 139–62; Rambousek, 1990.) The company has been controlled and directed by the same family – today the fourth generation – since the end of the nineteenth century.

In the nineteenth century Volkart experienced considerable growth and by the eve of the First World War its business was centred around the export of Indian cotton and coffee. The company was ranked third in importance as an Indian cotton exporter, after two British firms, and was also one of the main exporters of coffee. It also dealt in several other products, including the export of tea, oils and spices, for example, and the import of textile goods, chemicals and pharmaceutical products. Furthermore, the business functioned as an agency for several foreign firms, especially in the fields of insurance and seaborne transportation. Moreover, its network of subsidiaries encompassed India, Sri Lanka, today's Pakistan, Japan and Britain.

The company survived the First World War without great damage since the British authorities authorised its continued activities. What contributed to this decision, and to the relatively successful running of the business during the First World War, was the fact that in several regions of India, the local directors of Volkart also fulfilled the role of Swiss consuls, and were well integrated into British colonial circles.

The post-war years were among the most successful in the history of Volkart. The company benefited from the preservation of its trading infrastructure almost intact and also from the strength of the Swiss franc. At the beginning of the 1920s the company was ahead of the English firms, the previous leading exporters of Indian cotton. Subsidiaries were founded in Germany, China and the United States. In fact, the New York subsidiary quickly became one of the most important participants in the US cotton market.

Both the crisis of the 1930s and the Second World War resulted in a serious decline in business. Volkart lost two of its main markets – Germany and Japan – due to the war, although this loss was partly compensated for by the expansion of business on both the North and South American continents.

After the Second World War business picked up once more and Volkart remained as one of the main trading companies in the fields of cotton and coffee. This despite the loss of the Chinese market due to the Revolution in 1950 and the considerable decline of the Indian cotton trade caused by the measures of partial nationalisation taken by the Indian government in 1961. These two factors influenced the shift in the company's business concentration towards the American continent. At the beginning of the 1970s the company controlled between 5 and 8 per cent of the international cotton market and 4 to 6 per cent of the coffee market.

From the middle of the 1970s, however, things began to look ominous for Volkart due to the evolution of the coffee market. The merchants in this market were increasingly caught between the powerful circle of producers on the one hand, and a diminishing number of giant buyers – Nestlé, Procter and Gamble, General Foods – on the other. The outcome was a decrease in the margin of the trading companies and hence a reduction in their profits (Chalmin 1985: 241–7; *Die Weltwoche*, 27 April 1989).

This appears to be the explanation for the strategy adopted by Volkart from the middle of the 1970s. First, in 1975 the company diversified its activities by becoming heavily involved in the cacao trade. Ten years later Volkart was the second most important trading company in the field, having taken about 10 per cent of the international market. The company also became more involved in finance. In 1985, for example, it helped found, with a large injection of capital, the BZ Bank Zürich, an investment bank which experienced phenomenal growth. At the same time, Volkart tried very hard to strengthen its position in the coffee market. One of its strategies was an attempt to acquire Rothfos, at that time the leading company in the international coffee trade. Neither of the above strategies proved to be successful. First, the German government vetoed Volkart's intended purchase of Rothfos. Second, the profitability of the coffee operations continued to worsen and third, the cacao business proved profitable only to a very limited degree.

From the end of the 1980s, Volkart again changed direction. In 1987 the company sold off its cacao sector, and in 1989 disposed of the major part of its coffee sector, turning instead to cotton. This can be illustrated by the company's important purchases in the United States in 1990, and in Australia in 1997, both in the trading and processing of cotton. Thus, it is envisaged that Volkart will be one of the leading, maybe even *the* leading trading company, in this field (*Neue Zürcher Zeitung*, 3 July 1997). In addition to this, Volkart has continued to attach more and more importance to financial activities (*Bilanz*, May 1989, 232–4).

Trading companies established in Switzerland

Swiss trading companies, that is companies controlled by Swiss capital, were not the only ones which transformed Switzerland into an international trading centre. Those established in Switzerland – companies created in Switzerland by foreign capital – also played a significant role. It will, therefore, be of interest to investigate what attracted foreign trading companies to Switzerland. In fact, companies controlled by foreign capital which have, since they were established, based their registered office in Switzerland, are legally considered to be Swiss. Most of these companies are not simple brass-plate societies, but actually run their operations from Switzerland, and indeed have many top managers in the country. The Marc Rich Group, a brief description of which will be given below, is the best example of this type of company. In addition there are also the – often very important – branches and subsidiaries which many foreign companies have established in Switzerland.

To a very large extent, foreign companies are attracted to Switzerland for the same reasons which, in a general way, explain the success of the Swiss trading centre. Although these reasons will be emphasised in the concluding section of this chapter, it will be useful at this stage to highlight the two areas which are particularly important to foreign companies.

In the first place there is the clemency of the Swiss tax system. This can be illustrated by the case of Marc Rich who, when asked about his decision to locate in canton Zug, pointed out 'the good tax policy' (*Neue Zürcher Zeitung*, 26 May 1997). Furthermore, the company where Marc Rich served his apprenticeship – Philipp Brothers, the American giant in petroleum and metals – created and developed subsidiaries in the same canton of Zug during the 1950s, mainly for fiscal reasons (Waszkis 1987: 154–159). Another example from the 1950s is that of the American company Cargill. When Cargill decided to establish itself in Europe in order to extend its international activities, it chose Geneva, where it created the Tradax subsidiary, and again fiscal considerations played a very decisive role (Broehl 1992: 768–92). Two decades later, the directors of Cargill were able to judge to what extent their choice was judicious when, in 1975, they profited from favourable Swiss legislation by using Tradax in order to circumvent the new and more severe fiscal policy of the American Congress (Morgan 1980: 161).

The second attraction for companies can be identified with further reference to Marc Rich who, when discussing the canton of Zug, declared 'It is astonishing to see how much international business is done here' (*Neue Zürcher Zeitung*, 26 May 1997) and clearly this is the case. According to one expert, the number of foreign companies of all kinds attracted to Zug, principally by the benevolent tax policy adopted since 1945, is so high 'that not even the cantonal authorities seem to know what it is' (Van Orsouw 1995: 113). Yet Zug is a tiny place, and Switzerland a small country, that serves as the base for many international political and cultural organisations and associations. An area which is so limited and yet so densely occupied presents a substantial advantage to companies as secretive about their activities as trading companies tend to be. As Casson argues in Chapter 2, this increases the possibilities of establishing contacts and creating international networks thus allowing improved access to information. When it attains a certain level, this phenomenon probably tends to become self-supporting: the denser such an area becomes, the more this advantage increases and the higher will be the number of foreign companies attracted. This is probably what happened in Switzerland from the 1950s onwards.

The Marc Rich Group

Founded in 1974 in Zug, the heart of the Swiss tax haven, the Marc Rich company quickly became the largest among the Swiss trading companies and trading companies established in Switzerland. By the beginning of the 1990s, its turnover was estimated at about 40 billion Swiss francs. The group is ranked second, after the American company Philipp Brothers, in the world petroleum and non-ferrous mineral market. In fact, it is one of the very rare newcomers to have successfully entered the ever-decreasing circle of big trading companies.

Marc Rich, an American citizen, joined Philipp Brothers in 1954 (Copetas 1985, 1990; Waszkis 1987: 204–18; *Forbes*, 29 December 1986, 30–1 and 12 June 1989, 38–9; *The Economist*, 17 October 1987, 69–70; *Bilanz*, June 1990, 12–17, February 1992, 52–7; March 1992, 22–4; August 1995, 42–5; March 1997, 30–4). Rich, along with Pincus Green, specialised in activities in the petroleum field. Thanks to the efforts of these two employees, the loss of control of the oil market by the big petroleum companies and the rapid expansion of the 'free' market in black gold, Philipp Brothers expanded rapidly from 1970. It is important to note here that the petroleum business was, for fiscal reasons, based with the subsidiaries founded by the company in Zug.

In February 1974 Marc Rich left his employer and founded his own business in Zug. He acquired the initial capital for this venture in part from his father, a trader and banker, and in part from his wife's family, who were important footwear industrialists in the United States. However, the really important capital of the new company was, first, its expertise since Marc Rich succeeded in taking along with him not only Pincus Green, but six others of Philipp Brothers most experienced traders. Second was Rich's relational capital, the solid relations that he had established with the petroleum and mineral circles of Gulf countries, especially in Iran and Nigeria, during his years at Philipp Brothers. Thus, the new firm benefited from the beginning from the powerful support which these circles willingly gave in return for generous bribes and the opportunity to play the Marc Rich company off against Philipp Brothers in the international petroleum and mineral markets in order to raise their sales prices. The firm also profited from the 1970s petroleum boom, and from several operations which were very profitable if particularly dubious even when judged by the extremely slack criteria of the circle of traders. These operations were facilitated by the extreme discretion which the Zug company enjoyed in Switzerland, the very permissive attitude of the Swiss authorities and, finally, by Switzerland's non-membership of international organisations, notably the UN.

Between 1978 and 1988, for example, Marc Rich violated the United Nations' embargo against South Africa – an embargo widely adhered to by the petroleum-producing countries from 1979 – by providing, among other products, considerable petroleum imports to the South African government. (Shipping Research Bureau 1987.) This activity alone brought the company a profit of about 2 billion Swiss francs. Moreover, from the end of the 1970s the Zug company grossly inflated its petroleum sales prices in violation of American legislation and was also alleged to have practised gross tax evasion in the United States. Another example is that from 1980 the company delivered weapons to Iran in return for petrol in defiance of the embargo decreed by the United States government against Iran.

The group's growth has been spectacular. In 1980 its turnover was estimated at around 20 billion francs – two-thirds of which came from petroleum – with profits before taxation of about 600 million Swiss francs. The company diversified into the grain trade and also secured half the capital of Twentieth Century Fox, a leading American film producer. This latter purchase put Marc Rich in touch with Henry Kissinger, thus increasing his symbolic capital.

Between 1982 and 1984 the Zug company experienced a serious crisis when Marc Rich faced legal proceedings in the United States for a series of offences among which were tax evasion, racketeering and trading with the enemy. It was at this point that Marc Rich and his company fully benefited from the advantage of being established in Switzerland. The Swiss authorities defended the firm vehemently since, they argued, 'If Switzerland doesn't do anything to help this tax payer, it could whet the appetite of other countries' (*Tages-Anzeiger*, 18 August 1983). The American request for access to the files of the Zug company was refused on the grounds that it was contrary to Swiss legislation concerning business and banking secrecy laws. The American request to extradite Rich was also refused, because the offences he was charged with, specifically tax evasion, were not part of the American–Swiss judicial co-operation treaty.

Subsequently the Zug company were banned from carrying out its activities on US territory, a very heavy blow, especially since the alarmed American banks stopped their credit. The company suffered a considerable loss of business as a result of these actions. Indeed, the company's turnover for 1983 proved to be 40 per cent down on that of 1980, several subsidiaries were closed and hundreds of traders dismissed. Driven against the wall, Marc Rich was forced to settle and, in October 1984, agreed to pay the American government a fine of roughly 400 million Swiss francs, which he raised by selling his shares in Fox. Although this allowed his American subsidiary to take up its operations on US soil again, the deal did not concern Marc Rich personally, who was still indicted and therefore unable to return to the United States.

Despite this considerable setback, the Zug company managed to recover quickly, thanks mainly to the continued support of some rich, princely oil families from the Gulf countries (Chalmin 1985: 260). It is also likely that the Swiss banks played a role, willingly taking over the place left vacant by the American establishments.

Whatever the truth of the matter, the Marc Rich company began to grow steadily once more between the second half of the 1980s and the beginning of the 1990s. By 1990 the company's estimated turnover was about 30 billion Swiss francs, it employed about 300 top traders at its head office in Zug and almost 1,000 traders in the rest of the world, divided among 48 branches or subsidiaries. During this period the company made some important investments in industrial concerns linked to raw materials (petroleum and aluminium production, etc.). It also developed a considerable number of operations, often of a financial type, in the countries of the former USSR.

Finally, it is necessary to point out that in 1993 Marc Rich agreed to a managerial buyout and the company was renamed Glencore International in the following year. The company continued to grow with an estimated turnover of 46 billion francs in 1996. From what knowledge is available it is difficult to understand Marc Rich's actions. Even more so since, in 1995 he began to trade in raw materials again, at the head of a new group named after himself. Moreover, this business started out with just two traders, but already comprised 300 in August 1997 . . . (*24 Heures*, 22 August 1997).

Explaining the competitiveness of Switzerland as a trading centre

A number of factors seem to be decisive in explaining the 'success story' of the Swiss trading centre despite the lack of colonial possessions or access to the sea.

First, situated at the north–southern and east–western crossroads of medieval Europe's commercial channels, Switzerland developed important trading activities very early on in history. Swiss traders of the nineteenth and twentieth centuries could therefore draw on a tradition, a know-how and a centuries-old network of relationships.

Second, Swiss political neutrality, its military and political non-participation in the wars between the Great Powers and its absence of political transnational organisations, represent considerable advantages. First of all, since being considered as not very dangerous rivals, the Swiss companies were generally tolerated by the Great Powers and usually managed to follow in their wake. Thus, they benefited from the order established in the colonies without having to pay the price for it. Second, Switzerland was little affected by the twentieth century's two world wars, and came out of them with a strong currency and a reliable tax system. These are two important privileges, as will be seen below. Third, the Swiss companies and the companies established in Switzerland had a large leeway in their actions regarding decisions taken by international organisations, even larger, given the lack of Switzerland's visibility in international politics. This latter factor increased further the discretion that companies enjoyed. For example, when in the 1970s the United Nations requested permission to investigate André's violations of the embargo against Rhodesia, the Swiss government refused the request without further ceremony.

Third, the power of Switzerland's financial centre also represented a valuable asset. The Swiss trading companies and the trading companies established in Switzerland were able to profit from the abundant range of credit at an interest rate which was usually several points below that at the disposal of the competing companies in other countries. As early as 1935 the survey conducted by the association of Swiss trading companies underlined the importance of relations between its members and the Swiss banks (Mangold 1935: 16–17). Moreover, since the First World War the Swiss franc has been one of the most stable and strongest currencies in the world. Thus, during the twentieth century the Swiss government has never been in the situation of having to take measures of exchange control or restriction. This was a particularly profitable element in the operations of international trade. As the owner and director of Volkart put it when he declared in 1951 that

> It is absolutely clear to us what a fabulous advantage it has been for us that our company has had its headquarters in a country which has not had its currency weakened by war and, for this reason, the currency has not been limited in its freedom of movement.
>
> (Rambousek 1990: 146)

Fourth, particularly because of Switzerland's military non-participation in the two world wars, and the early and profound integration of the workers' movement, the Swiss economic and political elite succeeded in maintaining a tax system which satisfied companies, well-off residents and therefore traders. In fact, Switzerland and in particular certain of its cantons were, as shown above and also according to the biographer of Marc Rich, real 'havens' to anyone who could master the 'labyrinthine complexities of tax loopholes' (Copetas 1985: 21).

Fifth, Switzerland has been, for many years, marked by exceptional political stability. Largely this was the result of the great weakness of both the workers' movement and, more generally, of social movements critical of the ruling political and social order. In these surroundings, protected by banking and business secrecy laws as hermetic as the Swiss alpine granite, the Swiss trading companies and the trading companies established in Switzerland did not have to lift even a corner of the thick cloak surrounding their operations. However, it must be stressed that although Switzerland shares a tax paradise with them, it is neither Panama nor Liberia. When it came to the American legal proceedings against Marc Rich, the Swiss economic and political elite were quick to say that their country was not a 'banana republic' (*Die Weltwoche*, 29 September 1983). In fact, as the example of the Marc Rich affair illustrated, Switzerland has in its hands economic power and symbolic capital – the Red Cross, humanitarian policies, neutrality – which are important enough to permit it to oppose the biggest world power without great harm.

Each of the above factors provides a considerable advantage for trading companies, but in Switzerland's case they are mutually reinforcing. The plurality of these factors form an original combination, which offers a decisive advantage to an activity as uncertain and varying as international trading: that of making risk management a lot more comfortable (Weber 1977: 51–60).

Acknowledgments

The author would like to thank J. M. Schaufelbühl, University of Lausanne, whose help was invaluable for the elaboration of this chapter.

Notes

1 The author of the survey committed himself to destroying all questionnaires completed by the companies after having used them (Mangold 1935:2).
2 The business of leading Swiss trading companies established in Egypt between 1914 and 1922 performed well between 1923 and 1928 (Müller 1992: 93–6).
3 By 'relational capital', I mean the extent and quality of the network of personal relations a trader succeeds in establishing with suppliers, buyers, political circles, and so on.
4 The UTC Group is often referred to by the name of the holding which controls it, the Basler Handelsgesellschaft AG.

References

André & Cie (1977) *André & Cie SA 1877–1977*, Lausanne: André & Cie.
—— (1997) *André Group*, Lausanne: André & Cie.
Bammatter, E. (1958) *Der schweizerische Transithandel. Eine Darstellung seiner Struktur und ein Überblick seiner Entwicklung in den Jahren 1934–1954*, Lörrach: Buchdruckerei K. Schahl.
Bericht des Verbandes Schweizerischer Transit- und Welthandelsfirmen über das Geschäftsjahr. The annual reports of the Association of Swiss Trading Companies are deposited at the Wirtschaftsarchiv in Basel.
Bertolami, S. (1983) *Halbgötter, Giftkriege und Kondensmilch: Schweizer Agro-Firmen in der dritten Welt*, Basel: Z-Verlag.
Broehl, W. G. (1992) *Cargill. Trading the World's Grain*, Hanover: University Press of New England.
Chalmin, P. (1985) *Négociants et chargeurs. La saga du négoce international des matières premières*, Paris: Economica.
Chalmin, P. and El Alaoui, A. (1990) *Matières premières et commodités*, Paris: Economica.
CNUCED (1981) *Fibres et textiles: dimensions du pouvoir des sociétés transnationales*, Geneva: United Nations.
Confederation of Swiss Firms for World and Transit Trade (1990) List of Members, Company Portraits.
Copetas, A. C. (1985) *Metal Men: Marc Rich and the 10-Billion-Dollar Scam*, New York: G. P. Putnam's Sons.
—— (1990) 'Sovereign Republic of Marc Rich' *Regardie's*, February 1990: 47–57.

Eggenberger, J. (1987) *Das Haus Diethelm im Wandel der Zeit: 1887–1987*, Zurich: Diethelm Corp.

Gisel, P. (ed.) (1995) *Encyclopedie du protestantisme*, Paris/Geneva: Cerf/Labor et Fides.

Green, R. and Laurent, C. (1985*) Bunge & Born. Puissance et secret dans l'agro-alimentaire*, Paris: Publisud.

Guex, S. (1997) 'Der Wandel der Schweiz zum internationalen Finanzplatz', *Gegenwart. Forum für Kultur, Politik, Wirtschaft*, 3/4: 11–13.

Mangold, F. (1935) 'Der Schweizerische Transithandel. Ergebnis einer Enquete', *Journal de statistique et revue économique suisse*, pp. 1–29.

Morgan, D. (1980) *Les géants du grains*, Paris: Fayard.

Müller, A. (1992) *Schweizer in Alexandrien. Zur ausländischen Präsenz in Ägypten*, Stuttgart: F. Steiner.

Rambousek, W., Vogt, A. and Volkart, H. (1990) *Volkart. Die Geschichte einer Welthandelsfirma*, Frankfurt: Insel Verlag.

Ritzmann, H. (1996) *Historical Statistics of Switzerland*, Zurich: Chronos Verlag.

Schweizer-Iten, H. (1980 ?) *The Hundred Years of the Swiss Club and the Swiss Community of Singapore 1871–1971*, Singapore: Swiss Club.

Shipping Research Bureau (1987) *Shell, Marubeni, Rich: Crude Oil Deliveries to South Africa from Brunei*, Amsterdam: Shipping Research Bureau, January.

UTC International AG (1988) *UTC International AG*, Basel.

Van Orsouw, M. (1995) *Das vermeintliche Paradies. Eine historische Analyse der Anziehungskraft der Zuger Steuergesetze*, Zurich: Chronos Verlag.

Veyrassat, B. (1991) '1945–1990: bilan des recherches sur l'histoire du négoce international de la Suisse (18ème siècle-Première Guerre mondiale)', *Revue suisse d'histoire*, 41: 274–86.

Vogel, R. (1966) *Politique commerciale suisse*, Montreux: Editions du Léman.

Wanner, G. A. (1959) *Die Basler Handels-Gesellschaft AG 1859–1959*, Basel: Basler Handels-Gesellschaft.

—— (1960) 'Basel und die Goldküste, das heutige Ghana', *Basler Stadtbuch*, 97–116.

—— (1984) *Eduard und Wilhelm Preiswerk. Präsidenten der Basler Handels-Gesellschaft*, Zurich, Verein fur wirtschaftshistorische Studien.

Waszkis, H. (1987) *Philipp Brothers. The History of a Trading Giant 1901–1985*, London: Metal Bulletin Books Ltd.

Weber, H. W. (1977) *Führung, Organisation und Leistungen schweizerischer Aussenhandels-Unternehmungen*, Zurich: Schulthess.

Yonekawa, S. (1990) 'General trading companies in a comparative context', in Yonekawa, S. (ed.) *General Trading Companies. A Comparative and Historical Study*, Tokyo: United Nations University Press.

9 French trading companies in sub-Saharan Africa 1960–90

Hélène d'Almeida-Topor

The French trading companies that acted as major economic players in francophone black Africa have gone through fundamental changes over the last three decades. After a period of expansion linked to the independence of the colonial territories, the political orientations of the new states, as well as changes in the international market, led to their concentration and, at the same time, to a redeployment of their activities. The successive oil crises and the resulting economic depression reinforced these trends. In the second half of the 1980s, business circles acknowledged that Africa was going through a long-term crisis (CNPF-CIAN Report 1988: XVII). Africa was being marginalised in international exchanges: its significance as a producer as well as a market was limited. Yet, was it necessary to abandon the continent? In spite of the troubles, French enterprises continued and even increased their presence in Africa. How did they adapt? Did the concept of 'trading company' mean the same thing in the 1990s as it had in the 1960s? In order to analyse this evolution, this chapter adopts a 'macroeconomical' approach that allows a global image of the French commercial presence in sub-Saharan Africa, while also demonstrating the diversity of the situation regarding the different types of enterprises, activities and countries.

The main sources employed in this chapter are the *Annuaires des entreprises et organismes outre-mer*. This has been systematically checked every five years, from 1955–56 through to 1989–90. The exhaustive character of this publication has enabled the compilation of a sample that is very close to the reality of all the existing trading companies. Two criteria have been used to decide whether a company is a 'French trading company' or not: on the one hand, it had to have its registered office in France or, at least, where the owners were French, to have an office or a correspondent there whenever its head office was located in Africa. On the other hand, a company had to mention the word 'trade' (or a derivative) in its name or in the description of its activities. Insurance companies, banks and credit organisations as well as engineering companies have, therefore, been excluded. Similarly, local enterprises, even where they were French-owned, were not included.

To begin with, a list was compiled of the French trading companies dealing with Africa according to the *Annuaire des entreprises et organismes outre-mer*

(1960–61). Their evolution was then checked over five-year periods in order to make a comparison in 1990.

A partial renewal of the French companies

By the time of independence, 153 French companies corresponded to the definition given above. It was not possible to determine the exact date of creation of fifteen of these enterprises (9.5 per cent of the sample used) and these were, therefore, excluded from Figure 9.1. This figure is based on six-year periods related to major events (world wars, the 1930s crisis, decolonisation and so on). Sixty per cent of the trading companies were created after 1945 which shows how dynamic the post-Second World War period was.

Due to the development of an urban salaried population, Africa appeared, in the 1950s, to be a favourable field for the development of trade in the area of public equipment as well as current consumption. The chief executive of the SCOA trading company, René Carré, emphasised this favourable situation at the time (Carré 1956: 999–1001). In fact, as Figure 9.1 illustrates, Black Africa clearly attracted trading companies.

Starting in 1952, five to six companies were created per year with a peak of nine in 1954. This trend slowed down in 1956 and 1957 to three per year, and again in 1958, to just two new enterprises. French colonial events may have led to a certain amount of caution, but did not keep the existing companies from their activities. Decolonisation was, therefore, not incompatible with commercial development, even though independence became unavoidable (Marseille 1984; Pasquier 1992). The Fifth Republic, established in 1958,

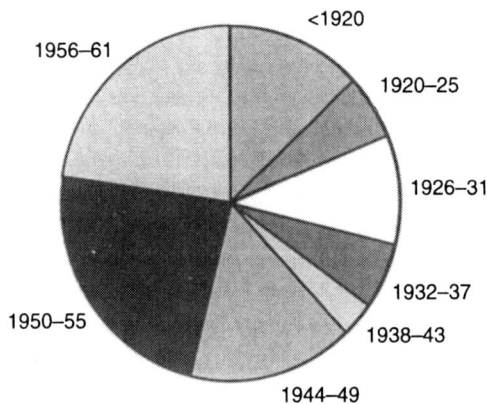

Figure 9.1 Date of creation of the French trading companies in Africa existing in 1961

appears to have reassured the business world because approximately ten new companies were established in 1959.

Besides these newcomers, there were older colonial companies whose relations with Africa had lasted for decades. Some of these were created in the early nineteenth century, such as Maison Devès & Chaumet from Bordeaux, founded in 1807, which became a publicly quoted company (SA) in 1927, and carried out import–export trade with Senegal and Soudan/Mali. Others dated from the end of the eighteenth century: Société Daniel Ancel & Fils, for example, created in Le Havre in 1782, whose limited liability company (SARL), traded in the Ivory Coast with three branch offices and a coffee factory. Their ability to adapt is the key to an explanation of both their longevity and their power. From among these old companies were included, in 1960, the biggest trading houses such as CFAO (1887), SCOA (1907), Compagnie du Niger français (1913) or Anciens Établissements Charles Peyrissac (which succeeded a company created in 1908) and was subsequently acquired by the Optorg Group.

The majority of the companies (85 out of 153) listed at the time of African independencies disappeared between 1962 and 1988, 69.4 per cent of them between 1966 and 1970. On the other hand, about twenty new companies were created and dissolved between 1962 and 1990, having lasted for an average of 15 years. By the end of the 1960s, the African trading landscape was partially redrawn: a large number of enterprises had stopped their operations while others were acquired by more powerful companies, following a concentration trend that was not confined to Africa (Suret-Canale 1987; Alibert 1992).

As a result, over three decades the total number of trading companies working with Black Africa was reduced by 38 per cent. In 1990, only 96 companies corresponded to our definition. Among these companies, 68 already existed in 1960–61, representing 70.8 per cent of the total, while 23 per cent were established between 1966 and 1975. They were either new companies or older ones which settled in Africa through new branches or joint ventures. From 1976, there were very few newcomers among those which remained active in 1990: one in 1977, two in 1980, one in 1983, and none at all after 1984. Moreover, in the period between 1985 and 1990, many trading companies were reorganised, which led to the closure of some of their offices or branches.

In France, companies began to consider whether or not the maintenance of a presence on the continent was worth their while. An article in *Marchés tropicaux* (2 January 1987) signed 'P. B.', explicitly asked: '1987: leave Africa, take Asia?' in reference to a policy, called for by the Minister of Finance, which would encourage French public or private companies to turn towards the Orient. The author of the article, who favoured a continued presence in Africa, argued that the attractiveness of one continent did not imply the abandonment of another. Should France divert from a continent whose share in French external trade was 10 per cent for a continent whose share was then only 6 per cent ?

In fact, and even though new trading companies were not attracted to Africa, the companies which were already in business there (mainly in the French-speaking area) considered that it was a 'valid market'. This conclusion was reached during the Premières Rencontres inter entreprises, organised in Libreville, 11–13 January 1987, on the initiative of the French Minister of Co-operation, in order to promote a Franco-African partnership (*Marchés tropicaux* 1987). Three years later, the publication of a survey by the National Committee of French Employers & Committee of Investors in Black Africa (CNPF-CIAN) among 470 branches of 39 French groups in 26 African countries reached the same conclusion (*Marchés tropicaux* 1990: 461–7). Only six groups out of the 39 in this sample represented the trade sector. Moreover, the study did not take into account either the oil companies or those French traders without branch offices, despite the fact that the latter constituted an important part of the trading companies, as is shown below. For this reason the results of the survey should be considered merely as indicators of the chapter's subject area. Regarding their medium-range plans, 52 per cent of the enterprises intended to invest in Africa over the next three years (1990–92) with the franc zone as a first choice in 84 per cent of cases. Moreover, 63 per cent had no plan to reduce their activities during the same period. However, 77 per cent of the enterprises involved had considered the redeployment of their activities outside Africa, in particular in France (31 per cent), in the rest of EU (31 per cent), in Asia (17 per cent), in Eastern Europe (13 per cent), etc. Indeed, as the authors of the survey emphasised, the sample represented groups that were able to undertake such an international redeployment, in contrast to the more modest type of companies, without branches.

Thus, the choice of remaining without further investments prevailed, but also with the concept of reinforcing the position in francophone Africa, and extending to other African regions as well as outside the continent. These general results showed that, at the very beginning of the 1990s, those involved were not in favour of a disengagement from Africa. Of course, in order to remain, they had been obliged to make major changes.

A necessary reorganisation

In 1960, French trade with Africa, mainly conducted by publicly quoted SAs (only 19.6 per cent of the firms were SARLs), was based on legal frameworks established during the colonial era and left unchanged after independence. However, the new states called for a certain 'localisation' of the foreign companies working in their territories, either through a public or a private participation in their capital, or the demand that some of the shareholders or executives would be local. Hence, the foreign companies had to reorganise their operations, move their registered office and, if necessary, create subsidiaries (which are not taken into account in the 96 companies listed in 1989–90).

Table 9.1 shows a switch in favour of France between 1960 and 1990. This

Table 9.1 Location of registered offices of French trading companies in Africa
1960–90 (percentages)

	France	*Senegal*	*Ivory Coast*	*Others*
1960-61	37.3	26.8	16.9	19.0
1989-90	49.0	17.4	12.2	21.4

trend, in place by the end of the 1960s, may have been caused by the uncertain political environment of several African countries. It can also be observed that the companies that kept their head office in Africa were spread differently, with a sharper decline of those located in Senegal and the Ivory Coast.

With regard to their actual operations in Africa, most of the trading companies worked through a chain of small shops in different areas of the countries in which they operated, with the management of their stocks and their turnover left to Africans (Durand-Réville 1970). Besides this 'Africanisation', which had already begun during the colonial period, the French companies began opening branch offices which complied with the local laws and thus complied with the requirements of the independent states. This type of adjustment began in the 1960s, accelerated at the beginning of the next decade until the mid-1970s and then slowed down (Larcena 1987: 8–9). Furthermore, as previously mentioned, the crisis resulted in the closure of several of these branches and local outlets from 1985 onwards. Thus, in 1990, the situation was less active. At that time, more than half of the companies (49 out of 96) had subsidiaries.

There are important disparities between companies having subsidiaries and those that had none (47 out of 96), and between those with only a few (30 out of 49 had two, three or four branches) and the more powerful companies, for example, 'the big four' – CFAO, SCOA, France-Niger, Optorg (Alibert 1992) – and also the oil group ELF, Les Grands Moulins de Paris or Brossette International from Lyon, which owned at least ten subsidiaries. In 1989, the subsidiaries of all kinds of business groups were believed to represent between 80 and 90 per cent of the French presence in African countries (CNPF-CIAN Report 1990). However, this share was certainly lower in the trade sector, although to what extent cannot be precisely determined because of the important number of companies which, as was noted above, had no branches.

Because of the lack of data concerning the turnover of all the trading companies, which was the sole reliable indicator of their scope and real influence on economic activities, the distribution of their share capital and its evolution over three decades has been analysed.

Table 9.2 emphasises the importance of small and medium trading companies in 1961 because 50 per cent of their total number had a share capital of 600,000 francs or less, and 75 per cent stayed within the 2 million franc range.

Table 9.2 Distribution of the share capital of French trading companies in Africa in 1961 and 1990

Constant Francs (1961)	In 1961 %	In 1990 %
-100,000	11.4	15.2
100,000 to - 300,000	14.2	17.1
300,000 to - 600,000	21.3	11.4
600,000 to - 1 million	11.4	5.7
1 million to - 2 millions	17.0	13.3
2 millions to 5 millions	16.3	11.3
+ 5 millions	8.4	26.0
TOTAL	100.0	100.0

Note: 1961 constant values obtained through the French GDP deflator – *International financial statistics*, IMF.

Big companies represented only a very small share of the total. In contrast, in 1990 there was a sharp tendency to an increasing share capital: half of the companies had a capital of 1 million 1961 francs or less, while more than a quarter exceeded the 5 million rank. This distribution confirms that a concentration of capital had occurred. It appears that at this time more capital was necessary to trade in Africa: the lowest share capital, in constant value, was five times more important in 1990 than it had been in 1961. Moreover, the scale of the share capital between the small businesses and the big trading companies reduced. In 1961, the ratio was 1 to 21,667 between Baraderie & Loustallot SARL (3,000 francs) and SCOA (65 million francs). In 1990, the ratio was 1 to 2,962.6 between the 100,000 current francs of Teisseire SARL and the share capital of SCOA (296,259 million current francs). At that time, however, SCOA was far behind other companies, for example, the oil company Total-CFP (1,816.310 million current francs) or L'Air Liquide SA, a producer and distributor of all kinds of gas (2,843.830 million current francs). Thus the decline in the number of French trading companies was accompanied by a growth in size of the survivors. In fact, the increase of capital corresponded to the increasing needs of the French trading companies due to their functional and geographical diversification.

Specialisation through diversification.

The comparison of the types of activities of the trading companies shows the major changes which occurred over thirty years. A first conversion, in the

Table 9.3 Activities of French trading companies in Africa, 1960 and 1990

	1960–61	1989–90	
	%	%	% of share capital
Specialised trade (a)	47.1	37.5	45.5
Import-export	40.5	19.8	1.8
Export (b)	7.2	7.2	1.5
Department stores	3.9	4.2	0.9
Diversified activities	-	22.9	41.9
Unknown	1.3	8.4	8.4
Total	100.0	100.0	100.0

Notes: (a) More than 95% import and also wood import-export (b) Tropical goods, wood

1950s, explains why the group of importers–exporters, which dominated the market until then is ranked only second in 1960–61.

It has been noted that a change had taken place in the trading methods which had made the fortune of colonial traders who exported raw material and imported manufactured goods:

> The traditional shop with its wire fencing counters, a true hotchpotch of the most varying goods, sold wholesale or retail, paid cash or on credit, did no longer have its place in the cities where buildings grew, as the entire country is changing.
>
> (Carré 1956: 999–1001)

The movement accelerated in the 1960s and it was observed in 1970 that, 'the colonial trade mechanism is broken' (Durand-Réville 1970). The number of French enterprises involved in general trade fell even more, falling to only 19.8 per cent in 1990. Most of these were small or middle-sized companies: on average, their share capital was 2.2 times less than that of export companies, 2.5 times less than department stores, 13.2 times less than specialised trade companies and 19.9 times less than the 'hybrids'.

Nevertheless, this sector perpetuated as modern department stores were created by the big metropolitan chains. As early as 1952, the Grands Magasins de l'Ouest Africain (GRAMOA) established stores in Dakar and in other cities of Senegal as well as in Bamako, Conakry and Abidjan. A few years later, every country of western francophone Africa had developed outlets connected to Prisunic or Printania such as SEMAG in Senegal, GUIMAG in Guinea, CIMAG in the Ivory Coast, etc. In 1974, the brand SCORE, belonging to the SCOA group, took over, and by 1990 owned up to fifteen stores in six countries (Alibert 1992).

What is striking about the trading activities in Table 9.3 is the first rank of specialised trade and the separation of import and export. Exports were gradually abandoned by most companies, even the biggest ones, for reasons of interference. First, there was the intervention of the African authorities, who controlled the marketing of local products either through *Caisses de stabilisation* (stabilisation funds), inherited from colonisation, or similar more or less compelling institutions, according to the policy of the independent states. Second, there was the transformation of the international markets such as petroleum (d'Almeida-Topor and Lakroum 1994: 121–4). Third, increased technical demands because of more complex packaging and transportation, required higher investments and professional skill. As a result of these factors there was a decrease in the number of operators benefiting from a *de facto* monopoly over a product and/or a region of origin or of consumption.

Conversely, the share of importers and/or representatives was increasing, creating competition that was not welcomed by the established traders or their spokesmen (Carré 1956; Durand-Réville 1970). In the following years, under pressure from the establishment of European firms in Africa, encouraged by the EU and the ACP Accords, the competition was even harsher.

All these firms specialised in the supply of various consumer goods (for instance, food, domestic electrical equipment, cars, etc.) and public equipment. The petroleum trade illustrated this revolution. In the 1950s, the oil companies installed an entire network of their own gas stations, taking away from other importers an activity that had previously belonged to them. At the same time, another new sector was created: the maintenance of electric household appliances, automobiles and heavy equipment.

Immediately after independence, a certain number of trading companies diversified their activities and participated in the industrialisation of the new states by creating their own production units or assisting local firms. Other companies enlarged the area of their activities, integrating new services or research departments. In 1990, this type of company along with approximately a quarter of all French trading companies, ranked second, before the import–export dealing with general trade, and took an important part of the total share capital (see Table 9.3). These included big companies such as CFAO, which had relinquished general merchandising and SCOA and the Optorg group, for which general trading activities had become residual (Suret-Canale 1987; Alibert 1992).

The wish to extend the activity to other areas accompanied geographical expansion.

Even if western francophone Africa kept its primacy, Table 9.4 shows that the companies which existed in only a few places tended to diminish to the benefit of geographically more diversified companies. This evolution confirms the results of the survey cited above concerning the plans of the French subsidiaries established in Africa. However, for more important groups, diver-

Table 9.4 Geographical diversification of French trading companies, 1960–90

	1960–61 %	1989–90 %
Located in:		
1 country	44.9	39.0
2 or 3 countries	18.8	6.3
Western francophone Africa (at least 4 countries)	6.7	9.5
Francophone Africa (west &/or centre &/or Madagascar)	18.1	23.1
Francophone Africa + other	11.5	22.1
Total	100.0	100.0

sification meant a smaller share of Africa in their total turnover. The examples of CFAO and SCOA illustrate the evolution over a long-term period. 'Pure trading companies' from the turn of the twentieth century until the 1950s, began diversifying and redeploying even before the independence of the African colonies (Coquery-Vidrovitch 1975). By 1990 they were full 'hybrid' companies: as they closed their general trade departments in French-speaking Africa, they became specialised in selling automobiles and in managing many transport services. CFAO, which was absorbed by the Pinault Group, also specialised in the public equipment trade in Africa, but the continent was only contributing 17 per cent of its total turnover, the major part of which consisted of international trade in electrical goods and in materials for factories, especially in Europe and in North America. The SCOA Holding also specialised in selling pharmaceutical goods; it had department stores in many African countries and an automobile factory in Nigeria. Africa's share of the SCOA total turnover was only 26 per cent (Alibert 1992).

In this period of crisis, French trading companies had to face international competition, which caused them some concern. The survey led by CNPF-CIAN in 1987 among 102 French enterprises indicated as major competitors: Germany, Japan, Italy, Canada, Brazil, USA, Belgium and Britain. In 1989, another survey among 470 subsidiaries of French groups still mentioned Germany as the main competitor, followed by Canada, Italy, Japan, Belgium, USA, Brazil, Britain, the Netherlands and South Korea. An additional source of anxiety was smuggling in sub-Saharan Africa. In the same study, 61 per cent said that they were affected by the increasing amount of illegal activities and 88 per cent considered that political action against this phenomenon was necessary.

Conclusion

During a period of three decades, French trade in Africa went through fundamental changes. The continent, today composed of independent states, still exports raw material and still imports manufactured products, but its share in international trade has fallen. It has been necessary for companies to adapt to the new political and economical conditions. Of course, the existence of the franc currency zone was an advantage, as was the French policy of cooperation which supported economic relations between France and African French-speaking countries. However, this was not sufficient to maintain the presence of the French companies: they had to change. Some of them were unable to do so and disappeared. Those who stayed were obliged to get more capital, to concentrate and to redeploy their activities in and out of Africa. The experience of the French companies between 1960 and 1990 provides a striking example of how trading companies 'reinvent' themselves over time. By 1990 the French trading companies in Africa were very different corporate entities than three decades earlier.

References

Primary sources

Annuaire des entreprises et organismes outre-mer (1960–1961), R. Moreux (ed.), Paris, 1955–56 à 1989–90.

Carré, R. (1956) 'L'évolution du commerce en Afrique française et ses perspectives', *Marchés coloniaux*, 31: 3.

CNPF-CIAN Report (1988) *Marchés tropicaux*, 24: 2.

CNPF-CIAN Report (1990) *Marchés tropicaux*, 16: 2.

Durand-Réville, L. (1970) 'Le commerce français en Afrique noire', *Marchés tropicaux*, 21:11.

P.B. (1987) '1987: lâchons l'Afrique, prenons l'Asie ?' *Marchés tropicaux*, 2: 1.

Larcena, D. (1987) 'Après 25 ans d'indépendance: où en est l'africanisation des entreprises ?' *Marchés tropicaux*, 23: 1.

Published texts

Alibert, J. (1992) 'Les mutations du grand commerce européen', nl spécial 'trente années d'Afrique', *Afrique contemporaine*, 164, October–December: 81–7.

Coquery-Vidrovitch, C. (1975) 'L'impact des intérêts coloniaux: SCOA et CFAO dans l'Ouest africain, 1910–1965', *Journal of African History*, 4 (6): 595–621.

d'Almeida-Topor, H. and Lakroum, M. (1994) *L'Europe et l'Afrique. Un siècle d'échanges économiques*, Paris: Armand Colin.

Marseille, J. (1984) *Empire colonial et capitalisme français. Histore d'un divorce*, Paris: Albin Michel.

Pasquier, R. (1992) 'Les milieux d'affaires face à la décolonisation (1956–1960) d'après quelques publications', in Ageron, C. R. and Michel, M. (eds) *L'Afrique noire: l'heure des Indépendances*, Paris: CNRS, pp. 297–314.

Suret-Canale, J. (1987) *Afrique et capitaux*, Paris: L'Arbre verdoyant.

10 Japanese general trading companies and 'free-standing' FDI after 1960

Ken'ichi Yasumuro

This chapter examines the historical evidence concerning the foreign direct investment (FDI) of nine Japanese *sogo shosha* or general trading companies (GTCs) in the 1960s and 1970s. It is argued that parallels can be drawn between Japanese FDI in this period and British FDI in the nineteenth century, which predominantly took the form of 'free-standing companies' (FSCs). There are good reasons for believing that foreign affiliates organised by Japanese GTCs usually have limited life cycles and often die at an early age. It is suspected that the major cause of such high mortality of the GTCs' foreign affiliates lies not in managerial failure, but is due to the strategic features of the projects. Based on this argument, the concept of FSC is expanded and the idea of free-standing style FDI is used to analyse GTCs' FDI projects. Finally, from the results of this analysis, it is asserted that free-standing type FDI will become common in service multinationals and that it is different from 'classic' MNE investment. Free-standing type FDI is classified as a market-making investment. Finally, it is suggested that research on free-standing type FDI is one of the most useful approaches to developing a new theory of service multinationals.

Patterns of free-standing type FDI: the issue of free-standing companies

Mira Wilkins (1988a, 1988b) first identified the importance of FSC at an international conference held at the European University Institute in 1983 (Ohtowa 1996). Wilkins suggested that the majority of British FDI from 1870 to 1914, especially those investments in the United States, Africa and Asia, were carried out by FSCs. According to her view, FSCs formerly classified as 'indirect' (portfolio) investments were in fact a form of FDI, as they involved managerial control from the home economy (Jones 1996: 33–6). British and Dutch FSCs were widely spread over the developing world, especially in the colonies (Jones 1996: 34). This type of firm registered and raised equity capital in London, or some other European financial centre, and owned overseas operations in a specific region, but undertook no domestic production operation whatsoever (Casson 1997: 217).

The unique characteristics of FSCs were defined by 'fragile' networks of business partners. Wilkins identified clusters of business partners which linked together various professional fields such as financial intermediaries, solicitors, accountants, mining engineers, merchant banks, trading companies and other influential individuals (Wilkins 1988a: 265; Jones 1996: 25). Major business activities of FSCs were property-related industries such as natural resource exploitation and infrastructure investments (Casson 1997). Management of local operations was performed by British expatriates or management agents, but controlled by head offices located in London or some other European city. While in some instances managerial control was exercised from a head office in the home country, in other cases managerial decision-making operated locally (Wilkins 1988a; Jones 1996,34).

When managerial control was exercised by the head office, FSC could well be classified as a multinational company (Casson 1997: 227). Yet the issues presented by Wilkins (1988a,1988b) have given rise to much academic debate as to whether or not FSCs can be really defined as multinationals.

Hennart argued that a FSC internalises equity markets and direct investment occurs whether managerial control is located in the home office or not. He characterised a FSC as an international financial system to transfer equity capital from London to developing areas (Hennart 1994a,b). On the contrary, Casson argued that Hennart's interpretation of internalisation theory was incorrect. He claimed that for a start capital is a factor of production and not an intermediate product. According to internalisation theory it is intermediate product markets that are internalised, and not factor markets (Casson 1997: 220, 224).

Casson classified four types of FSC according to export of technology and information. Table 10.1 shows the typology of free-standing firms defined by Casson (1997: 227).

Casson argued that the type A firm which exports both information and technology is qualified as both a direct investor and as a multinational firm. The type B firm exports information but not technology. It is a direct investor because the information exports are encoded in the form of orders, but it is not a multinational because its headquarters do not qualify as a separate activity. The type C firm exports technology or project management services, but without the responsibility for co-ordinating them, and is classified as quasi-multinational. The type D firm exports neither technology nor information and maybe classified as a trusted investment (according to the author) where assets are managed by other people (Casson 1997: 226–9). Casson classified Hennart's FSC as type D.

On the other hand, Geoffrey Jones claimed that a FSC was a different entity from the American-type classic MNEs, which evolved from manufacturing giants (Jones 1996: 33). He placed great weight on the networks linking many FSCs, suggesting that there were interesting parallels with the complex cross-border relationships which developed in international business in the 1980s and 1990s. This might suggest that in periods of fast and deep

Table 10.1 Typology of free-standing firms

Export of information	Export of technology	
	Yes	*No*
Yes	A multinational direct investor	B direct investor
No	C quasi-multinational	D ★ ———

Source: Casson 1997: 227
Note: ★ indicates 'trusted' investment

globalisation, flexible networks of firms have advantages over firms with clearly defined boundaries (Jones 1996: 35).

The perspective which is presented by Jones (1996) can contribute to the development of a theory of service multinationals, even though control by ownership and organisation structure are ambiguous compared with the classic MNE model.

In summary, it is suggested that FSCs are a different form of direct investment when compared with classic multinationals. Although the prototype of a FSC originated in Britain and some other areas of Europe, the basic rationale of the entity is universal. The nature of FSCs comes from a collaborative service network. The major feature of FSCs, though their types are diverse, stems from the human relations of the founders and collaboration of business experts. The organisation of a FSC is personal network-oriented, rather than the hierarchical stratum typical of formal organisations.

Where managerial control from head office exists, a FSC can be classified as a MNE. However, if collaboration is made without any equity investment, control without ownership will be the norm rather than the exception. As a result, the boundary between direct and indirect investment will be ambiguous and fluid. When a FSC is defined as a MNE, it can be explained by the internalisation theory. In such a case, transaction costs reduction occurs when intermediate product markets are internalised, but does not occur when factor markets such as equity capital are internalised. The free-standing type investment is made when intermediate product markets are internalised. Moreover, the internalisation of intermediate product markets is the key to understanding the FDI of Japanese GTCs.

Japanese GTCs as free-standing investors

Foreign affiliates of Japanese GTCs

Japanese GTCs were the leading companies to undertake Japanese outward investment in the early post-Second World War period, especially in the 1960s and early 1970s (Yasumuro 1984). GTCs used credit (finance) capability extensively to finance overseas business and investments and eagerly performed the role of financial resource suppliers to developing countries. In this context, GTCs could be conceptualised as free-standing investors which conveyed financial resources to less developed countries.

In contrast to Britain, Japan had no managing agency system or the like in developing countries. The overseas branches of GTCs, however, undertook similar functions to those performed by British managing agencies (Yoshino and Lifson 1986: Chapter 12).

In such cases, Japanese GTCs could not export production technology because of their commercial orientation. If GTCs needed to transfer technology to a foreign affiliate they had to collaborate with manufacturing companies in order to organise a joint venture. At the same time, to establish sales channels in local markets, GTCs often had to collaborate with local sales agents. Where local market entry was prohibited or restricted by local government, joint ventures with local commercial firms were an indispensable feature. Thus, Japanese GTCs needed business partners both inside and outside of their home country. Besides the supply of their plentiful financial resources, GTCs often achieved information on export (control) by dispatching managerial talents to foreign affiliates. When GTCs decided to engage in direct investment, they organised an international collaborative network as a part of this operation. This led to the argument that there was a distinctive 'Japanese-style' form of multinational enterprise. The strongest advocate of this view was Kojima (1982) who praised 'Japanese-style' FDI and criticised 'US-style' FDI, because the former was based allegedly on the concept of free competition, whereas the latter, he argued, stemmed from the monopolistic behaviour of large enterprises (Buckley 1983: 1992).

Export promotion for intermediate products

As trading companies, GTCs exported finished goods to foreign countries, but sometimes their export activities were restricted or prohibited by host governments due to protectionism. Most of the prominent restrictive measures adopted by governments were the import substitution policies introduced by many developing countries between the 1960s and 1970s. Therefore, GTCs were forced to establish local assembly plants to overcome trade barriers.

At this time, unfortunately, local firms which produced the finished goods were few in number and immature. As a consequence, local authorities requested foreign importers to establish joint ventures with local partners and it was expected that the transference of technology would take place. Japanese

GTCs, as the largest importers, negotiated to organise jointly owned affiliates between Japanese manufacturers and local firms.

This promotion strategy of organised joint venture companies in the developing countries was advantageous to GTCs. To meet the needs of economic development in these countries, especially in South East Asia, GTCs attempted to export intermediate products such as chemicals, synthetic materials, metal products, electrical parts and components, and electronic devices. The technology of local firms was, however, at a level below that required to absorb modern industrial technologies, and access to licences was unavailable. The intermediate products market was immature and contained much uncertainty due to its early stage of industrial development. Thus GTCs had to build manufacturing capacities into the local markets. GTCs also organised collaborative production affiliates within the local markets to promote exports of intermediate products and sold a large amount of intermediate products to jointly owned foreign affiliates. As an investor, GTCs monopolised intermediate product markets by the internalisation of local assemblers.

In short, foreign affiliates organised by GTCs were a strategic response to uncertainty in transactions and an attempt to reduce those transaction costs incurred through imperfections in the industrial systems of the less developed areas. When GTCs internalised intermediate product markets by applying this measure, their export sales of industrial goods continually increased. GTCs usually treated these FDIs as business expenses or running costs associated with the maintenance of their exports. For this reason GTCs owned hundreds of minority-owned foreign affiliates and also applied this minority ownership policy widely to reinforce long-term contracts with resource suppliers.

Current discussions of the FSC issue, typically the one based on Hennart's view of a financial institution, have concentrated upon financial resource transactions. However, the focal point must be placed instead on the internalisation process of intermediate products. In this sense, foreign affiliates organised by GTCs can be characterised as market-making investments (Casson 1997: 90–7). Thus, Japanese GTCs' FDIs can be classified as free-standing type FDIs, although collaboration with Japanese manufacturing firms in the export of technology was a necessity.

Disadvantages of the investment life cycle

The evidence, although insufficient, suggests that the similarity between British FSCs and Japanese GTCs' foreign affiliates lies within the disadvantages of their investment life cycle. That is, free-standing-type investment was usually short-lived when compared with that of classic FDIs. This was because free-standing-type investment was organised within a relation-based network encompassing personal relations and collaboration of interests between partners. On the other hand, the classic multinational firm organised relations by ownership policies and hierarchical principles. As a consequence, free-standing-type investment was more fragile than classic-type and market-making investment was particularly short-lived when intermediate product markets were organised by local governments. When free-standing-type investment had a short life cycle, viability of FDI would be low and mortality correspondingly high. This life-cycle assumption is examined in the following section.

Viability of GTC foreign affiliates

Destiny of GTC foreign affiliates: exist, decease, or withdraw?

To verify the assumptions discussed above, a database was constructed using nine Japanese GTCs' foreign affiliates established (or in operation) by 1980. Using the 1980 edition of *Facts and Figures of Japanese Foreign Direct Investment* (Japanese edition, Toyo Keisai Shinpou Publishing Company, Tokyo, 1981), 1,414 FDIs made by nine Japanese GTCs were identified. The data for each foreign affiliate was made up of such items as affiliate name, country, year established (or operation start-up year), ownership (percentage), amount of equity capital (both local currency and Japanese yen), number of employees, number of expatriates, industry or product items and joint venture partners (both Japanese and local firms). Out of 1,414 FDIs, 76 had multi-GTC investors – that is, more than two Japanese GTCs invested in the same project. Consequently, the actual number of foreign affiliates owned by Japanese GTCs in 1980 was 1,338.

The next step was to examine these 1,338 affiliates in turn to establish whether or not they were still in existence. For this purpose, data was collected from the 1995 edition of *Facts and Figures for Japanese Foreign Direct Investments*, which allowed an adequate time lag of fifteen years to test the relatively short investment life cycle. Where the same affiliate name was listed in the 1995 GTCs' FDI list, it was defined as 'survivor' and, alternatively, where the name was not listed a double-check was made in the partner's FDI list. If the affiliate name did not appear in either list, it was defined as 'deceased', although it could not be confirmed that the business had, in fact, been liquidated or that succession had not gone to local partners. In a situation where the affiliate name had disappeared from the GTCs' list but appeared in the partner's list, it was defined as 'withdrawn'.

The methodology applied here was simple but practical. It was the most effective because of the difficulties faced in researching the details of each of the 1,338 affiliates when GTC managers did not welcome investigation into the facts behind the dissolution of foreign affiliates. Hence, the method offered an effective approximation of the mortality of Japanese GTCs' FDIs.

Table 10.2 gives the fate of an aggregated number of foreign affiliates of nine general trading companies. Table 10.3 shows the 'real' numbers (excluding the case of multi-investors). From these two tables it can be seen that out of the 1,338 GTCs' affiliates which were established before 1980, 527 (39.5 per cent) were still in existence in 1995. On the other hand, 760 foreign affiliates had disappeared by 1995, a mortality rate of 56.8 per cent. Foreign

Table 10.2 Fate of nine GTCs' foreign affiliates established before 1980

GTC Name	Survivor (%)	Deceased (%)	Withdrawn (%)	Total
Mitsubishi	86 (39.3)	119 (54.3)	14 (6.4)	219 (100)
Mitsui	120 (43.3)	149 (53.8)	8 (2.9)	277 (100)
Itochu	9 (26.9)	152 (69.4)	8 (3.7)	219 (100)
Sumitomo	48 (38.7)	73 (58.9)	3 (2.4)	124 (100)
Marubeni	77 (34.8)	140 (63.4)	4 (1.8)	221 (100)
Nissho Iwai	59 (54.6)	43 (39.8)	6 (5.6)	108 (100)
Tomen	50 (53.8)	42 (45.2)	1 (1.0)	93 (100)
Nichimen	28 (36.4)	47 (61.0)	2 (2.6)	77 (100)
Kanematsu	25 (32.9)	44 (57.9)	7 (9.2)	76 (100)
Total	552 (39.0)	809 (57.2)	53 (3.8)	1,414 (100)

Note: The number of survivors as based on 1995 data. the ranking order of the GTCs is based on annual sales volume for 1995 (Fortune 1995).

Table 10.3 Fate of nine GTCs' foreign affiliates established before 1980, excluding multi-investors

Number of Affiliates	Survivor (%)	Deceased (%)	Withdrawn(%)	Total
	527(39.5)	760(56.8)	50(3.70)	1,338(100)

Note: The number of survivors (or not) is based on 1995 data.

affiliates which had disappeared from the GTCs' 1995 list but were still included in the Japanese partner's list amounted to 50, thus GTCs' equity withdrawal from the affiliates accounted for 3.7 per cent.

Around 60 per cent of GTCs' affiliates which were established by 1980 had deceased or withdrawn. This figure implies that GTCs' affiliates disappeared at a rate of 4 per cent per annum between 1980 and 1995. A key question here is whether or not the 60 per cent mortality rate was abnormally high.

Unfortunately, with the exception of a few studies, comparable data concerning Japanese foreign divestment is unavailable. Horaguchi (1992) has estimated the rate of Japanese foreign divestment per year, but the data used was inappropriate.[1] Using Japanese government data, he estimated the extinction (number of equity disposal and divestment) rates and concluded that

16.31 per cent per year was an adequate approximation of the extinction rate, although he has made many other estimates (Horaguchi 1992: 115). A simple, but most reliable, estimate derived from government data was 12.6 per cent (simple average value of extinction from 1973 to 1986) (Horaguchi 1992: 108). While these estimations were 2–3 times larger than GTCs' average mortality as defined by 'deceased' plus 'withdrawn' in the above analysis, comparison of numerical values between different data is meaningless and open to misinterpretation.

In general, the mortality rate of GTCs' affiliates would be expected to be higher than that of classic multinationals. Multinational manufactures were able to transfer production technology swiftly to foreign affiliates, thus the viability of affiliates was improved. On the other hand, GTCs which lacked technological ability were unable to support their affiliates in this manner. Moreover, where Japanese partners were small in size and unable to continue to export technology, the viability of affiliates worsened. For all of these reasons, the mortality rate of GTCs' affiliates was higher than that of the classic multinationals.[2]

A detailed examination of Table 10.2 reveals the differences in mortality among Japanese GTCs. Itochu's mortality rate was the highest – 73.1 per cent – while Nishow Iwai had the lowest rate of 45.4 per cent. Table 10.2 also demonstrates that the largest GTCs, such as Mitsubishi and Mitsui, also suffered relatively high mortality rates of 60.7 per cent and 56.7 per cent, respectively.

Thus it can be said that, in general, each Japanese GTC experienced relatively high mortality rates. Yet the above discussion has clearly indicated that the reason for this high mortality was not always the result of managerial failure.

Causes of high mortality

There are five factors which seem to have affected the survival of GTCs' foreign affiliates. These are the ownership percentage of the GTC; the size of the affiliate measured by number of employees and amount of equity capital; the industrial category of the foreign affiliate; the location (region) of the affiliate; and the establishment year of affiliate. These factors will now be examined.

Ownership percentage of GTCs and viability of foreign affiliates

Table 10.4 shows the relationship between ownership percentage of GTCs and the fate of their foreign affiliates. As can be seen, GTCs tended to hold a minority ownership. Indeed, GTCs owned less than 20 per cent of their affiliates in 47 per cent of cases. When it is assumed that ownership is fundamental to the control of FDI (Casson 1997), then majority ownership or wholly owned affiliates should be higher in viability relative to minority ownership.

Table 10.4 shows that ownership percentage in every category exhibited a mortality rate of over 60 per cent. Where the percentage of ownership was

Table 10.4 GTC ownership percentage and fate of foreign GTC affiliates

Ownership (%)	Survivor (%)	Deceased (%)	Withdrawn (%)	Total
0–9	38 (20.2)	140 (74.5)	10 (5.3)	188 (100)
10–19	111 (42.1)	143 (54.1)	10 (3.8)	264 (100)
20–29	71 (39.9)	100 (56.2)	7 (3.9)	178 (100)
30–39	31 (31.9)	61 (62.9)	5 (5.2)	97 (100)
40–49	51 (45.1)	58 (51.3)	4 (3.6)	113 (100)
50–59	16 (20.8)	57 (74.0)	4 (5.2)	77 (100)
60–69	12 (46.2)	14 (53.8)	0 (0.0)	26 (100)
70–79	7 (36.8)	11 (57.9)	1 (5.3)	19 (100)
80–89	9 (36.0)	16 (64.0)	0 (0.0)	25 (100)
90–99	6 (28.6)	15 (64.0)	0 (0.0)	21 (100)
100	(60.6)	106 (39.4)	0 (0.0)	269 (100)
n.a	12 (21.3)	39 (63.9)	9 (14.8)	61 (100)
Total	527 (39.5)	760 (56.8)	50 (3.7)	1,338 (100)

small, however, mortality tended to increase. Interestingly, in the case of the wholly-owned affiliates the mortality rate only amounted to 39.4 per cent. Included in this category were not only the wholly-owned foreign affiliates but also the wholly-owned overseas branches.

Apparently, GTCs applied different policies to their activities dependent on whether or not they were foreign operations, wholly-owned branches or minority-owned affiliates. The reason for this was simple: GTCs treated branches as internal organs but joint ventures were treated as business-promotion devices. Consequently, if foreign branches are excluded from the wholly-owned category, the mortality rate of this category is at the same level as other ownership categories.

Size of affiliates and viability

Table 10.5 shows the relationship between the size of foreign affiliates (measured by number of employees) and their fate. Small affiliates which employed less than 49 employees accounted for 42 per cent of total affiliates, while relatively large size affiliates which employed more than 500 employees, accounted for only 172 (15.9 per cent) of the total 1,338 affiliates. It was expected that a positive correlation would exist between the size of affiliates and the rate of existence, since larger affiliates were richer in resources than the smaller ones and, therefore, more likely to survive the effects of a business depression. Yet, Table 10.5 gives no indication of any positive relationship between size and viability. In fact, the affiliates, whether they were small, medium or large, experienced almost the same mortality (45–60 per cent). The one exception occurs in the largest one (more than 5,000 employees), where the mortality was extremely high (85.7 per cent). In short, it can be concluded that the mortality rate of foreign affiliates has no correlation with size as measured by number of employees.

Table 10.5 Size of foreign affiliates (by number of employees) and fate of GTC foreign affiliates

Number of Employee	Survivor (%)	Deceased (%)	Withdrawn (%)	Total
0–49	174 (38.7)	260 (57.8)	16 (3.6)	450 (100)
50–99	77 (54.2)	60 (42.3)	5 (3.5)	142 (100)
100–499	129 (40.6)	171 (57.8)	18 (5.7)	318 (100)
500–999	40 (38.8)	60 (58.3)	3 (2.9)	103 (100)
1000–4999	24 (38.7)	36 (58.1)	2 (3.2)	62 (100)
5000–	1 (14.3)	6 (85.7)	0 (0.0)	7 (100)
n.a.	83 (32.4)	167 (65.2)	6 (2.4)	256 (100)
Total	527 (39.5)	760 (56.8)	50 (3.7)	1,338 (100)

Next, the relationship between the size of foreign affiliate as measured by equity capital (converted into yen at the 1995 level) and their fate was examined.

Table 10.6 reveals that the smallest size category (less than 10 million yen) exhibited the highest mortality (78.8 per cent), followed by the largest size category (more than 1 billion yen) where mortality was 63.6 per cent. Other categories exhibited almost the same mortality rate (50–60 per cent). Again, no meaningful correlation could be identified, in this case between size and mortality (or viability) of foreign affiliates.

Industrial classification and viability

In this section, the relationship between industrial classification and outcome is examined.

Table 10.7 shows, that the largest number (46 per cent) of foreign affiliates belonged to manufacturing industries, followed by commercial affiliates (31 per cent), and service industries, excluded commercial industries (168, 12.6 per cent); finance (12), insurance (4), real estate (17), transport (49), warehouse (21), other services (36), stock holding (9) and others (20). Finally, natural resources development industries (114, 8.5 per cent): agriculture (26), forestry (10), fishery (23) and mining (55). There is also an independent category, the construction industry, with 26 affiliates. The manufacturing industries, textiles (143) and chemicals (143) had the highest numbers, metal products (mainly processed steel products) and machinery (including electric machinery) were also a large group. In short, as a diversified trader, GTCs invested directly in all industries, though manufacturing and commerce were the main focus.

As can be seen from Table 10.7, the following industries experienced relatively high mortality rates: agriculture (77 per cent), forestry (100 per cent),

Table 10.6 Size of foreign affiliates (by equity capital) and fate of GTC foreign
affiliates (millions of yen)

Capital	Survivor (%)	Deceased (%)	Withdrawn (%)	Total
Less than 10	25 (31.2)	91 (77.1)	2 (1.7)	118 (100)
10-49	68 (33.8)	125 (62.3)	8 (3.9)	201 (100)
50-99	67 (48.2)	70(62.3)	2 (1.4)	139 (100)
100-199	66 (37.9)	98 (56.4)	10 (5.8)	174 (100)
200-299	72 (49.7)	66 (45.5)	7 (4.8)	145 (100)
300-499	58 (41.7)	73 (52.5)	8 (5.8)	139 (100)
500-999	67 (41.6)	91 (56.5)	3 (1.9)	161 (100)
1000-4999	80 (43.5)	98 (53.3)	6 (3.2)	184 (100)
5000-9999	11 (45.8)	11 (45.8)	2 (8.3)	24 (100)
10000-	12 (36.4)	20 (60.6)	1 (3.0)	33 (100)
n.a.	2 (10.0)	17 (85.0)	1 (15.0)	20 (100)
Total	527 (39.5)	760 (56.8)	50 (3.7)	1,338 (100)

fisheries (74 per cent), mining (81.8 per cent), foodstuffs (85.7 per cent),
finance (91.6 per cent), transport (87.8 per cent) and stock holding (88.9 per
cent). These industries were either primary or tertiary industries and this is
unsurprising since it has been shown that free-standing companies tended to
engage in these fields (Davenport-Hines and Jones 1989). Even though affiliates in manufacturing industries could survive longer than those in other
industries, their mortality rate was also high. In fact, as Table 10.7 shows, the
existence figure for manufacturing affiliates was only 38.5 per cent. In short,
mortality of the GTCs' foreign affiliates was high in any industry.

Location of foreign affiliates and viability

Table 10.8 shows the relationship between location of affiliate (region) and
the viability conditions. The viability of affiliates located in ASEAN (49.3 per
cent), Oceania (46 per cent), the EU (47.4 per cent) and Latin America (42.9
per cent) was rather good. However, mortality in North America (74.6 per
cent), Middle, Near East and Africa (73.5 per cent), East Asia (72.0 per cent)
and other European countries (100 per cent) was extremely high.

As a whole, although there are some differences, the mortality rate of
each region accounted for more than 40 per cent. Here also, meaningful
differences between host regions and the viability of affiliate companies
cannot be identified.

Table 10.7 Industrial classification and fate of GTC foreign affiliates

Industries	Survivor (%)	Deceased (%)	Withdrawn (%)	Total
Agriculture	6 (23.0)	20 (77.0)	0 (0.0)	26 (100)
Forestry	0 (0.0)	10 (100)	0 (0.0)	10 (100)
Fishery	6 (0.0)	16 (69.6)	1 (4.4)	23 (100)
Mining	10 (18.2)	44 (80.0)	1 (1.8)	55 (100)
Construction	10 (38.5)	12 (46.2)	4 (15.3)	26 (100)
Manufacturing	237 (38.5)	353 (57.4)	25 (4.1)	615 (100)
Foodstuffs	7 (14.3)	42 (85.7)	0 (0.0)	49 (100)
Textiles	56 (39.2)	83 (58.0)	4 (2.8)	143 (100)
Chemicals	69 (48.3)	72 (50.3)	2 (1.4)	143 (100)
Metal products	48 (41.4)	64 (55.2)	4 (3.4)	116 (100)
Machinery	36 (33.0)	60 (55.0)	13 (12.0)	109 (100)
Miscellaneous	21 (38.2)	32 (58.2)	2 (3.6)	55 (100)
Commerce	214 (51.6)	185 (44.6)	16 (3.8)	415 (100)
Finance	1 (8.3)	10 (83.3)	1 (8.3)	12 (100)
Insurance	2 (50.0)	2 (50.0)	0 (0.0)	4 (100)
Real estate	9 (52.9)	8 (47.1)	0 (0.0)	17 (100)
Transport	6 (12.2)	43 (87.8)	0 (0.0)	49 (100)
Warehouse	11 (52.4)	9 (42.8)	1 (4.8)	21 (100)
Other service	8 (22.2)	28 (77.8)	0 (0.0)	36 (100)
Stockholding	1 (11.1)	8 (88.9)	0 (0.0)	9 (100)
Others	7 (35.0)	12 (60.0)	1 (5.0)	20 (100)
Total	527 (39.5)	760 (56.8)	50 (3.7)	1,338 (100)

Establishment year and viability

According to our short life-cycle hypothesis, older foreign affiliates will exhibit higher mortality than younger affiliates. Table 10.9 shows the relationship between establishment year and their fate.

GTCs had established four foreign affiliates before 1950, sixty affiliates during the 1950s and a further 218 affiliates in the 1960s. Although these numbers are small, nevertheless GTCs led Japanese FDI in this period. GTCs showed their real ability, however, in Japanese FDI of the 1970s: GTCs established 591 affiliates between 1970 and 1974, and 342 in the period 1975

Table 10.8 Location and fate of GTC foreign affiliates

Region	Survivor (%)	Deceased (%)	Withdrawn (%)	Total
East Asia (except China)	37 (28.0)	89 (67.4)	6 (4.6)	132 (100)
ASEAN	168 (49.3)	158 (46.3)	15 (4.4)	341 (100)
Southwest Asia	17 (37.8)	28 (62.2)	0 (0.0)	45 (100)
Oceania	46 (46.0)	53 (53.0)	1 (1.0)	100 (100)
EU	72 (47.4)	71 (46.7)	9 (5.9)	152 (100)
Other Europe	0 (0.0)	4 (100)	0 (0.0)	4 (100)
North America	62 (25.4)	172 (70.5)	10 (4.1)	244 (100)
Latin America	108 (42.9)	137 (54.3)	7 (2.8)	252 (100)
Middle, Near East & Africa	18 (26.5)	48 (70.6)	2 (2.9)	68 (100)
Total	527 (39.5)	760 (56.8)	50 (3.7)	1,338 (100)

Table 10.9 Establishment year and fate of GTC foreign affiliates

Year	Survivor (%)	Deceased (%)	Withdrawn (%)	Total
Before 1950	1 (25.0)	3 (75.0)	0 (0.0)	4 (100)
1950–54	8 (57.1)	6 (42.9)	0 (0.0)	14 (100)
1955–59	29 (63.0)	14 (30.4)	3 (6.6)	46 (100)
1960–64	39 (52.0)	35 (46.7)	1 (1.3)	75 (100)
1965–69	63 (44.0)	69 (48.3)	11 (7.7)	143 (100)
1970–74	205 (34.7)	364 (61.6)	22 (3.7)	591 (100)
1975–79	125 (36.5)	208 (60.8)	9 (2.6)	342 (100)
1980–★	6 (40.0)	9 (60.0)	0 (0.0)	15 (100)
n.a.	52 (48.1)	52 (48.1)	4 (3.8)	108 (100)
Total	527 (39.5)	760 (56.8)	50 (3.7)	1,338 (100)

Note: ★ including establishments which were permitted by local government

to 1979. In short, 69.7 per cent of GTCs' foreign affiliates were established in one decade from 1970 to 1979. Accordingly, Japanese FDI led by GTCs in the 1970s was an epoch-making event (Yasumuro 1984). After this date, however, the number of newly established GTCs' foreign affiliates decreased rapidly. A new peak period did appear in the early 1990s but further discussion of this lies beyond the boundaries of this chapter.[3]

One interesting finding was that a relatively large number of old affiliates established in the 1950s survived. Those established in the 1950–54 period, for example, had a 57.1 per cent survival rate, whilst those in the 1955–59 period had 63 per cent survival rate. The foreign affiliates established in the 1960s also had a longer life with 52 per cent recorded for the years between 1960 and 1964, and 44 per cent in the period from 1965–69.

In contrast to the above, foreign affiliates established in the 1970s showed unfavourable viability: those established in the 1970–74 period show 34.7 per cent survival rate, and those established between 1975 and 1979 showed a 36.5 per cent survival rate. Table 10.9 reveals that viability of GTCs' foreign affiliates decreased year after year, thus the life-cycle hypothesis is not appropriate. Some of the affiliates found their niche successfully and established collaboration with local partners. Yet the majority of them could not maintain the collaborative interests between partners, and their partnerships were dissolved. A successful collaboration between partners will, therefore, be a key to the maintenance of GTCs' foreign affiliates.

To summarise the analysis, it can be concluded that the mortality of the GTCs' foreign affiliates established before 1980 was generally high in any classification such as ownership, size, industrial category and establishment year. No special factor has been identified to explain the high mortality of the GTCs' foreign affiliates.

Market-making investment to create intermediate product markets

Organising intermediate product markets

More than 50 per cent of the GTCs' foreign affiliates established before 1980 extended the termination of their operations from a ten to a fifteen-year life cycle. This period overlapped with the payback of investment. When investors have collected the profit from investment, the aim of the collaborative venture comes to an end. However, GTC agreed on additional investment if the venture proved profitable.

What was the aim of the venture to be achieved within the period that investment yielded a return? Probably the answer lies in the foundation of reliable transaction of intermediate products. In the 1960s and 1970s, host governments of developing countries introduced import restriction and substitution policies. GTCs exporting finished goods to the less developed countries were thus faced with difficulties in the maintenance of market share. As a result, they decided to organise assembling and processing facilities within the country using Japanese small manufacturing firms and local interest groups. Since these ventures consumed a large amount of intermediate products constantly, they contributed to the raw materials and industrial products exported by GTCs. In this situation, GTCs internalised intermediate product transaction vertically through FDI.

Comparisons with British free-standing companies

When industrial markets are immature and imperfect, export of intermediate products contains unexpected transaction risks. Unlike consumer products, transaction of intermediate products requires some technical expertise and professional information, such as specifications, explanatory leaflets, manuals, technological instructions, etc. A complex production facility is usually exported by the turnkey project method. If the industrial capacity of the accepting country is insufficient, GTCs must create an industrial market. FDI becomes a strategic measure.

In this way, GTCs organised the manageable markets and replaced trade negotiations with production planning. As a result, GTCs eliminated the uncertainty which accompanied the export of intermediate products to the less industrialised countries. This is a further factor which explains why GTCs' FDIs were relatively short-lived and unsuccessful in advanced countries such as the United States, where industrial markets already existed.

Another reason which explains the short life of the GTCs' ventures was the limitation of ability to export technology to foreign affiliates. The resource dependence of foreign affiliates upon their partners lessened as the foreign affiliates matured and became independent. As soon as the required intermediate products were standardised and could avoid the GTCs' import channel, local partners and managers sought enthusiastically for cheaper materials, parts and components in the international markets by arm's-length price. Where this occurred, the GTCs' FDI was classified as type B of Casson's typology (Casson 1997: 224).

When the joint venture became independent, local partners and managers procured information for themselves, thus the GTCs' information export also declined. Where a GTC's ownership was inferior to the local partner, the execution of control from headquarters became difficult. Here the case can be classified as type D. When the investment finally arrived at type D, that is, the trusted investment stage, the GTC decided on divestment. Now the GTC could be divested, the affiliate dissolved and their transactions switched to external markets.

Conclusion

Though dissimilarities exist in the historical background and the constituent of clusters of business, many similarities existed between British free-standing companies in the nineteenth century and Japanese GTCs' FDI in the 1960s and 1970s. The analysis can be summarised under the following four points.

First, free-standing-type FDI was based on the human side of business, that is, the interpersonal networks of international business. The logic behind the organisation of free-standing ventures may well have been different from the logic of classic-type investment. Free-standing-type FDI was directed towards a horizontal network and often managed by control without ownership. On the other hand, classic-type FDI was directed towards vertical integration (hierarchy) and pursued control by ownership. Moreover, free-standing-type FDI was open and flexible compared to classic FDI.

Second, trading companies were required to proceed before large manufacturing companies intent on entering foreign markets. Furthermore, if GTCs failed to take the lead, they lost advantages. In contrast to the export of finished goods, export of intermediate products required manufacturing companies which consumed a large amount of industrial goods and services periodically. However, where sufficient local manufacturers did not exist, GTCs had to organise production capacities at their own expense. GTCs also had to internalise local production facilities in order to protect market share from manufacturing multinationals. In this context, service multinationals, such as GTCs, followed the transaction theory paradigm when in competition with other GTCs and manufacturing multinationals.

Third, the major business of GTCs was still in the field of international trade with their profit arising from commercial transactions. As a consequence, they did not expect too much in the way of dividends from foreign affiliates, but expected much from trade surplus. They adopted international transfer prices for intra-company transactions, with profit accruing from trade between foreign affiliates. Preference was for a micro-ownership position (less than 5 per cent) in the joint venture, even where they could have chosen a more advantageous position. The purpose of micro-ownership policy was clearly to solidify relations with local partners and here, long-term contract and micro-ownership policy shared the same ground. GTCs' managers have often called micro-ownership an association or friendship investment and that expresses well the purpose of the policy.

British free-standing companies increased from 1870 and prospered until 1914, just one hundred years ahead of Japanese GTCs' FDI. It is notable that the period of disappearance of British free-standing companies overlapped with the rise of Japanese GTCs. From this viewpoint, it can be asserted that the free-standing type of FDI was not obsolete in Britain, but instead handed over the baton to the Japanese general trading companies. The rationale of free-standing investment was still effective and active.

Fourth, the high mortality of a GTC's foreign affiliates was a logical outcome of its market-making strategy and externalisation of internalised markets – i.e. a shift from transfer pricing policy to arm's-length price. In this context, high mortality does not necessarily mean managerial failure. Very often, the decline of British FDI, especially free-standing companies, has been explained as mismanagement by incompetent British expatriate managers and their weak management structures (Chandler 1990: Chapter 7). However, from the above discussion it can be seen that this is misleading in some cases.

In the early stage of FDI, the market-making type of investment provided indispensable groundwork for the industrial market, especially intermediate product transactions. Service industries, such as Japanese GTCs, have led the classic-type manufacturing multinationals (Yasumuro 1984). When the stable industrial market was completed, classic type MNEs were able to enter into developing countries.

It is necessary to divide FDI phenomena into two categories: service MNE and manufacturing MNE (Boddewyn *et.al.* 1986; Dunning 1988,1989; Enderwick 1989; Jones 1996: 163–6). Some authors have tried to develop a theory of service multinationals by applying the classic theory of manufacturing MNEs (Boddewyn *et.al.* 1986; Dunning 1988,1989). However, an entirely new theory of service MNEs is badly needed. Studies of free-standing companies and GTCs' FDI lead us to the fertile territory of the history and theory of service multinationals.

Acknowledgements

I am most grateful to Geoffrey Jones for suggesting that I write on this topic, and to Geoffrey, T. A. B. Corley, and Mark Casson for illuminating discussions on the subject. I would like to thank Geoffrey Jones for his comments on this chapter and correction of the English.

Notes

1   Ministry of Finance and Ministry of International Trade and Industries (MITI) do not disclose divestment data; parent company name, affiliate name, location of affiliate and amount of equity capital withdrawn, etc., are unknown. Consequently, we cannot obtain the current amount of investment which is defined as divested capital subtracted from the aggregated FDI of the year. The government only discloses aggregated FDI so both net FDI and divestment are unknown in Japanese statistics.

   The only available but unreliable data is the number of equity devolution and investment from 1973 to 1986 (except 1981 because it was not investigated in this year). Accordingly, the data cannot properly represent divestment because, even if the parent company disposed of a part of its equity and still held control of the affiliates, government data counted it as one divestment case. Consequently, government data is inadequate for academic use.

2   The Harvard study group on MNEs estimated divestment rate as follows: the largest US companies had until 1968 abandoned 292 manufacturing affiliates in the EU (15 per cent of their local number of liquidated and expropriated firms), and the largest non-American MNCs had until 1971 withdrawn 306 subsidiaries in the EU (19 per cent of their total number of liquidations) (Bulcke *et.al.* 1980: 2). When we compare GTCs' data with the Harvard study group's classic MNEs' data, the difference is clear.

3   For example, Itochu had nearly 230 affiliates in China by 1997. Of these, 115 affiliates are not yet in operation because most of the affiliates were established or invested after 1990. Another eight GTCs were also invested directly in China and Vietnam after 1993.

References

Boddewyn, J. J., Halbrich, M. B. and Perry A. C. (1986) 'Service multinationals: conceptualisation, measurement and theory', *Journal of International Business Studies*, 16 (2): 41–58.

Buckley, P. J. (1983) 'Macroeconomic versus international business approach to direct foreign investment: a comment on Professor Kojima's interpretation', *Hitotsubashi Journal of Economics*, 24 (1): 95–100.

Buckley, P. J. (1992) *Studies In International Business*, London: St. Martin's Press.

Bulcke, D. Van Den, Boddewyn, J. J., Martens, B. and Klemmer, P. (1980) *Investment and Divestment Policies of Multinational Corporations in Europe*, New York: Praeger.

Casson, M. (1994) 'Institutional diversity in overseas enterprise: explaining the free-standing company', *Business History*, 36 (4): 95–108.

—— (1997) *Information And Organization, A New Perspective on the Theory of the Firm*, Oxford: Clarendon Press.

Chandler, A. D., Jr (1990) *Scale and Scope: The Dynamics of Industrial Capitalism*, Cambridge, Mass.: Harvard University Press.

Davenport-Hines, R. P. T. and Jones, G. (eds) (1989) *British Business in Asia since 1860*, Cambridge: Cambridge University Press.

Dunning, J. H. (1988) *Explaining International Production*, London: Unwin Hyman.

—— (1989) 'Multinational enterprises and the growth of service: some conceptual and theoretical issues', *The Service Industries Journal*, 9 (1): 5–39.

Enderwick, P. (1989) 'Some economics of service-sector multinational enterprises', Enderwick, P. (ed.) *Multinational Service Firms*, London: Routledge.

Hennart, J.-F. (1994a) 'International financial capital transfer: a transaction cost framework', *Business History*, 36 (1): 51–7.

—— (1994b) 'Free-standing firms and the internalization of markets for financial capital: a response to Casson', *Business History*, 36 (4): 118–31.

Horaguchi, H. (1992) *Foreign Direct Investment of Japanese Firms: Investment and Divestment in Asia* (Japanese edn), Tokyo: University of Tokyo Press.

Jones, G. (1996) *The Evolution of International Business*, London: Routledge.

Kojima, K. (1982) 'Macroeconomic versus international business approach to direct foreign investment', *Hitotsubashi Journal of Economics*, 23 (1): 1–19.

Ohtowa, T. (1996) 'Whether a free-standing firm is multinational firm or not?' (in Japanese) *Shougaku Kenkyu* (Kurume University): 137–71.

Yasumuro, K. (1984) 'The contribution of sogo shosha to the multinationalization of Japanese industrial enterprises in the historical perspective', in Akio Okochi and Tadakatsu Inoue (eds) *Overseas Business Activities*, Tokyo: University of Tokyo Press, pp. 65–92.

Yoshino, M.Y. and Thomas, B. L. (1986) *The Invisible Link, Japan's Sogo Shosha and the Organization of Trade*, Cambridge Mass.: MIT Press.

Wilkins, M. (1988a) 'The free-standing company, 1870–1914: an important type of British foreign direct investment', *Economic History Review*, 41 (2): 259–82.

—— (1988b) 'European and North American multinationals, 1870–1914: comparisons and contrasts', *Business History*, 30 (1): 8–45.

11 Is efficiency compatible with history?

Evidence from Japanese general trading companies

Tom Roehl

The new economic history argues that firms and individuals attempt to create new institutional forms when the existing forms are no longer an efficient way to organise their transactions relationships (North 1994). These approaches have been applied by other scholars to the establishment, but not the continued existence, of trading firms (Jones and Ville 1996). It is often argued that the old forms sometimes trap economic actors as the environment changes, making them incapable of adjusting to new environments. Yet institutional forms are often surprisingly durable. Many Japanese general trading companies (GTCs) were formed well over a century ago, and remain important actors on the world economic scene in the 1990s, a period of very rapid environmental change. How can we explain such a phenomenon? It is tempting, especially in the light of the current Japanese economic troubles in the late 1990s, to agree with those who say the GTC and its trading partners are trapped in an institutional relationship which is no longer appropriate, but they simply see no way to disengage.

This is a familiar story, since Japanese authors have been forecasting the demise of these economic institutions for several decades (Misono 1974). Other chapters in this volume also present a similar story to these pessimistic analysts. In some chapters, the colonial past traps a trading firm in the trading rights of that area – trapped in either geography or commodity. It is not able to adjust to the new reality when firms have open access to geographical or commodity markets. Yasumuro in Chapter 10, this volume, on Japanese GTCs also comes in this group, since he argues that the Japanese investments in the United States are not likely to persist as the conditions change. Alternatively, authors of other chapters argue that the only alternative is to ignore history totally, taking the leap from trading to retailing or other downstream activities, taking primarily the profits from the trading company operations. This approach, what strategic management theorists call 'unrelated diversification', implies a strange combination of extreme efficiency and flexibility of the firm: a firm can give up all its old traditions and relationships and yet be successful in a very different area against seemingly more appropriate institutional forms. These approaches seem to ignore the middle ground. Far from guaranteeing success, history can still provide important experience and information a firm can use to create new, and to extend existing relationships. History should be more likely to reward this type of behaviour on the part of economic actors than either of the alternatives: a firm desperate to maintain its monopoly position or a firm willing to attempt, with only the financial support of its earlier successes, moves into entirely new sets of activities.

The Japanese GTC is an example of an institutional form which has been able to utilise this middle road. The Japanese GTC story presented in this chapter, which stands in marked contrast to the other trading companies presented in this volume, is based on this different view of history. For the Japanese general traders, history is *information*, not rights. The information can be about markets it controls (often Japanese domestic markets), as in the colonial market descriptions. But more often, it is information about the markets they *participate in* rather than ones they manipulate, and about clients they *serve* rather than clients they control. Variety in the portfolio of these relationships has value. This is due to the increased flow of information which should result. This is consistent with the analysis in Chapter 12, this volume, by Hennart and Kryda, which finds substantial variety in one kind of GTC relationship, joint ventures in the United States. Close observation of the transactions managed by these Japanese institutions indicates that they are using their history to adapt to the changing needs of the next century. The information 'embedded' in their history (Granovetter 1985) is the basis of their ability to adapt and change.

Trading company history

Japanese GTCs began after the country was opened to the west in the late nineteenth century. There is a rich literature on the history of GTCs. In particular, studies by Yamamura (1976) and by Daito (1976) explain their origins in economic terms, while Yonekawa and Yoshihara (1987) give rich historic detail. Several points are salient in understanding how the Japanese trading companies have been able to accumulate their experience. In international markets, most Japanese firms began from a base in a specific industry. Building on that base in either metals or textiles, the firms gradually built up the variety of activities in which they are now engaged. The path to their 'generalness' thus allowed for a variety of approaches, and a different mix of products for each company and for a company over time.

The second important element is the nature of the trade. Contrary to many of the other trading companies discussed in this volume, the Japanese trading firms were able to develop all three types of trading relationships: domestic, import to Japan and export from Japan. These relationships were already in evidence early in the development of the companies. Even before the turn of the century, Japanese firms dealt in cotton imports from India, managed the often complex relationships within Japan that turned the cotton into apparel, and then sent the final product to European markets. Futures markets were utilised, even in the early stages. As Japanese futures markets were already well developed, participation required less learning than might have been expected. Financial relationships were also necessary, since monies from sales in Europe had to be transferred back to Japan and to India to buy future cotton supplies. The variety of relationships which thus developed, even with transactions involved with a seemingly simple product like textiles, shows the importance of this variety to the companies.

Does Japanese nationality matter?

The bulk of the analysis in this chapter is at the level of the firm, arguing that firms are only able to continue to prosper if they create efficient trading structures that their partners can use. Yet Japanese nationality does matter. The nature of the Japanese market, and the nature of the transactions which the trading companies were allowed to manage *inside* Japan, both make it more likely that we would find this type of trading company in the Japanese economy. History on a country level matters here, though it is only supportive rather than sufficient. Competition and rules both encouraged firms to act to create and maintain these structures.

Competition

The Japanese market has always been large enough for multiple players to find profitable business opportunities. No single firm needs to dominate in order to achieve trading on a world scale. Even within the industrial groups in Japan (what Japanese call *keiretsu*), there was no need to buy all the raw materials or sell all of the output through a single trading channel. In the days before the First World War, Mitsui and Company traded very strongly in cotton and textiles. Yet even at that time, there was another trader of textiles and cotton within the same Mitsui group of companies. Also, Mitsui and Company sold its first large-scale bulk carrier to the United Kingdom shipping line, P&O, not from its own *keiretsu* company, Mitsui Shipbuilding, but from Hitachi Shipbuilding, which had better technology in the late 1950s. From large steel companies to small log processors, the custom of having at least some transactions with competing traders is a long-established pattern in the Japanese market. Even the long-term relationships that the Japanese favour highly are tempered by concerns for competitive prices and service. While Japanese traders would certainly desire the same sort of monopoly position often described in other chapters in this volume, they were seldom able to create such a position, nor hold it for long, in this type of market.

The development of Japanese GTCs predated any government regulations to promote this economic institution. Any firm could take advantage of any export incentives offered by the government. In many other Asian markets, governments often limited the number of trading companies that had access to the export market. This is equivalent to the geographical rights that are often described in other chapters in this volume. While some Japanese firms may have chosen to specialise in particular commodities (Mitsui in the early days, in cotton) and in particular areas of the world (Nichimen, in Eastern Europe), there was no government or other guarantee that automatically gave companies those rights; they had to earn them. Thus firms constantly had to pay attention to potential competitors.

Nor were there any regulations concerning the participation of the GTCs in particular types of transactions. If trading companies are limited in their participation in the domestic market, both efficiency and asset-building will suffer; fewer opportunities to construct useful transactions relationships are available to such a firm. If denied access to the local market for textiles, can a firm easily forecast the local demand for cotton? If a GTC does not know about the skills of various metal-processing firms in the steel industry domestically, how can it be sure that it is a suitable choice when its partner chooses to subcontract some of the work on a ship to these domestic players? Japanese GTCs were fortunate in that the transactions in imports, domestic processing and export of products from Japan had always been available to them throughout their history. Thus, the lack of regulation, and the very lack of trading rights which other chapters in this volume emphasise, are what forces the Japanese GTCs to view history as information. Competition forces each firm to seek efficiency in the management of their transactions relationships or lose the business.

In contrast, many other trading companies described in this volume concentrated only on one geographic area, and often on a narrow range of products. Other trading companies in the United States and in Asian countries which mimicked Japan, limited the types of transactions which the trading firm could handle. US laws allowed anti-trust exemptions only for export transactions. Korean trading firms were developed to compete with their Japanese counterparts (Cho 1987). Korean traders were not, however, allowed to participate in the domestic market in their own country (Fields 1989). Roehl shows that the difference in rules required in Japan and Korea required firms to structure their transactions in different ways (Roehl *et al.* 1984). Chinese firms have only been allowed to partake in this range of activities in the last few years (Wang 1995). Thus, it is not so much history *per se*, but the *richness* of the historical experience that the Japanese firms were allowed by the structure of the Japanese market and by government policy that is important. This Japanese environment makes – or forces – GTCs to be able to effectively use the experience of history for increased business efficiency.

History, efficiency and competitiveness

How can the information embedded in history allow Japanese GTCs to escape from being trapped by their history? Ironically, to achieve this, firms have to be future-oriented. They must not be satisfied with their established position and the established geographical areas in which they currently operate. Once a trading company views its history in this light, the role of the GTCs is in stark contrast to the alternative view of profiting from and protecting existing positions described in many other chapters in this volume. Companies must constantly prove to their trading partners that they are performing efficiently. Yet at the same time, they must use information based on their historical experience to search for new places and new products where they can use that very information. They must also replenish the system that constantly supplies that information.

Efficiency

Now suppose that firms search for efficiency in their transactions relationships. Will this define a different kind of trading institution than when trading rights define the transactions relationship? In this alternative view based on efficiency, a firm does not have the goal of protecting and expanding its trading monopoly rights. Rather, it has quite different goals. First, it must be able to carry out the exchange at the lowest possible cost. Competition for the business forces this concern. A firm with trading rights has to worry less about this issue. Yet lowered cost is not sufficient. We have to drop the assumption that parties must trade with the trading firm, since it has no trading rights. Thus the trading company performs a second function; it must also find a way to structure the exchange so that all participants feel that the exchange was an equitable one. It is often the second concern that requires a trading company to enter a transaction. The trading company's history of relationships, and the commitment of the trading company to 'create' history by pledging to continue relationships frequently allows the trading company to perform these dual functions necessary for transactions efficiency.

Japanese trading companies are usually called *general* trading companies because they handle a wide variety or products ('from missiles to *ramen* (instant noodles)'). Yet when we consider their role from an efficiency perspective, seeking the effective management of trading relationships, the companies are 'general' in another important sense. They manage a wide variety of 'transactions types' effectively, using and creating history in the process.

Oliver Williamson's distinction of transactions types (Williamson 1979) helps us to understand the variety of GTC transactions relationships. Market transactions and subsidiaries (keeping the entire transaction within the firm) are familiar to everyone, but Williamson adds two additional intermediate types which are more important in the role played by the GTC.

The first is *bilateral governance*. Here a firm creates a repetitive transaction when the alternative would be 'once only' transactions between trading partners. This repetition allows more complicated transactions to occur because of the repeated deals. This is more than a search for scale economies. With both sides carrying out transactions together many times, the firms are more confident that the deal is appropriate. Prior experience may allow the trading company to establish a long-term relationship: you don't make long-term deals with people you don't know. So history matters here. History is also created as the trading company establishes a record of consistent trading through this commitment to the long-term relationship.

The second intermediate form, *trilateral governance*, also requires the trading company to use its experience to create a transactions relationship that makes both sides confident of an equitable exchange. Williamson identifies a set of transactions that require a third-party monitor to make sure that both sides will see the deal as being equitable. This happens most frequently when there are large players on both sides of the transaction, or when each side has some ability to influence the distribution of the returns. In the case of trading companies, this could be large suppliers of raw materials and large users of the same materials. It could also be a local firm with strong political connections making a deal with a Japanese supplier. Able only to block the other side, they need to identify an outsider who can, through its commitment to the relationship, make sure that the relationship develops smoothly. Note that in this transaction type, history is again going to be important. Why would you choose an outsider that you don't have confidence in? The commitment also requires that the third-party monitor makes a commitment to the relationship. Without that decision, how can the GTC provide a credible commitment that it will stick around to manage the ongoing repetitive relationship? Here again, a trading company must create history as well as utilise it in its business relationships. Thus, both bilateral governance and trilateral governance are only effective when history can be both used and created by the trading companies as they develop and manage their relationships.

Competitiveness

If trading companies are not automatically given the right to trade, but must continuously earn it, then we need to have a way of analysing how firms develop and exploit their competitive position. A good way to do this is to use a concept from the business strategy literature, the *resource-based* theory of the firm. Good reviews of this line of research can be found in Barney (1976), Mahoney *et. al.* (1992) and Conner (1991). From this point of view, firms need to find ways to develop and maintain their competitive position. Assets that can be duplicated easily by others are not the source of competitive advantage. The firm must somehow find assets that are not easily imitated, even if, as the firm already knows, all assets will inevitably be copied in the future. Itami and Roehl (1987) call these resources 'invisible assets', and assert that only assets based on the flow of information can produce this ability to forestall imitation. The flow of information between the firm and its suppliers and customers, and the flow of information within the firm, are the basis for these assets. Creating a similar source of information flow takes much longer than any other competing source of advantage. The flow of information is also able to be used simultaneously without being used up. Utilisation is necessary to maintain the value of the information flow and the system that maintains it. The information can be used for one activity at one point in time, and also for something quite different over a period of time as well. These invisible assets are what makes a firm attractive in managing the stream of transactions.

History fits in very smoothly with this discussion of invisible assets as well. The experience of the trading firm gives an opportunity to develop the necessary information flow for invisible assets to be built up and maintained. Viewed in this way, history no longer necessarily traps the firm. History has the potential to give the firm the opportunity to develop new relationships and handle new types of transactions based on the historical information background. Thus, the historical experience is a kind of organisational as well as a product 'data base' that the trading company can draw on to continue to play a role in a fast-changing business environment. Obviously, a firm can destroy the value of its invisible assets. Yet a trading company is no longer, in this view, destined to decline. It can use its invisible assets and continue to find new uses for them and new ways to further strengthen its information base.

In the sections that follow, we show how Japanese GTCs have used these principles to maintain a significant position in Japanese trading relationships over time.

Japanese GTC trading relationships: building on history

Japanese GTCs have demonstrated an ability to change the nature of their activities, both in products and in the nature of the transactions they handle, as the Japanese economy and the world economy has evolved. They have used the experience gained from their history to develop new ways to maintain and expand their customer base. We can see good examples of this using both the Williamson transactions efficiency approach and the invisible asset approach.

Using history for transactions efficiency

Markets can make redundant more complicated, personal relationships. Yet, as more efficient markets develop for many of the products handled by the traders, we do not see the GTC role diminish that significantly. Instead, trading companies combine markets and relationships, using their knowledge of both.

Financing has become a rather efficient market, and we would thus expect history to be of less value to the GTC in handling financial transactions. A financial transaction is often a combination of several markets, however. With no formal market for used aircraft, one GTC can use its historical experience serving JAL to develop a new product that prices the used aircraft at the end of a lease. Even when there are efficient markets operating in most of the areas where firms want to put together a complex transaction, if one inefficient market exists, that inefficient market creates the potential for a new role for the GTC, a role that is based on the GTC's historical experience, and helps all sides structure the complex transaction.

Markets often pressure firms to increase their transaction efficiency. Small domestic steel firms, faced with low-cost competitors from abroad, want to search for ways to remain competitive. A firm in south Japan and one in north Japan could have customers near one another's plants. They could reduce transportation and improve delivery by serving each other's customers. They are unlikely to know about the opportunity. Trading companies, knowing both firms and their customers, can suggest the exchange, and help structure the exchange so that both sides will benefit. Their thorough knowledge based on the history of trading with both firms allows the GTC to suggest the appropriate terms for the exchange.

Sometimes markets allow the trading company and the customers to ensure that the trade was carried out properly by the GTC. Steel companies allow several GTCs to buy tin for them in Malaysia, where there is an established market. They then check the prices in the Penang market over the month and see which GTC got them the best prices on average, rewarding the one that got the best prices with a bigger share next time. The steel firms get both the benefits of markets and the benefits of their historical relationships with the GTCs. Here markets give a 'history' to help assure performance.

Williamson's bilateral governance often requires information from history also. To make these bilateral relationships work, they must have what Williamson calls 'durability'. The GTC provides durability with its long-standing relationships with the parties, and with the commitment to further develop them. The GTC makes a commitment to buy coal from Australian mines. Without the experience of dealing with the steel companies in Japan and also with the shipping companies that would ship the coal, the GTC would not be able to make a bid to buy the coal.

Trading companies are becoming increasingly involved in selling electric power, instead of merely supervising the sale of power plant equipment around the world. The former relationship of selling plant equipment makes the traders worry about their performance in this new area. The trading company can turn the relationship into a more durable one by participating in the ongoing sale of power. Having done this, the power plant sale is easier to manage. If it doesn't work, the GTC does not sell any power. Its knowledge of markets in several countries, and its experience with all the players in power plant construction, allows the GTC to make a credible promise to potential customers.

Trilateral governance, however, gives the most opportunity for the GTC to use the knowledge from the history of transactions relationships. The more conventional neutral mediator has no say in the outcome. In contrast, the GTC uses its knowledge of the entire relationship to create an outcome that both sides can have confidence in. When the transaction monitoring requires substantial knowledge of the deal, a history of dealing with the parties, as opposed to strict neutrality, becomes more important for monitoring.

When two rival companies wish to establish closer relationships, the trading company may be able to help them establish these ties. Two chemical firms in one industrial group were of relatively equal size, but both were not particularly competitive in the global marketplace. The GTC helped them to jointly purchase a foreign plant. The two firms learned to work more closely together in the process. The increased competitiveness due to the closer cooperation led to higher GTC trading commissions. The long experience in dealing with both firms helped the GTC to mediate with the inevitable problems in the new venture. Note that if the venture fails, the GTC has lost valuable trading rights in the chemicals market, so there is strong incentive for the GTC to make it work.

When participants cannot check in the markets to find out the appropriate price for the things they want to exchange, someone needs to guarantee the quality of the unfamiliar product, firm, or product characteristic. With CIS metal from former Soviet Union smelters, the output is unpredictable. Trading companies guarantee, using various metal market contracts, that the manufacturers of aluminium products will be able to serve their customers when they use CIS metal. GTC utilise a long history of relationships in aluminium around the world to make their offer of monitoring credible.

Another trading company developed a system to send songs via satellite to *karaoke* bars. It had US experience in developing chips capable of compression. It has developed those chips to speed up its entry into the CATV market in Japan. The GTC had worked with software companies in Japan that added the necessary experience in Chinese characters. Telecommunications equipment vendors were familiar to the GTC as well, via its CATV activities. The GTC would get paid at least in part by transmitting the songs to the *karaoke* bars, so that if the system does not end up being competitive, its return from the venture would be low. Using its knowledge from working with the various partners, the GTC was able to carry out the venture.

For all types of transactions, a trading company can build on its history of trading relationships to make complex transactions feasible. The history itself enables the company to ensure that the relationship is handled properly. A new entrant or a market is not always able to match the value of those a GTC offers to its customer.

Trading company history and competitive advantage: building and using information assets

Trading companies will often lose the specific trading rights which they have initially developed. Plant equipment firms that have repeated transactions in a single country may find that their partners deal directly with them. Trading relationships in the export of textiles may disappear as the Japanese supplier becomes less competitive in the market place. Thus firms must (a) find ways to build up new assets; and (b) find new ways to use the information flow from their historical operations. Without these efforts, the trading rights will be as ephemeral as the trading monopoly rights described in other chapters of the book.

Trading companies have been able to use their information-flow assets in different geographical areas and in different product areas over time. Each time they lay down a new set of information-based capabilities for future use.

By the late 1980s, most GTCs had substantial experience in developing joint ventures and in buying foreign companies. As other firms followed them to foreign markets, their partner firms needed advice on investments in foreign manufacturing. One trading company set up a company to provide advice on a fee basis to utilise their knowledge base on structuring market-entry strategies. Not only did they find customers for the service, but they expanded their knowledge base by working with American customers as well, and also by expanding their relationships with investment bankers. The unit, once established, could bid on work related to privatisation in the former Soviet Union. The company's earlier interests in energy in that area gave them the information basis to participate in these activities. Ironically, this service is now finding more business in selling Japanese subsidiaries to foreigners, but here again the experience of the GTC, which aggressively sold off non-performing subsidiaries earlier, provides an information base for the investment advisory service unit. Trading led to management services, which allowed for contacts with a new customer base, both in the United States and in Eastern Europe.

In its raw materials sourcing units, GTCs have always been involved in the major commodity exchanges, hedging exposure and operating on their own account. This experience has enabled at least one GTC to become involved in the management of a commodities mutual fund for individual investors. The knowledge which was originally used to serve industrial customers is thus simultaneously used to develop a new customer base.

One trading company had a worldwide reputation in textiles going back over many decades. So when the market for textiles moved from exporting to importing into Japan, this company was able to use its information network abroad to find ways to structure a new set of transactions. Knowledge of foreign suppliers was important in the extremely seasonal garment business in the domestic market. This company had always handled products with the other company's name in the overseas export market to provide timely delivery of complex textile products to the US and European markets. With the information from these relationships in hand, they could identify the appropriate firms to produce for the now open Japanese garment market. The company committed itself to using the production facilities of these firms, which were mostly based in China. It then found orders to match its contracted capacity. Their reputation and their experience in managing international production of textiles gave local Chinese firms the confidence to deal with them. The GTC was thus able to assure access to low-cost reliable production for Japanese firms they had not served before. The new relationships built in China will enable the firm to continue to play an important role in its traditional arena in textiles, even as the flow of goods reverses and trade between third countries becomes increasingly important.

History does not always enable the companies to develop new assets. This is especially true when the trading rights are assigned to a trading company. Trading companies were given the quota rights to import beef into Japan. Because of these rights, the firms were always able to get business. Without the incentive to expand volume, and with profits guaranteed, there was less investment in the information-based assets that would let the GTC develop new businesses. When the quotas were dropped in the early 1990s, the companies were not able to develop new or innovative relationships to match the new environment. Political change due to US pressure made the asset base easy to imitate, and thus vulnerable. Here history mattered, but because of the undeveloped nature of the information flow in the earlier period, the trading companies were not able to expand their business in the new environment. Their historical assets have much less value in the changed environment, and their role is primarily limited to logistics, with correspondingly smaller profits.

Conclusion

History, rather than necessarily restricting trading, can be the source of new competitive advantages for firms which 'learn' from their experiences and search for new ways to utilise the experience of history for their trading clients. The continued existence of Japanese GTCs is strong evidence that the value of the information embedded in history has important economic and competitive value for the firms which make the effort to build on that history. Neither markets nor alternative economic institutions are able to duplicate the information this history provides to conscientious participants. In the battle for the trades of the twenty-first century, it is dangerous to underestimate the value of information accumulated in the past. Markets and new institutions do not have the baggage of history, but sometimes the baggage includes some well-hidden, even invisible, competitive information-flow weapons that will keep old institutions competitive in the new environment.

Acknowledgements

Support for this chapter was provided by the Center for International Business Education and Research, College of Commerce, University of Illinois, Urbana Champaign and the Department of Agricultural Economics, University of Illinois at Urbana Champaign. I would also like to thank the ESRC for contributing towards my travel and other expenses to attend the Reading Conference.

References

Barney, J. B. (1996) 'The resource-based theory of the firm', *Organization Science*, 7: 469–76.

Cho, D.-S. (1987) *The General Trading Company*, Lexington, Mass: Lexington Books.

Conner, K. R. (1991) 'An historical comparison of resource-based theory and five schools of thought within industrial organization economics', *Journal of Management* 17: 121–54.

Daito, E. (1976) 'Why are they general trading firms?' *Japanese Economic Studies*, 4: 44–62.

Fields, K. J. (1989) 'Trading companies in South Korea and Taiwan: two policy approaches', *Asian Survey*, 1073–89.

Granovetter, M. (1985) 'Economic action and social structure: the problem of embeddedness', *American Journal of Sociology* 91: 481–510.

Itami, H. and Roehl, T. W. (1987) *Mobilizing Invisible Assets*, Cambridge, Mass: Harvard University Press.

Jones, S. R. H. and Ville, S. P. (1996) 'Efficient transactions or rent-seeking monopolists? The rationale for early chartered trading companies', *Journal of Economic History*, 56: 898–915.

Mahoney, J.T., Pandian, T. and Rajendron, J. (1992) 'The resource-based view of the firm with the conversation of strategic management', *Strategic Management Journal* 13: 363–80.

Misono, H. (1974) 'Shosha shayoron: sairon', *Ekonomisuto* 42: 6–20.

North, D. C. (1994) 'Economic performance through time,' *American Economic Review*, 84: 359–68.

Roehl, T. W. (1983) 'A transactions cost approach to international trading structures: the case of the Japanese general trading companies', *Hitotsubashi Journal of Economics*, 24: 119–35.

Roehl, T. W., Chee, P.L. and Cho, K. R. (1984) 'Patterns in Asia–Pacific trading structures: testing marketing and transactions cost approaches in an Asia–Pacific context', in Moxon, R., Frederick Truitt, J. and Roehl, T.W. (eds) *International Business Strategies in the Asia–Pacific Region*, New York: JAI Press: 67–118.

Wang, Y. (1995) 'China's first sogoshosha', *Beijing Review* 38: 32.

Williamson, O. (1979) 'Transactions cost economics: the governance of contractual relations', *Journal of Law and Economics*, 22: 233–61.

Yamamura, K. (1976) 'General trading companies in Japan: their origins and growth,' in Patrick, H. (ed.) *Japanese Industrialization and its Social Consequences*, Berkeley: University of California Press.

Yonekawa, S. and Yoshihara, H. (eds) (1987) *Business History of General Trading Companies*, Tokyo: University of Tokyo Press.

12 Why do traders invest in manufacturing?

*Jean-François Hennart and
Georgine M. Kryda*

Why do traders invest in manufacturing? In this chapter we argue that the manufacturing investments of traders result from their efforts to secure the custom of manufacturers. As markets mature and information diffuses, trading companies risk being bypassed by their customers. One defence is to take an equity stake in them to guarantee their trading rights. Because the goal of these investments is to tie customers, not to exploit advantages, such stakes are likely to be minority ones.

A second defence for trading companies faced with the decreasing value of their contribution as industries mature is to orchestrate the development of new value chains whose trade they will handle. The superior intelligence of trading companies gives them a comparative advantage in this task. Their broader viewpoint and their ability to structure the whole chain reduce the risk they face in financing new businesses. Setting up the chain will lead them to invest strategically in selected stages of the chain. All of these investments will serve to support trading.

As markets in these value chains mature, trading companies will sell their minority stakes to their manufacturing partners, either because they are in danger of losing the trade of their affiliates, or because they can cash in on their investment while still safeguarding their trading rights. The resulting pattern of trading company investments in manufacturing should be one of short-lived minority investments that are eventually sold back to their majority joint venture partners.

This chapter checks this story against the pattern of stakes taken by Japanese trading companies in all manufacturing affiliates that were active in the United States in 1980. We find that, compared to the stakes taken by non-trading Japanese investors, trading companies had a preference for minority stakes. The manufacturing stakes of Japanese trading companies were also shorter lived and more likely to be sold to their majority partners than was the case for non-trading investors.

We start this chapter by considering the fundamental logic of trading companies, and how this logic leads them to invest in manufacturing. The second section describes the investments made by 1980 by Japanese trading companies in US manufacturing subsidiaries and finds support for our speculations. In the third section we trace these investments to 1989 and find that they are shorter lived than those of non-trading Japanese investors. Our conclusions are presented in the fourth section.

Why do trading companies invest in manufacturing?

Trading companies are brokers who link buyers with sellers. Traders can also be resellers when they take title to the underlying commodities or goods. In Chapter 2, this volume, Mark Casson describes the types of activities into which trading firms (either brokers or resellers) can integrate (e.g., production, transportation, financial services), and the range of markets, defined by product and/or geography, over which they can diversify their operations. Here our concern is why they integrate into manufacturing.

The business of trading companies can be described in static and dynamic terms. In terms of statics, trading companies attempt to satisfy buyers' demands for goods and services and to identify customers for existing output. To fulfil this function, traders typically invest in a sophisticated proprietary intelligence network that allows them to identify exchange opportunities at lower cost than would be available to individual manufacturers. Trading companies often manage and finance the actual transportation of products from seller to buyer. They often own transport infrastructure (ships, trucks, docks, warehouses) and play an important role in the financing of exports and of new projects. Often they take equity stakes in their suppliers and customers. Why they take such stakes in manufacturing firms can be understood by considering the central characteristics of trading.

One fundamental aspect of the trading company's business is that it is continually threatened with extinction. Once traders reveal their information by pairing a buyer and a seller, the clients can deal directly with each other. Direct interaction between buyers and sellers, especially in stable markets, can save on trading commissions. The bargaining position of the trading company thus becomes weaker as clients become better informed, and they will be forced to accept lower commissions if they want to keep the business. In late 1996 and early 1997, for example, Japanese steel companies (Kawasaki Steel Corp., Sumitomo Metal Industries, Ltd., Nippon Steel Corp.) lowered their commission payments to their respective trading companies and reduced their interest payments by cancelling prepayment arrangements with the traders ('Steelmakers . . . ', *The Nikkei Weekly*, 2 September 1996, 34 (1738): 9). These steel companies and other manufacturers who are the principal clients of Japanese trading firms 'increasingly deal directly with customers and handle import procedures and domestic sales' (T. Anzai 'Holding companies by any other name', *The Nikkei Weekly*, 20 January 1997, 35 (1757): 9). The threat of replacing traders provides these firms with enough bargaining power to negotiate lower commissions.

Faced with this threat to their livelihood, trading companies have four main defences. First, the minimum efficient scale of trading is sometimes larger than that of manufacturing. This was one of the reasons for the emergence of Japanese trading companies. The small textile firms for which they handled exports were too small to afford and to make full use of an exclusive network of sales agencies abroad. Trading companies could efficiently pool the exports of many small textile firms and handle them at much lower cost than those that would have to be paid by each firm if they handled their exports on their own.

A second defence is for the trading company to gain a stronghold on distribution infrastructure in order to prevent buyers and sellers from bypassing them. For example, in autumn 1990, the Japanese trading company Mitsui allied with the Japanese trucking firm Tonami Transportation to buy a US $40 million stake in Airborne Express (USA). With a credit line from Mitsui of up to US$100 million for aircraft financing, Mitsui, Tonami and Airborne Express created Airborne Express Japan. Airborne provides Mitsui with a global air cargo network (Brazier 1994).

Third, trading companies can take an equity stake in both suppliers and customers so as to be able to veto being dropped as an intermediary. This rationale for taking equity positions in upstream and downstream activities appears systematically in the company histories of trading firms (in the case of Metallgesellschaft in Chapter 4). Japanese trading companies have followed the same strategy. For example, the Japanese trading company Marubeni owns 65 per cent of a yarn-making company in Shanghai and 50 per cent of the company that dyes the yarn. Marubeni has smaller stakes in both a blanket manufacturer and another yarn supplier in China (Sender 1996a).

A more radical defence is to abandon mature, stable industries and to orchestrate the creation of new value-added chains. Trading companies can then get commissions for the trade flows that will be generated by these new businesses. This was the strategy followed by nineteenth-century British trading companies when they took the lead in developing South East Asia rubber plantations: the trading companies acted as selling agents for the rubber of the companies they helped set up and as exclusive importing agents for the inputs the plantations needed. We can observe Japanese trading companies doing the same thing. Consider the role played by the Japanese trading firm of Mitsubishi in setting up Kentucky Fried Chicken Japan. In the mid-1960s, Mitsubishi was the leading Japanese importer (and domestic distributor) of animal and chicken feeds made of corn and milo.

> Mitsubishi took the initiative in starting large broiler farms in Japan, at first mainly as the captive customers of Mitsubishi corn and milo feeds. In order to find captive markets for their increased chicken feed business, the trading firm continued to open broiler farms around the major cities in Japan. . . . Mitsubishi broiler farms continued to increase the supply of broilers so much that by around 1967 the trading firm was saddled with surplus broiler meats. One logical way around this problem was to create an expanding and new demand for broilers.
>
> (Tsurumi 1977:249)

Mitsubishi's headquarters in Tokyo cabled its Chicago office to obtain suggestions for increasing chicken consumption in Japan and requested that it identify the largest consumer of chicken in the US. The Chicago office found that this was Kentucky Fried Chicken (KFC) and contacted the firm. It took three years for the two parties to reach an agreement, but in 1970 KFC Japan was founded with Mitsubishi and KFC each owning 50 per cent (Tsurumi 1977). In the following two decades the joint venture opened more than 900 outlets in Japan. In August 1990, 36 per cent of the company was sold at a handsome profit on Tokyo's stock market ('The Giants that Refused to Die' *The Economist*, 1 June 1991, pp. 72–3).

There are two points to note in the preceding example. First, setting up new industries requires an ability to see the big picture, to look at the whole value chain from upstream suppliers to downstream customers, from corn growers to fast-food patrons. The vast intelligence networks of Japanese trading companies allow them to view the entire value chain in a way a bank may not. Second, even if individual buyers and sellers are aware of the profitability of the new value chain, they may not possess sufficient internal resources to fund the new venture. They would have to approach banks for loans. For reasons we now consider, trading companies are in a much better position than banks to finance these new value chains. This comparative advantage of trading companies in funding new, speculative activities explains their integration into financing, and, more to the point, their strategic minority investments in manufacturing ventures.

Traditional neoclassical economics ignores the intermediation role of trading companies because it assumes perfect information and enforcement, i.e., zero transaction costs (see Chapter 2, this volume). The same assumptions of zero transaction costs must be dropped if one is to understand the role played by trading companies in financing new, speculative businesses.

Lending money is characterised by high transaction costs because, in contrast to many other transactions, the two parts of a lending transaction are not simultaneous. Money is lent today to be repaid in the future. Money is also fungible and can be used for purposes that differ from those approved by the lender. Finally, incentives in a loan transaction are not symmetrical. The lender bears the brunt of default costs if the venture fails. A borrower's loss of reputation is supposed to curb such dishonesty, but in the case of lending, such reputation effects are weak because it is often difficult to know whether the borrower's default was due to dishonesty or ineptitude and/or to poor business conditions.

With perfect information, lenders could screen out risky ventures and dishonest or incapable borrowers. Perfect enforcement would discourage borrowers from taking undue risks and defaulting. In the real world, lenders will be forced to fall back on three second-best strategies: screening borrowers and projects, controlling the use of borrowed funds and securing collateral.

By screening out risky projects and unknown applicants, lenders concentrate on safe projects presented by well-known borrowers with solid track records. The chances of securing a loan are practically zero for the potential borrower who has a less than sterling record or who is not personally known by the lender.

Restricting the use of funds to purposes specifically authorised by the lender is another possible strategy, but it has two limitations. First, banks in some countries can only control expenditures *ex post*. Second, banks may have insufficient knowledge of what expenditures are necessary to carry out the proposed business. The more unconventional the proposed business and the more volatile its environment, the more likely that tight bank monitoring will be ineffectual.

Banks could require the borrower to pledge collateral that will be forfeited should the borrower fail to repay the loan. That collateral may consist of assets held by guarantors or of the assets financed by the loan itself. Prospective borrowers may vary greatly in their ability to get wealthy individuals to serve as guarantors. Projects will also vary greatly in the extent to which they provide collateral (Williamson 1988).

Return now to our earlier example, and consider the situation of an individual who seeks in the early 1960s to borrow money from a Japanese bank to raise chickens in Japan. If the prospective borrower has not had prior (successful) dealings with the bank, then he or she will have almost no chance of passing the screening process. Raising chickens is a new business to the bank, so the bank is unable to specify appropriate uses for its funds. Hen houses are poor collateral because they have few alternative uses.[1]

A trading company will be in a better position than a bank to lend to this individual. It will look at the business that will be generated by the chicken grower, its purchases of grain from the trading company and its sales of chicken to its fast food business. The traders' strong international network of contacts in upstream and downstream activities provides them with deeper and broader perspectives on the industry than those of banks. For example, trading companies can tap the expertise of their US affiliates to get information on the prospects and success factors of raising broiler chickens on a large scale. Through participation in all stages of the value-added chain, from grain trading to restaurants, a trading company can configure the chain to minimise risk. It can structure its loans, monitor the use of its funds and construct contingency plans more effectively than a bank. Hence, the trader's outlook on growing chickens will be better informed than the bank's (Roehl 1983).

The costs of using collateral will also be lower to the trading company than to the bank because the trading company could operate the business itself, at least for a while, should the lender default. Last, a trading company can take an equity stake in the business to which it lends in order to get inside information. Hence, we would expect trading companies to be in an excellent position to provide financing to help develop newly emerging industries.

It is also important to consider the point of view of our prospective borrower. The entrepreneur's reward is the difference between the return and the repayment obligation, so the venture requires customers as well as capital.

This problem of creating demand is especially acute in the case of new products for which uses are not yet established. A trading company can motivate the borrower by guaranteeing customers. The trader can support these guarantees in two ways. First, repayment of the loan can be contingent on effective sales to the trader.[2] Second, the trader can take equity in the supplier.

The amount of the trading company's equity investment required to assure the supplier is inversely related to how well established the business is. At one extreme, if the venture is extremely risky, the trading company may have to supply all of the equity. The need for such reassurance (i.e. equity holding) by the trader decreases with time and with the supplier's increasing familiarity with his customers and with the market. At the same time, the trading company will also want to reduce its stake in the supplier so as to be able to redeploy its resources towards emerging fields and more diffident suppliers. Selling its stake will allow the trading company to cash in on its foresight.

The preceding section suggests that trading companies will take equity in suppliers and customers for the three main reasons surveyed above: (1) to prevent their customers from bypassing their services; (2) to monitor the use of funds they have lent to them; and (3) to incite suppliers and/or customers to start new businesses.[3]

How much equity would we expect trading companies to take? Trading companies make money on commissions earned on the trade they facilitate, so their goal is to generate new trade or to consolidate their hold on old trade, not to earn money on their manufacturing investments.[4]

Taking majority or full equity positions would have two deleterious effects for trading companies. First, the more resources devoted to one affiliate, the less that can be invested elsewhere. Second, taking a 100 per cent ownership stake in a manufacturing firm weakens the incentives for the former owners, as they no longer have a strong claim on the profit stream for which they would otherwise be responsible. The less the trader knows about the business, the greater the opportunity for the employees to shirk. Hence, it makes sense for the trading company to own as little as possible of any given manufacturing firm.

On the other hand, the trading company will want to hold enough of the manufacturer's shares to retain the contract to buy from and/or to sell to that firm. Trading companies will also want to hold enough of the stock of new suppliers to persuade them to produce the needed supply. Last, trading companies may end up owning more of their manufacturing suppliers/customers than they like because the traders took the firm as collateral or because they are unable to sell off their shares in emerging firms and recover their capital.

The manufacturing investments of Japanese trading companies in the United States

The crux of the preceding argument is that trading companies invest in manufacturing to: (1) safeguard their right to handle the trade of existing manufacturing customers; and (2) help establish new manufacturers who will need their services. Because their goal is to secure trading rights, not to invest in manufacturing, the traders' stakes should typically be minority ones. Their stakes in manufacturing firms are likely to decrease with the passage of time for two main reasons: first, because their stake in emerging firms is especially crucial at initial stages, but can be safely sold when the business takes off; and second, because their role as trade intermediary loses its importance as markets become more established and having a stake in a customer may no longer be sufficient to guarantee them trading rights.

The preceding suggests that we should observe systematic differences between the stakes taken in US manufacturing firms by traditional manufacturing multinationals and those taken by trading companies. Stakes taken by trading companies should be principally minority ones, while a higher percentage of those of manufacturing multinationals should be full ones. The evolution of these stakes should also be different. Traditional manufacturing firms enter foreign countries through minority stakes to learn about foreign markets from their local partners. Once they acquire this knowledge they typically transform these partial stakes into wholly-owned subsidiaries. On the other hand, the typical evolution of the manufacturing investments of trading companies should be one of stability or decrease. When stakes of traders are wound up, they should be through a sale to the former joint venture partner. Minority stakes of non-trading firms are more likely to disappear because of the bankruptcy of the affiliate, or because of the sale of the stake to a third party.

Table 12.1 shows the distribution of the 370 Japanese equity stakes taken at entry in the 313 Japanese-owned affiliates that were manufacturing in the United States on 31 December 1980.[5] Seventy-one of these stakes (19 per cent of the total) were held by Japanese trading companies and 299 (81 per cent of the total) by Japanese non-trading investors. Mitsui was the trading company with the largest number of US manufacturing stakes (27), followed by Marubeni (10) and Mitsubishi (7). 61 per cent of the equity stakes taken at entry by Japanese trading companies were minority ones, compared to 20 per cent for Japanese non-trading companies. Thus, the pattern of manufacturing investments by Japanese trading companies differs significantly from that of their non-trading counterparts in so far as it consists principally of minority equity stakes. Table 12.2 shows the ownership patterns of the 54 equity stakes Japanese trading companies took in US manufacturing affiliates in 1988–89. Trading companies were even more apt to use minority investment in this later period.

What is the logic of these trading company investments? Most of them are joint ventures with Japanese and/or American firms. All of them have been made to expand trade: trade between Japan and the US, and increasingly between the United States and the rest of the world. Japanese trading companies have invested in US manufacturing firms to expand or to replace traditional Japanese exports to the United States. Typical of this first category

Table 12.1 Japanese equity stakes at entry, affiliates in business in 1980

Equity Stake at Entry	Trading Company		Non-Trading Company		Total	
	no.	%	no.	%	no.	%
Minority	43	60.6	61	20.4	104	28.1
50	6	8.4	22	7.4	28	7.6
Majority	7	9.8	36	12.0	43	11.6
100	15	21.2	180	60.2	195	52.7
Total	71	100.0	299	100.0	370	100.0

Table 12.2 Japanese trading company equity stake at entry for affiliates in business in 1980 and for new entries in 1988–89

Equity Stake at Entry	1980 population (at entry)		Entries in 1988–89	
	no.	%	no.	%
Minority	43	60.6	40	74.0
50	6	8.4	2	3.7
Majority	7	9.8	0	0.0
100	15	21.2	11	20.4
Unknown★	0	0.0	1	1.9
Total	71	100.0	54	100.0

Note: ★ The one unknown entry in 1988–89 is Mitsubishi Freestate Class

are their investments in steel service centres and in steel mini-mills. In the 1970s Japanese trading companies helped Japanese steel manufacturers establish steel mini-mills in America and took a minority stake in these investments. Examples in our database are Auburn Steel in Maine (Sumitomo and Kyoei Steel) and Tamco in California (Mitsui and Tokyo Steel). Setting up mini-mills in the US was a clever way of avoiding trade barriers, as they made use of two inputs, electricity and scrap metal, that were cheaper in the United States than in Japan (Christelow 1995:95). Later, in the early to mid-1980s, Japanese trading companies, occasionally with minor participation by Japanese steel companies, set up in the United States a number of steel service centres to cut and blank steel imported from Japan or made in Japanese-owned plants in the US. These centres supply the trading companies' automotive customers, both Japanese transplants and the US Big Three (Kenney and Florida 1993:184–5).

A second reason for the stakes taken by Japanese trading companies in US manufacturing was to develop American exports to Japan. Japanese trading companies, well aware of Japanese needs and of US cost conditions, were in a position to link US firms with Japanese customers. To stimulate American exports, they have taken strategic stakes in US firms. Aluminium production is energy-intensive. Japanese firms have typically relied on oil-fired power plants, while US producers have used hydroelectricity. The 1974 oil shock hit domestic Japanese producers harder than their American counterparts. Consequently, Mitsui and Nippon Steel purchased half of the aluminium business of Amax, an American firm, and set up Alumax as a joint venture to supply their Japanese customers with primary aluminium and other aluminium products (Christelow 1995:95). Similarly, Japanese trading companies, such as Marubeni, set up in the 1970s fish canneries and freezing plants in Alaska (Wilkins 1994). These plants tap abundant stocks of previously unused fish, such as pollock and arrowtooth flounder, to produce *surimi* and other fish products for Japanese and other customers (Chojnaki 1997). More recently, Japanese trading companies have taken strategic stakes in American high-tech firms. Mitsui, for example, has set up a joint venture with a Massachusetts manufacturer of high-tech medical devices and secured approval of the Japanese Ministry of Health for imports of that firm's medical lasers into Japan (Carlson 1989).[6]

The pattern of Japanese trading company investment we observe in the US thus fits the logic described earlier. Japanese traders have taken minority equity stakes in US and/or Japanese concerns to protect their trading rights and to motivate suppliers and customers to invest in new value chains.

Evolution of trading company manufacturing investments

As industries mature, suppliers gain confidence, clients deal directly with each other, and the trading company identifies new areas for investment, we would expect equity holdings by Japanese trading companies in US-based manufacturers to decrease. In contrast, conventional foreign direct investment theory would predict that Japanese non-trading investors would joint venture to tap the locals' knowledge of the host country and, eventually, would take full control of the venture (Stopford and Wells 1972). The general trend for traders should be to hold or divest their equity whereas non-trading investors should generally increase their stakes.

Table 12.3 shows the evolution of equity stakes of both trading and non-trading investors. We define decrease or increase in the level of the ownership stake as passage to a different ownership category with the categories defined as follows:

Zero	=	under 5 per cent
Minority	=	5 per cent and over, but less than 49.5 per cent

50	=	49.5–50.5 per cent
Majority	=	over 50.5 per cent and less than 95 per cent
100	=	95–100 per cent

For example, a stake that goes from 48 to 50 is coded as increasing, while one that jumps from 10 to 48 is coded as unchanged. This is consistent with the fact that the impact of ownership level on control is highly discontinuous across ownership levels (Hennart 1991).

Japanese trading companies did decrease their equity stakes.[7] The sharpest difference between the two categories is in the proportion of equity stakes that goes to zero, 41 per cent in the case of trading companies versus only 17 per cent in the case of non-trading investors.[8] Adding the number of decreases across categories that are shy of complete divestment to the number of complete exits, the results are 40.8 per cent for trading companies versus 18.4 per cent for non-trading investors. Inversely, the percentage of ownership links that increased was higher in the case of non-trading (10.0 per cent) than in the case of trading companies (8.5 per cent). [9]

What explains the large number of Japanese trading company stakes going down to zero? The simplest explanation is that the affiliate in which the trading company has a stake experiences difficulties, and must be liquidated. Trading companies may also end up selling their stake to their majority

Table 12.3 Changes in Japanese equity stakes in US manufacturing affiliates, from entry to 1989

Change in Equity, Entry-1989	Trading Company		Non-Trading Company		Total	
	no.	*%*	*no.*	*%*	*no.*	*%*
To Zero	29	40.8	51	17.1	80	21.6
Decrease across categories	0	0.0	4	1.3	4	1.1
Subtotal, Decrease across categories	29	40.8	55	18.4	84	22.7
No change across categories	36	50.7	214	71.6	250	67.6
Subtotal, Decrease or No change across categories	65	91.5	269	90.0	334	90.3
Increase across categories	6	8.5	30	10.0	36	9.7
Total	71	100.0	299	100.0	370	100.0

partners. There are three possible scenarios here. Trading companies may be 'booted out' when their expertise is no longer needed (Hayashi and Robock 1982). Trading companies may also find that the investments they made to secure sources of supply are no longer needed, and that they can sell back their equity stake to their partner and still safeguard their trading rights. This divestment also liberates funds for investments in new ventures. Hence Mitsui sold its 45 per cent stake in Alumax back to Amax in 1986 and replaced it with a long-term supply contract (see Chapter 11, this volume). While a trader could sell its stake to a third party, we would expect that most trading companies will divest by selling their stake to their majority joint venture partner. This is because the majority partner probably has the right of first refusal on the trading company's shares and because the trader will seek to continue to handle the trade of its erstwhile partner. This would be more difficult if the stake were sold to a third party.

In contrast, and as was stated above, the non-trading Japanese investor is more likely to increase ownership in affiliates. Exit is more likely to result from adverse economic conditions or from errors made at entry. Hence, we expect a higher proportion of non-trading company exits to be due to liquidation/bankruptcy and a lower proportion to be due to sales than will be the case for trading companies.

Table 12.4 shows how minority equity stakes in our database were unwound by their parents. A higher percentage (87.1 per cent) of the minority stakes held by trading companies were sold to their majority partner than in the case of non-trading Japanese investors. Only one of the 21 stakes (4.3 per cent) sold by trading companies was sold to a known party external to the joint venture, compared with six out of 28 (19.4 per cent) in the case of non-trading investors. These statistics are therefore consistent with our story.

Conclusions

Why and when will trading companies invest in manufacturing concerns? Trading companies, be they brokers or resellers, invest in manufacturing, at least initially, to support trade, not because they have special expertise in manufacturing. When they take equity stakes in their manufacturing suppliers and customers, it is for two main reasons. Trading companies take stakes in existing customers to prevent them from dealing directly with each other and doing without their services. Traders thrive on ignorance and chaos. As markets mature, buyers and sellers will forge direct links. Because the existing business of trading companies is continually threatened by extinction and its margins are so thin, traders are continually motivated to find new areas in which they can play their role of intermediator. These new value chains will require financing, which the trading company, because of its broad vision and superior intelligence, and because of its ability to configure the whole chain, is in a privileged position to provide.

Table 12.4 Divestment of Japanese minority stakes

1989 Status of Minority Stake at Entry	Trading Company		Non-Trading Company		Total	
	no.	%	no.	%	no.	%
Liquidated	1	4.3	1	3.2	2	3.6
Sold to joint venture partner	20	87.1	22	71.0	42	77.8
Sold to third party	1	4.3	6	19.4	7	13.0
Sold to unknown	1	4.3	2	6.4	3	5.6
Subtotal, Sales	22	95.7	30	96.8	52	96.4
Total	23	100.0	31	100.0	54	100.0

Trading companies will thus take strategic equity stakes in both mature and emerging value chains, but their stakes will be mostly minority ones. In mature businesses, these stakes will be just sufficient to assure them trading rights. In newly established value chains, the stakes will have to be large enough to reassure suppliers and customers and to make up for the lack of traditional bank financing.

As value chains mature, the manufacturing stakes of traders will go down, both because traders will lose their role of intermediators, and because they will be able to reduce the stakes they have taken to set up manufacturers in new value chains. By selling these stakes, traders will cash in on their foresight, and will obtain the resources necessary to start a new set of emerging value chains. Trading company stakes in manufacturing will therefore be, on average, short-lived. Divestment, an unintended consequence for non-traders, is part and parcel of trading company strategy.

A careful look at the 370 stakes taken by Japanese trading and non-trading parents in US manufacturing affiliates shows that Japanese trading companies exhibited a greater preference for minority stakes than their non-trading counterparts. These stakes were invariably taken to support their trading business. Over time, trading companies were also more likely than Japanese manufacturers to reduce their stakes, and when these were unwound, to do so by selling them to their former joint venture partners.

While our observations are limited by the specificities of time and place, they seem consistent with the findings of business historians who have studied the investment strategies of British and German traders (see Chapters 3, 4 and 6, this volume; Drabble 1973; van Helten and Jones 1989; Miller 1994)[10]. Why and when traders invest in manufacturing, and whether these investments follow a general logic that is applicable to all trading firms will, however, continue to pose a challenge to business historians.

Acknowledgments

We thank Thomas Roehl for providing crucial help in tracking down several Japanese investments. Danchi Tan and Ming Zeng contributed excellent research assistance. Thomas Roehl and Jana Sereghyova made insightful comments as did participants in the Fourth Workshop in International Business at the University of Vaasa in August 1997 and at the Conference on Trading Companies in Theory and History at the University of Reading in September 1997. Financial support from the University of Illinois Research Fund, the University of Illinois Center for International Business Education and Research, and the Carnegie Bosch Institute is gratefully acknowledged.

Notes

1 '[I]t's the classic problem of the small businessman. People are queuing at the door to take his product but he does not have the working capital to make the thing and commercial banks are very unsympathetic. They want assets, they want a balance sheet, which has no relation to the business a company can generate' (Carlson 1989).

2 This has been called 'loan and import'.

3 A fourth reason why a trading company may find itself owning equity in a supplier/customer is that the latter has gone bankrupt and the trading company has picked up the enterprise as collateral for its loans. We would expect this situation to be transitory and the trading company to eventually sell off all or part of the affiliate.

4 According to Arthur Clauser, adviser to the president of Mitsui USA: '[T]rading companies aren't so much interested in a high return on investment as they are on increasing trade flows. To the extent they can do this, they're quite content to get a return on investment of 1 to 2 per cent' (Carlson 1989). With the exception of Mitsubishi, that has made good returns on its investment in Brunei natural gas, most Japanese trading companies have earned very low rates of return on their equity investments (Kojima and Ozawa, 1984: 24).

5 The unit of analysis is the equity stake in a Japanese-owned US manufacturing affiliate. An affiliate that has two Japanese parents will generate two stakes. This census of manufacturing plants wholly or partially owned by Japanese firms in the US was compiled mainly from secondary data published by the Japan Economic Institute (JEI). Other sources such as the *JETRO Directory of Japanese Affiliates in the United States and Canada* were consulted. Mail, Fax and telephone inquiries were made of the subsidiaries or of their Japanese parents. We are confident that our database is very close to being a census of all Japanese equity stakes in US manufacturing at year-end 1980.

6 This investment, like many others made by trading companies in the US high-tech sector in the late 1980s, is not included in our database.

7 Information on the change in equity stakes was obtained from *Mergers and Acquisitions, Predicasts' F & S Index of Corporate Change*, the *Lexis–Nexis* database, and numerous phone and mail inquiries to the subsidiaries and their parents. In the case of discontinued affiliates, we confirmed this event with the City Hall, the Post Office, and/or the Chamber of Commerce of the last known location. Our results are robust to other definitions of ownership change. For example, if we look at changes across ownership deciles, 44 per cent of the stakes taken by trading companies declined, 46 per cent stayed within the same decile, and 10 per

cent increased. The figures for non-trading companies were 19 per cent, 69 per cent and 12 per cent, respectively.

8 Our findings answer the question raised by Yasumoro (Chapter 10, this volume) as to whether the investments of trading companies have a higher mortality rate than those of traditional Japanese investors. In our case they do.

9 Because our data form a census, no significant tests are necessary to establish the presence of statistically significant differences. One explanation for increases in trading company stakes is that our unit of observation is the affiliate, not the project. A given affiliate may be the institutional structure for more than one project. We would expect the trading company stake in the affiliate to remain stable or to increase if the trading company and its partners are using the subsidiary to undertake new projects. We are indebted to Tom Roehl for this suggestion.

10 The number of equity stakes in our database, while large enough to allow us to generalise, is small enough to be influenced by specific events, such as Mitsui Trading and Nippon Steel's sale of 27 minority equity stakes to Amax in 1986.

References

Brazier, R. G. (1994) 'Airborne in Japan', *Directors & Boards*, Winter, 18 (2): 45–6.

Burton, F. and Saelens, F. (1983) 'Direct investment by sogo-shosha in Europe', *Journal of World Trade Law*, May–June: 249–58.

Carlson, E. (1989) 'Japanese Bankroll Small U.S. Firms' *The Wall Street Journal*, Nov 2: B1.

Chojnacki, S. (1997). 'Alaska's Exporter of the Year finds success in bucking trends', *Alaska Journal of Commerce*, 16 June, p. 1.

Christelow, D. (1995) *When Giants Converge: the Role of US–Japan Direct Investment*, Armonk, N.Y.: M. E. Sharpe.

Drabble, J. H. (1973) *Rubber in Malaya: 1876–1922*, Kuala-Lumpur: Oxford University Press.

Hayashi, K. and Robock, S. H. (1982) 'The uncertain future of the Japanese general trading companies', *Kajian Ekonomi Malaysia*, 19 (2): 45–67.

Hennart, J.-F. (1991) ' The transaction costs theory of joint ventures: an empirical study of Japanese subsidiaries in the United States', *Management Science*, 37: 483–97.

Hertner, P. (1993) 'The German electrotechnical industry on the Italian market before the Second World War', in Jones, G. and Schroter, H. (eds) *The Rise of Multinationals in Continental Europe*, Aldershot: Edward Elgar.

Japan Economic Institute (JEI) (various years) *Japanese Manufacturing Investment in the United States*, Washington, D.C.: JEI.

Japan External Trade Organization (JETRO) (various years) *Directory of Japanese Affiliates in the United States and Canada*, Tokyo: JETRO.

Kenney, M. and Florida, R. (1993) *Beyond Mass Production*, New York: Oxford University Press.

Kojima, K. and Ozawa, T. (1984) *Japan's General Trading Companies: Merchants of Economic Development*, Paris: Organization for Economic Cooperation and Development.

LEXIS–NEXIS on-line database. Division of Reed Elsevier, Inc. Dayton, Ohio.

Mergers and Acquisitions (various years) Philadelphia: MLR. Enterprises.

Miller, R. (1994) 'British free-standing companies on the West Coast of South America', unpublished paper presented at the 11th International Economic History Congress, Milan.

Predicasts' Funk & Scott Index of Corporate Change (various years) Cleveland, OH: Predicasts.

Roehl, T. (1983) 'A transaction cost approach to international trading structures: the case of the Japanese general trading companies', *Hitotsubashi Journal of Economics*, 24: 19–135.

Sender, H. (1996a) 'Japan Inc., Let me introduce you, the shosha are making it easier to set up in China', *Far Eastern Economic Review* 159 (5): 51.

—— (1996b) 'Japan Inc., The sun never sets' *Far Eastern Economic Review* 159 (5): 46–8, 50.

Stopford, J. and Wells, L. (1972) *Managing the Multinational Enterprise, Organization of the Firm and Ownership of the Subsidiaries*, New York: Basic Books.

Tsurumi, Y. (1977) *Multinational Management*, Cambridge: Ballinger.

Van Helten, J.- J. and Jones, G. (1989) 'British business in Malaysia and Singapore since the 1870s', in Davenport-Hines, R. P.T. and Jones, G. (eds) *British Business in Asia since 1860*, Cambridge: Cambridge University Press.

Wilkins, M. (1994) 'More than a hundred years: a historical overview of Japanese direct investments in the United States', in Abo, T. (ed.) *Hybrid Factory*, New York: Oxford University Press.

Williamson, O. (1988) 'Corporate finance and corporate governance', *Journal of Finance*, 63 (3): 569–98.

Index

establishment in South America 102, 103–6; evaluation of South American companies 119–21; free-standing companies compared to Japanese 197, 198; interwar decline 10; management and organisation 113–17; slow death of trading in South America 106–9; South America post-war 15–14; Swedish trade 136; trade pre-eminence in 19th century 5

British India Associated Steamers 59, 61

British India S. N. Company 53

British marketing organisation 117

brokers: compared to resellers 24–7; multinational 27, 29, 33–4

broking 2

Brossette International 177

Bunge y Born 3, 13, 103

Calcutta and Burma S. N. Company 52, 53

Californian Oilfields Ltd 7

capital: as factor not product 184

Cargill Company 1, 3; family ownership 18; post-war 13

Carré, René 174, 179

cartels: metal traders 78–9

Casson, Mark 17; defining 'trading companies' 86; on Hennart's internalisation theory 184; integration 131, 214; pure and hybrid companies 2–3, 86; trader as speculator 98; types of free-standing companies 184

Cathay Pacific Airways 15–16

Cebeco-Handelsraad 88

Ceteco 15

CFAO 177, 180–1

Chandler Jr, Alfred D. 18, 113; *The Visible Hand* 87

Chapman, Stanley 48, 49–50; investment groups 7, 102

Chile 7, 105; economic crisis and British traders 117–18; government co-operation with British traders 110

China 204; British post-war companies 15; British trade in late 19th century 6; and Switzerland 164; trade with Japan 210–11

coal and coke 8, 10, 87, 208; Mackinnon Group 54, 61

Coca Cola 15, 16

cocoa and chocolate 7; Ghana and

Switzerland 162–3; South American trade wanes 110

coffee 5, 7; Brazil 109–10, 111; Volkart Group 158, 164–5

Cohen, Philipp Abraham 66

colonial trade: barter and interest rates on credit 42–4; decline 45; developing export trade 38–41; Dutch 91–3; The Netherlands 87–90; resource exploitation 39–40

commodities: barter 44; British in South America 104; Dutch colonial trade 88; effect of war 10, 107; fluctuations 95; post-war 13; shipping food 29–30; South America 107–8; strategy of British traders in South America 109–11

Compagnie des Minerais, Liège 71

Compagnie du Niger français 175

Compagnie Française de l'Afrique Noire (CFAO) 7

Compagnie Métallurgique franco-belge de Mortagne 73

Compañia Minera de Penoles 75

Compañia Minerales y Metales 71

competition: Japanese trading companies 203–4; market pressure on transactional relationships 207–9

competitiveness: general trading companies 206–7; satisfying customer demand 214; using company history to build information assets 209–11

construction: FDI from Japan 193

Continental 13

cotton 7; India 52m 54–5, 57, 202–3; Mackinnon Group 57; US Civil war creates Indian boom 52; Volkart group 164

countertrade *see* barter

Cuendet, Yves 159

cultural factors 26–7, 45, 159

Daito, E. 202

decolonization 14

defalcations 115

Deloittes 115

demand: seasonal or fashion fluctuation 24, 25–6

developing countries: barter and interest rates on credit 42–4

Diethelm, Wilhelm 161

Diethelm-Keller Group 98;

232 *Index*

Lightning Source UK Ltd.
Milton Keynes UK
UKOW04f1955141113

221123UK00007B/378/P